T0284823

"With its roadmap of skills and dynamic challenges to invigorate your career development, *The Zebra Code*, and its encouraging mentor Andrew LaCivita, guides all employees from emerging professionals to senior leaders on their professional journeys. It is hands-down simply the best resource you'll find when it comes to accelerating your career."

—**Paula Christensen**, Professional Resume Writer and Interview Coach, Founder of Strategic Career Coaches

"You don't have time to learn career skills the hard way. *The Zebra Code* lets professionals "stand on the shoulders" of a wise mentor, enabling them to effectively navigate the ambiguity of career development with confidence and clear purpose."

—**Chuck Peruchini**, Author of *Selling Professional and Financial Services Handbook*

"In a world where being unique is crucial, *The Zebra Code* provides a complete resource for professionals seeking to elevate their career trajectory."

—**Andrew Seaman**, Senior Managing Editor, LinkedIn

"In the world of professional advancement, the age-old adage "Different is better than better," reigns supreme. Andrew's teachings in *The Zebra Code* embody this philosophy, guiding savvy professionals on the art of "being a zebra, not a horse." Grounded in the belief that clarity, creativity, and focus are the pillars to career success, *The Zebra Code* presents a refreshing perspective. It doesn't just aim for improvement; it champions uniqueness and distinctiveness in the job market."

—**Sarah Johnston**, Founder of Briefcase Coach

"*The Zebra Code* is an indispensable tool, especially for those in the military and veteran communities. This book emphasizes the criticality of mastering brevity and inquisitiveness to make a mark. It's a direct and well-organized compilation of fundamental skills, applicable to professionals across all stages, irrespective of their background, expertise, or rank. It resonates with everyone since, in one way or another, we are all navigating through various transitions in life."

—**Jan Rutherford**, Founder of Self-Reliant Leadership®

THE
ZEBRA
CODE

A Step-By-Step Guide to Mastering Career Skills That Make You a Standout Professional

Andrew LaCivita

POST HILL
PRESS

A POST HILL PRESS BOOK

The Zebra Code:
A Step-by-Step Guide to Mastering Career Skills That Make You
a Standout Professional
© 2024 by milewalk, inc.
All Rights Reserved

ISBN: 979-8-88845-044-4
ISBN (eBook): 979-8-88845-045-1

Cover design by Jim Villaflores
Interior graphics made by Daniel Paterno, PaternoGroup
Interior design and composition by Greg Johnson, Textbook Perfect

Post Hill Press
New York • Nashville
posthillpress.com

Published in the United States of America
1 2 3 4 5 6 7 8 9 10

To all those I've helped, your desire to improve yourselves has made me a better teacher. A piece of you has found its way into this book. It's as much yours as it is mine.

Contents

Part Seven: The Visionary

Part Eight: The Satellite View

Part Nine: Draw Your Own Map

Part Ten: Before You Go

Appendices

A Preface with Thanks

Today, we live in a fifteen-minutes-of-fame, get-rich-quick-with-selfies-on-the-internet world. While the planet still rotates at the same speed it did on the day you were born, nowadays, people seem to want to zip through their twenty-four-hour day faster. Oddly, people don't technically move faster as much as want everything faster.

Why can't I get same-day delivery? Why am I not promoted yet? Why is this video on YouTube ten minutes and not four? Now that I think of it, why isn't it a short? I'm sure he can get that down to sixty seconds and still teach me all I need to know!

Against this pervasive sentiment, I took a bunch of time to write this book for you. I waited even longer for someone to publish it. It makes no difference how many hours I spent working on it or how many months it took to make its way to the "bookshelves." It definitely doesn't matter how many consecutive days I wrote in the dark hours of the morning while most people in my time zone were still sleeping. I enjoyed the journey because I genuinely believe the joy is "in the doing." I first wrote this book as a gift to me. Now, I want to make it my gift to you.

I mention this not because I'm looking for a pat on the back. In fact, it's you I'd like to congratulate and thank. I want to congratulate you on taking a step to better yourself. I also want to thank you for getting this book and taking the time to read this sentence. At this moment, that's all I can thank you for even though I'm sure there will be lots more for us to virtually high-five about. I know we'll be cheering soon because I can already tell a lot about you even though we've likely never met.

You might wonder how I could possibly know anything about you. On the surface, that seems like a lucid thought. It's amazing, however, how much you can *know* about a person based on their behaviors. For example, even though we've never met, I know you purchased this book or received it as a gift. Being that this is a career skill-building book and it's in your hands, whether by your own actions or someone else's, I can draw several conclusions with a great deal of certainty.

First, the fact you have this particular book, actually flipped it open, and are reading this sentence means you have aspirations to grow.

But wait, I can tell even more! You're not only reading sentences in the book. You're reading sentences in the Preface section. This is a good indication you have patience and want to take it all in. By not skipping the upfront matter to "get right into it," I can tell you want to go through the steps.

I'll keep going and say you're an observer. You know there are hidden meanings in all the nooks and crannies of life. You believe there are lessons to be learned everywhere as long as you have your eyes open and ears stretched.

I'll also go out on a limb and say it's a good bet you're willing to put in the time necessary to get what you want. You know anything truly worth having in this world takes time because no shortcut ever gave you what you deserved. This last part makes you the rarest of all, which is one of the biggest reasons I know your zebra stripes imminently await. When you're finished with this book and the effort it'll take to earn them, wear them with pride.

—*Andy*
December 22, 2022
...while it's still dark this morning.

Introduction

There's this woman named Elizabeth. On January 19, 2021, I had the good fortune of meeting her, via Zoom, for the very first time.

I'm guessing by the way she said "Hey!" as her face lit up my computer screen, she probably raises the temperature in any room she walks into. She's special. Of this, I'm sure, and it's not because she's a pediatric doctor and works in hospitals. It's also not because she's an editor-in-chief for a prominent pediatrics journal or that her Curriculum Vitae includes stints as an Associate Professor, Advisor to the United States Department of State, and a bunch of other things I'll omit for brevity.

On that day, she and I got together because she wanted help achieving one of her career goals, which was to work at a Harvard-affiliated medical facility. She felt working for a hospital in this healthcare system with its pedigree, teaching practices, and opportunities to learn and contribute would truly help her grow.

After she said "Hey!" and I said "Hey," I went through a quick introduction to set up the structure for our coaching session. Then I asked her about her goals for our session.

She said, "My goal is for you to get me into Harvard."

I asked, "And?"

She responded, "That's it."

I continued, "As in no other options?"

"No."

At this point, some other coach might be concerned, but I was thinking, *I love it! The honesty. The clarity. The drive. The ambition. The focus. My day just got better.*

A few minutes into our discussion, I discovered there are fewer than twenty of these Harvard facilities. As if this wasn't going to be challenging enough, we needed to dismiss 90 percent of them due to their geographical locations. Moving her family to take a new job was not an option because, well, that would have made our task too easy for us. Basically, we had two shots left.

To cut a short story shorter, I gave her my advice and the tactics she needed to employ. A few months later she began working at the number-one ranked Harvard facility. I know this because she and her daughter, Lily, sent me a thank-you card in the mail. This was not just any thank-you card, but one they had handcrafted with my very favorite coaching message on the cover—a zebra.

While Elizabeth and I actually met for the first time during that coaching session, she knew from following my online teachings that I've long used the analogy to "be a zebra, not a horse." That way, you'll stand out from the crowd.

I especially love the irony, in her case, as a doctor. In medical school, students are often taught, "when you hear hoofbeats, think horses, not zebras." This is their guidance to consider the most likely possibility first when forming a diagnosis of a patient. For you, in the corporate world, I want just the opposite. Be a zebra, not a horse.

At this point, you might be thinking, *Well, that was easy for Elizabeth, who has scholarly credentials. What's the big deal if some smart, accomplished person got a job at one of the best hospitals in the world?*

Let me offer this. In just the last five years, I've coached—individually—more than 3,000 people. They range in age from twenty-two-year-old recent college graduates with exactly zero hours of professional experience to people in their seventies who've worked for five decades. I can tell you from these interactions, as well as those I've had in the previous three decades of my career, being a zebra and standing out from the crowd has little to do with your credentials and much more to do with your drive, dedication, discipline, focus, creativity, and willingness to make failure part of your everyday life.

Zebras know that failure leads to success because confidence is not found in the quality of their talents, but in the quality of their thoughts. Confidence has more to do with your relationship with failure than success. When all goes well and we win, it's easy to believe in ourselves. Failures, on the other hand, can negatively impact our confidence levels if we don't design and interpret them properly.

What I didn't share with you in the story about Elizabeth were the failures she accrued before she met me. I didn't mention all the attempts she made that taught her lessons, one of which, I'm assuming, was to enlist a coach. There were other lessons about being consistent, iterating, and adjusting her job-search process based on what she learned from her "failures."

The truth is, no matter who you are, what you do professionally, or what goals you have, you can become whoever and accomplish whatever you want. Inside this book, I've packaged the formula for you to do just that. It'll require hard work, so let's just get that out of the way. This is no get-rich-quickly scheme. There are no shortcuts inside, but there are loads of accelerators. There are zero easy days, but there are many rewarding days.

The gift that keeps on giving...

To make it a little easier, before you turn the page and dive in, I want to share how to get the most out of this book. Whenever I offer an online training program, I include a video on how I'd go through my own training. Here's a book version of that for you.

The book, as I intended, is a **working manual**. You'll learn a **methodology** to help organize your skills development so you can enjoy your career and advance as quickly as possible. The better we are at something, the more we enjoy it.

In addition to the overall methodology, there are **fifteen detailed lessons** which cover wide-reaching skillsets every professional needs to build. Each lesson has a "reflection" and "challenge" exercise so you can evaluate your "current state" and implement the lesson through practice and real-life execution.

The last portion of the book includes a more thorough **self-evaluation** of your skills and a step-by-step process to **build your skills development plan** as it relates to your profession.

As you progress in your career, you'll need to adjust your career plan. As you become more proficient in certain skills, you'll be able to build higher-level skills. This fluid nature requires constant nurturing and attention. That's why I designed this book so you can continually refer back to it throughout your entire career. Consider it your very own "career bible."

Here are the seven major steps I'd take with my book!

Just read and notate. Read the book straight through. This might sound silly of me to say, but once you get into the book and see its structure, there's a good chance you'll be tempted to try to work the lessons! Hold off on your first pass through the book. Just take in the concepts. Highlight what you like and note which parts to revisit. You'll thank yourself for making these notations.

Review the exercises. As part of your first pass through the book, read the "challenge exercises," but don't actually do the challenges. The challenges are each one month in duration. That means there's some effort involved! You won't get the return on your investment if you're haphazardly working the lessons without taking into account your personal and professional priorities. You'll create a structured plan in one of the later steps.

Take the self-assessment. After you read and review the methodology and lessons sections of the book, you'll have a deeper understanding of the framework and respective skillsets. Then, you can take the skills assessment to surface your strengths and opportunities to fine-tune or build new skills.

Create your starting point. After you take the skills assessment, you can use the Track Your Progress Worksheet I've included in the appendices as a starting point to identify your strengths, include the most relevant skills for your profession, and note timing considerations so you can develop a plan that prioritizes your most-needed skills for the short and long terms. (This is why I don't want you to work on the challenges until you have an ideal, prioritized sequence.)

Build your skills development plan. With the information from your self-assessment and Track Your Progress Worksheet, you'll be armed to take the remaining steps to complete the first iteration of your skills development plan. This involves identifying your professional goals and all associated components to achieve those goals including the required skills, lessons, tools, coaches, schedule, metrics, and tracker.

Work the challenges. According to your overall plan, you can start working the lesson exercises (i.e., challenges) in an order that focuses on your short-term needs and long-term goals. Of course, you'll make adjustments based on your schedule and priorities.

Update your tracker. As you complete the challenges, update the Track Your Progress Worksheet and any additional tools you're using such as a diary, journal, or corporate career development model to update your progress.

If you follow this approach, you'll be able to maximize your time and results. I'm sure you can't wait to dive in as much as I'm eager to share this with you. Let's get to it!

Photo courtesy of Andrew LaCivita

Luck. ('lək).

noun

Working tirelessly behind the scenes before appearing for the final act to deliver magical results; typically viewed by an audience who watches in amazement questioning why they can't achieve the same simply by attending the show.

Source: *Andrew LaCivita's Professional Dictionary*, 3rd ed. (milewalk Inc., 2007).

PART ONE

Wisdom Is Expensive

CHAPTER 1

The Tuition Bill
You Never Stop Paying

1969 was a great year for fashion.

I'd like to bring you back to December 1969 when I received my very first sign you'd be holding this book right now. Over fifty years ago, it was in the cards we'd meet this way.

As a person who loves to reflect, I try to attach proper meaning to any experience. I like to say, "Experience is not what happened to you. It's the meaning you attach to what happened to you."

Experience is not what happened to you.
It's the meaning you attach to what happened to you.

In that spirit, whenever we experience a present moment, we aren't able to know whether it's a high or low. You might feel good or bad about what's occurring, but you can't possibly know something wonderful or catastrophic is happening until you look back with hindsight. Hopefully, no matter what it is, you attach a positive lesson to it.

As I look back, it doesn't surprise me, based on the way I behaved as a three-year-old, that I'd eventually engineer something to help you.

I was always in a hurry. It didn't matter what it was. I'd want to put the Legos together in a blur. When I was of school age, I'd do my homework as quickly as possible. As a three-year-old, I didn't have many tasks that required speed, but getting dressed seemed to be one of them.

I decided it would be smart to get my clothes out the night before even though I didn't have any major appointments the next day. My dad did this, so that instantly made it cool. He'd hang his suit on the bedroom doorknob. With my entire 1,000 days of life experience, who was I to question this tactic? I figured I'd just follow his lead.

Always looking to improve on what I observe, I had an idea. It struck me that if I laid out my clothes, not just in a neat, folded pile like a well-adjusted adult might do, but in the actual shape of a person, that would somehow expedite my ability to slide into them and get on with my busy day working at my Playskool Workbench.

There I laid the inventory of clothing in a flat, two-dimensional plane on the floor. Being a mere three feet tall, this made complete sense. I placed my shirt at the top and connected my pants before finally dropping each sock at the bottom of the pantlegs. The days Mom tossed out the sweater vest or little blazer presented some challenges.

I've always looked for the formula. *How can I do this faster? How can I do this better? How can I do this more vigorously?* (My dad says I even rest intensely. Like everyone's dad, he's right about this and everything else.)

As you might imagine from a beginning like this, I went on to study engineering. When I finally held that shiny degree in my hand, I realized my real passion was never about formulas. It's always been about helping people. From my first memory, I've wanted to support others. One of the ways I do this now is by building them better ways to advance their careers.

That fastidiously dressed little boy who wished he had arms big enough to hug the whole world grew into the man who will always put people first, results second.

Don't worry. I'm on a pitch count as they say in baseball, so I'll skip a handful of decades and get onto the whats and how-tos so you can become a zebra and stand out from the pack. In the meantime, feel free to use my lay-out-your-clothes technique if it'll save you a few minutes each morning. Maybe it'll help you create some space to work on the skills I'm about to teach you in this book!

Let's fast forward five decades and, out of thin air, voilà…

Here we are many years after I graduated from my Playskool Workbench. During this time, my love of supporting people has become an obsession. Don't take that the wrong way. Obsessed not in the you-need-to-get-a-restraining-order sort of way. Obsessed in the how-can-I-help-you-solve-your-problems-or-achieve-your-aspirations sort of way.

Throughout my thirty-six-year professional career, I've focused on building systems that enable businesses and individuals to realize their maximum potential. I've channeled experience across three distinct careers as an information technology consultant, executive recruiter, and career coach and packaged it into easy-to-follow, skill-building lessons. The lessons are wrapped into a structured framework you can use throughout your entire career to manage your professional development, impact, and enjoyment.

This is not an academic book filled with theories. There are absolutely zero laboratory studies using rats. I've never been one to design anything from sitting at a table inside a room with four walls and no windows. Don't fret. I've built models and run surveys and practiced in live situations with actual, willing participants I endearingly call human beings.

These methods and practices have been designed, built, practiced, tested, and optimized during my work as a corporate leader, serial entrepreneur, author, blogger, speaker, board of directors' member, angel investor, and international career coach.

They have been adapted using data captured from corporate personnel who know best and my personal experience consulting to more than 350 companies and coaching over 100,000 professionals. I'm confident what's inside will be applicable to you as a professional.

I paid how much for that degree?
And I still have to learn all this other stuff?

Before I share with you my skill-building concepts and all the elegant "systems" to help you become a zebra, stand out from the pack, and enjoy your career to the fullest, let's talk about why something like my methodology—and this book—are necessary and how it will help you.

Whatever you call yourself or wherever you are in your career, probability says you paid for some, if not a lot, of formal schooling. While education is wonderful and any accompanying credentials are something no one can ever take away from you, oftentimes, that education taught you a trade skill. That is, you learned to become an engineer, accountant, or computer programmer. (You literally learned to *become one* as opposed to actually being one, which requires a much larger set of skills.)

The biggest issue with our colleges, universities, and adult-learning programs is they typically teach you *only* the trade. Sure, they might have you squeeze in an off-trade elective like the economics or sociology classes I took on my way to an electrical engineering degree.

What is absent, however, from just about any curriculum you'll find, are the capabilities and foundational skillsets required to not only succeed in this world, but enjoy yourself in the process. These capabilities are traits and skills that not only transcend your specific trade, but also make you better at your specific trade. They are what will make you uniquely special inside and outside. They'll be your differentiators that make you the best of the best if you learn and practice them.

Colleges and universities aren't the only culprits when it comes to robbing you of opportunities to learn these skills that matter most in business and life. Corporations perpetuate this dysfunctional way of learning and growing. They don't mean to. I believe employers would love to teach their employees these skills, but based on my experience consulting to them and recruiting for them, I'm not sure they know what those capabilities are or how to teach them.

In *The Hiring Prophecies: Psychology behind Recruiting Successful Employees*, I defined these capabilities, in a recruitment context, as a person's demonstrated capacity to effectively perform an activity (or collection of responsibilities) without previously experiencing it.

As an example, consider a project manager. If a job candidate or employee demonstrated strong organizational, planning, customer-service, and team-building skills, you'd likely consider this person a good bet to be a great project manager even if this person was never previously a project manager. That's because the person has the capabilities which make a great project manager a great project manager irrespective of which type of project the person is managing.

Companies generally struggle with recruiting people with these capabilities in large part because they want to hire someone who knows "how to do the job." There is often little thought given to evaluating whether the job candidate is a great long-term bet thanks to the person's foundational skillsets. Once hired, the company does very little, if anything, to teach the employee these capabilities because the employer spends its time teaching the trade (i.e., how to do the job).

From an individual employee's standpoint, the problem is much worse. You, as perhaps an aspiring or current project manager, might not be sure what those foundational capabilities are, how to build them, what order to build them, and which matter most. In turn, your daily performance doesn't improve at the rate that it can and your career drags along.

Most people learn their trade, build the widgets, and punch the clock. After a while, one realizes you can only solve so many engineering problems, accounting problems, and computer problems before you become bored, your performance wanes, and your personal and professional growth plateaus.

There must be more. There is. The problem is most people don't know which capabilities to learn. Even if they do know, it's difficult to find effective lessons to learn the capabilities and build them. The lessons available in schools or on the internet generally offer only pieces. Until now. The formula is in your hands.

"Hard work" aren't two four-letter words.

You might be wondering, *Okay, the book is in my hands. Now, what exactly will it do for me?* The answer is nothing if you don't put in the work. If you simply read it and discard it, it won't change your life.

These techniques need to be integrated into your professional and personal life to improve your mindset, attitude, outputs, and enjoyment of anything you do. This will require hard work, practice, mistakes, and adjustments.

Some people aren't willing to do the hard work because they don't care enough. Let's not cover those people because you're still reading this, which means you're not one of them.

Those who care about building a better career and life but don't attain it usually fail because they don't know the steps or how to perform them. Hard work in the wrong direction won't work.

You need to know which skills and traits matter, why they matter, and what order to build them to get the greatest compounding return for your effort. You also need to know how to track your progress and make the necessary adjustments so you stay on your path. The great news is that's exactly what this book will teach you. It's broken down into sections to provide you a career-long, skill-building framework, fifteen detailed lessons on the most vital skills, and a formula to build a plan that works for you.

Before we dive in, I'd like you to keep something in mind. School teaches us concepts, but to truly learn and experience them, we need to go out into the world and apply them. To truly understand most things in life, we can't simply read them in a book. We need to experience them. The opposite is also true. There are things in life you'll have difficulty fully experiencing until you have the proper instruction or, dare I say, read them in a book. This particular book is a map, not the territory. I'm providing you, through my actual experience, steps that might work for you to gain the best experience and realize the most enjoyment out of your career and life. When you're finished reading, you'll have the structure and lessons to draw your own map and enjoy *your* terrain.

This particular book is a map, not the territory.... When you're finished reading, you'll have the structure and lessons to draw your own map and enjoy your terrain.

Photo courtesy of Andrew LaCivita

CHAPTER 2

The Technical Set

Swim, bike, run, repeat.

I do Ironman triathlons. If you're not familiar with these borderline-insane events, they are a ridiculously long sequence of swimming, biking, and running. That's all together and the clock doesn't stop, not even when you're changing your clothes and shoes. The lifestyle I've built for myself so I can "enjoy" these events requires a significant amount of practice and training.

Because I value the function of healthy limbs, I enlisted a coach to teach me the best techniques, manage my workloads, and everything else associated with getting me across the finish line upright and with a smile on my face. She lays out my training schedule every week. I won't share it with you for fear you think me not of sound mind and possibly worry you're reading the words of a crazy person.

Part of that schedule includes three swim workouts. She designs every one of those workouts to include four phases. There's a warm-up, technical set, main set, and cool down. Even if you're not a swimmer, I'm guessing you can follow along with the analogy I'm about to make: everything in life seems to follow these steps.

As a career coach and long-time professional, I've observed many people rushing through their day. They roll out of bed, take a shower, and grab the coffee (their warm-up). Then, they race right into their work (main set) and commute home (cool down). Most people skip the technical set entirely.

9

The technical set is one of the most important sets because it's designed to help you practice and—execute—correctly. During the technical set of my swim workouts, I often use tools and drills designed to help me improve my form, focus, and position in the water. This makes it easier to concentrate and practice effectively. Then, when I transition into the main set, where the goal is to build stamina, I'm in a better position to execute the process correctly as I work on my endurance.

Regardless of your profession, it's helpful to integrate "technical sets" into your daily routines. These sets provide frequent opportunities for you to practice and concentrate on building skills that will make you a better professional at your trade.

I even have a technical set each morning before I start my workday. I open my journal to the first page and review a list of ten reminders of how I want to conduct myself that day and every day. This helps me start the day in the right frame of mind. The list includes reminders to be responsible for my energy, be appreciative of this day, have faith I'm being prepared for bigger achievements whenever I struggle, and not complain, to name a few. I have other technical sets I perform before my writing sessions, live shows, and coaching sessions.

Many people skip these technical sets because they either don't make the time, don't know what to practice, or don't know how to practice. This book is all about helping you develop and execute a plan for your professional technical sets.

Even this book has a technical set. I want to share it with you now so you have "drills," which I've labeled "reminders," to help you get the most out of each and every one of your reading sessions. It's my hope you'll flip back to this chapter to review these so you get your mental form and focus in order before you take in the lessons. After all, where your mind goes, your body will follow. I don't want your body doing a bunch of hard work in all the wrong directions. If we can keep your perspective, effort, approach, and bias for action in order, you'll be amazed at what you can accomplish. We get really good at what we practice. Let's practice correctly.

Wisdom is expensive. Perspective is cheap.

Wisdom is expensive because you need to learn it by living it. Every experience you'll go through in life, you'll learn from it. The valuable lessons will be the most painful because no education is free and true value often costs more. Unlike college, there are no scholarships in real life. You'll need to pay the full freight.

For example, consider the lessons in this book. Imagine the years of experience it takes to learn the right skills and routines. How about the additional time to package and write them for you?

The lessons in this book are easy to read, but even reading them takes your time. Practicing them will take more of your time. You'll make mistakes and adjust. That requires more time. That's life and becoming an ace at anything takes time.

Now, think for a moment. What are you a master of? How long did it take you to become that? I'm sure it took lots of time and expense.

One thing that isn't expensive and doesn't require a lot of time, however, is perspective. It's around us all day every day, but we lose sight of it often. Why? Because we've grown accustomed to our comforts and routines and knowledge.

Lack of perspective is one of the biggest thieves that robs us of the wisdom we work so hard to attain. When we lose perspective, it makes us behave in a way that's inconsistent with our personal experience. This lack of perspective is what prevents us from using our wisdom when we need it the most.

Here's a little story. On March 11, 2021, I was fifty-seven minutes into my weekly Live Office Hours show I conduct every Thursday on my YouTube channel. My wife, Lynda, was home that day and was about to run an errand. She peeked into my office and I stopped the show so I could get up and give her a hug and kiss goodbye. I didn't want her to leave the house without knowing I care for her. We have no idea what's going to happen to any of us at any moment. This might sound like a morbid thought, but that doesn't make it any less true. When I sat back down on my Swiss ball to return to the lesson, it was the first time I shared my view on the relationship between wisdom and perspective with my community.

I shared how I practice keeping perspective in everything I do. A great example is before every one of my live coaching shows, I sit for five minutes and remind myself *God brought me to these people at this moment because they need my help. I get to teach them right through the camera. If they knew what I know, they wouldn't need to be here.* (Hey, there's another one of my technical sets!)

I consider it an absolute miracle that someone on the other side of the planet can learn from me. I never want something that amazing to become common to me. I've done more than 1,200 live shows and often get asked the same questions.

Many viewers ask, "How is it possible you are so polite and never get bored answering the same questions?"

To which I usually respond, "Because I constantly remind myself the person who asked the question may have recently discovered me. They needed me today. They didn't need me yesterday."

I feel the same way about you as a reader. If you recently discovered me, I'm so glad because perhaps you needed me today. Whoever you are and wherever you are in this world, I want you to know I appreciate you are reading this book. I genuinely want it to be valuable and for you to use it to become the very best version of *you* you can be.

I wrote this book so in a matter of hours you can add my years of experience and wisdom to your own. That, to me, is as much a miracle as teaching someone over the internet through a camera.

Don't let what was once a miracle become common to you. If you do, you'll become great at overlooking all of the good things in life.

> Reminder #1: Perspective keeps your wisdom intact and available when you and others need it most.

Skills are cheap too. Effort is not.

If you want to be the best at your craft or live the good life or get the brass ring or attain whatever is your holy grail, it won't be easy and it will take time.

I have my own definition of the word time. It's the most often-used excuse for people to rationalize why they haven't accomplished something they don't want badly enough.

When I speak of time, I consider it two ways. There is, of course, the length of time in terms of months and years it will take you to keep building and practicing your skills to become adept.

More importantly than becoming overwhelmed by the long journey ahead, we have bigger issues related to time. That is, creating time (technically, creating space) in your calendar today and next week and the week after simply to learn the skills you need to build and practice.

You might be wondering why you can't just learn these skills on the job. It's because corporations don't explicitly teach you the skills in this book. They focus more on the making-the-widget skills. You get to learn and practice those between 9:00 AM and 5:00 PM.

When will you get to work on the skills I'm teaching in this book? Let me answer that with a story about the first time I applied what it takes to get what you want.

I went to an all-boys high school filled with a bunch of type-A personalities. There were 365 boys who started in the freshmen class and 244 of those boys graduated from that school. You get the idea. There was no messing about.

When I started as a freshman, I received my class schedule. It began at the 02 period and finished with 08 period. One of those periods was my lunch break and another was gym class. That left five actual classes.

The inquisitive child I was, I wondered, *Why I am I starting at 02 and not the 01 period?*

After I was there one week, I meandered into the principal's office to ask. There was a nice gentleman there and I said, "Hi. My name's Andy and I have a question."

He said, "Sure young man, shoot."

I asked, "I noticed my schedule starts at 02 period. Is there any reason it doesn't start at 01?"

He responded, "The 01 period is for an extra class for the 'advanced' kids. They can elect to take classes like chemistry, biology, and other advanced classes we don't offer during the regular periods."

I asked, "Can anyone take those?"

He said, "Sure. We can sign you up for an extra class next semester."

Now, I really started thinking. *If the ambitious kids show up at the 01 period, maybe there's a zero period.*

I asked him, "Is there a zero period? Are there classes before the first period?"

He replied, "No. That's when teachers come in to get ready for the day."

I asked, "How early does the school open?"

He said, "The facilities man opens the doors at 5:30 AM."

I asked, "Can anyone come into the building?"

He said, "Sure."

I asked, "Can I do anything I want in the building? Can I use the strength-training room?"

He said, "I don't see why not."

I asked, "I want to make sure I have this straight. I can get in the school at 5:30 AM. I could strength train, run up and down the basketball court, grab a shower, take an extra class, and then everybody else starts?"

He said, "That's right."

I said, "See you in the morning!"

Whenever I coach people who are looking to become a high achiever, I ask them to share their goals and assess their current abilities in relation to those goals. Then I ask, "Can you please show me your calendar for the week?"

In nearly every case, there is not one minute allocated to building the skills necessary for them to achieve their goals. I often ask, "Where have you allocated the time to work on the skills and practice them so you're able to achieve your goals? How do you expect to attain those heights if you don't actually work at it?" If you show me your calendar, I'll tell you your future.

Occasionally, people ask me to assess why they haven't currently achieved goals they thought they should. In these situations, I don't assume they cannot. In fact, the person is usually already equipped to attain those goals. In these situations, I ask, "What were you unwilling to give up in order to attain that goal?" It goes straight to the heart. If you didn't achieve your goal, that's the only question you need to ask yourself. We all have our limits. Maybe you didn't want to get out of bed earlier or give up social outings with your friends. Maybe you didn't want to go into debt. Any of these reasons are certainly okay.

Most of the time, however, it's because you didn't want to invest the time. I assure you; change is not a function of ability. It's a function of desire. If you want to grow, you'll need to put in the time. That means, making the time.

For you to be successful in implementing the lessons in this book, you'll need to create time in your calendar to learn the skills and practice them.

I teach people the first place to start when attempting any goal is to focus on the sacrifices they'll need to make to create the space in their lives to work on those goals. Addition by subtraction is the key.

> Reminder #2: Change is not a function of ability. It's a function of desire. Desire starts with the willingness to create space in your life to work on the skills you need to achieve your goals.

Short-timers focus on wins while long-timers study their plans.

An ambitious reader like yourself who would even think of picking up a book like this probably has some lofty aspirations. As such, you might have designated goals you want to achieve. People who have designated goals often focus on outcomes. That is, the exact number or metric. The how-fast-was-my-marathon-time with little regard for the weather on race day or the diligence in how well they adhered to their running plans.

I see this often in my line of work. The thirty-year-old employees who want to race up the ranks in their corporations and wonder why they don't have their six-figure salaries or corner offices yet.

I would argue expectations are our greatest source of stress. Much of the expectations I speak of are related to outcomes people think they should attain on their attempts.

The flip side to this is enjoying the journey and falling in love with the process. The joy is in the doing. The reward is in the daily steps. Then, on your figurative race day, you do your best and have complete trust in the process because you know you put in the work.

Remember this: when it comes to outcomes, short-timers focus on wins while long-timers study their plans. What do I mean by short-timers? They're people who quit because their focus was on a short-term win or outcome that didn't go their way. They're worried about that victory right out of the gate. The biggest problem with this is you are never more at risk of throwing in the towel than at your first stumble. Short-timers get discouraged if they don't get those early wins and that's what leads to quitting.

Long-timers are mainstays because they build lasting power through the development and execution of their plans. The secret to their successes is not only having a plan, but also where they focus their attention, which is on the process of executing the plan.

Much like change is not a function of ability, long-term success has more to do with where you place your attention than any outcome you do or don't achieve. Part of executing the plan includes evaluating what went well during a particular step as well as the opportunities for improvement. It's all part of the process and their attention is on the process. They focus on their trajectories and what they're learning more than where they are at any snapshot in time.

They fall in love with the planning process as opposed to the designated plan itself. This is a crucial way to approach it because after you take a step, you know so much more about what you're doing. On any given day, you're simply working on a puzzle piece of your overall plan.

A long-timer's reaction to anything sounds a lot like *Okay. I now have experience with that. I understand it might not have turned out how I would've liked, but it's just a step in the overall process.*

Don't stick to your plan if you know you need to alter it based on new information. Stick to your overall strategy and modify your plans according to the newest information. The longer-term you think, the better short-term moves you'll make.

While this may sound obvious, a plan is put together based on history and not current events. The moment you take your first step, you know more than you did when you put the plan together. Why would you ignore the experience you just gained?

To get the most out of the lessons in this book, it will be important to build your own professional development plan. I will walk you through the exact steps to do that. I hope you shoot big because nothing grand ever came from small thinking.

I like to say, "Big plans, tiny steps, fulfills dreams."

Reminder #3: Build a plan, fall in love with the planning process, and remember, the joy is in the doing day in and day out.

Realize you are always a WIP
and MVPs will make you successful....

This will seem very obvious after you read it, but I challenge you to think about this day in and day out. When you consider yourself, do you realize you're always a WIP? You are always a work in progress. The problem for most people is they don't think of themselves this way. Worst of all, they don't treat themselves this way.

Consider when you meet people for the first time. It can be anyone. Perhaps they're friends of a friend. The moment you see them for the first (or any) time, it's natural to think of them as "finished products." Even though they've gone through years of evolving, at the moment you meet them, they seem "completely assembled" to you. They are truly nothing more than versions of themselves at snapshots in time.

If you discovered me on YouTube or television or a stage, I probably looked like a finished product to you as I gave a lesson. Even the lesson itself might seem like a finished product. As you read this book, you might consider it a finished product because it's packaged and will help you build new skills. It's a product on a bookshelf in a store or e-tailer, but it's far from finished regarding the lessons and mediums by which I share them today. In fact, these words you're reading were written eighteen months before the book was released. I'm sure today I'm using additional examples, pointers, and platforms to share these lessons. This entire method of learning will continually evolve because everything is constantly in a state of change!

Whenever we build something in our lives, as we go through the creative process, that "product" will transform greatly. A masterpiece will never look like a masterpiece when you're in the middle of it. As I write these words, I assure you, this book does not feel like a bestseller as it sits in the Word document. Even so, "doing the work" is what makes it a masterpiece to me.

I often say, "The plagiarizer never sees the invisible work that makes the masterpiece a masterpiece." The copiers, they might be able to mimic your "final" product, but they will never get to appreciate the "joy in the doing." For you, I hope the internal work and your journey becomes a masterpiece—for you.

A masterpiece, however, can never truly be a masterpiece unless it benefits someone else. It cannot benefit someone else unless it's breathing. That means, you need to build it and get it out into this world preferably as quickly as possible. That'll be easier if you have a bias for action.

The easiest way to become comfortable with a bias for action is to think of your outputs (masterpieces-to-be of course) as Minimum Viable Products (MVP). That is, spend the least amount of time and least amount of effort to get something livable and breathable into this world. This could be a white paper, book, training program, or any "deliverable" you create for your work or life.

I don't mean to hurry or be sloppy. I want you to focus on getting your version 1.0 up and running so to speak. It, just like you, is a WIP! You can always work on version 1.1 or 2.0. I (and I'm sure many others) like to say, "You can't scale version zero, but you sure can scale the heck out of version 1.0."

The longer you wait and more you ruminate before releasing your outputs, the more stressed and worried you become. Keeping a bias for action will help you stay in motion and continually produce. This will, in turn, positively affect your self-image as you watch yourself and your outputs constantly improve.

> Reminder #4: You are constantly changing and the easiest way to see your progress is through creating MVPs.

As a reminder, feel free to turn back to this technical set from time to time. It'll help you keep perspective and also serve as a nice warm-up when you practice the lessons.

Now, let's get on with the main set.

PART TWO

Skill-Building Codified

CHAPTER 3

The Career Syllabus

"Andy, see if you can find those instructions.
They should be somewhere in the garbage can."
—Dad

Every child enjoys getting presents. As a kid, I didn't just get the joy out of ripping off the wrapping paper that draped my birthday and Christmas presents. I was also blessed with the gift of entertainment as I watched my father put these complicated contraptions together without the aid of the instructions. It wasn't as if the toymakers didn't properly insert them into the boxes. They simply were the first item Dad kicked to the side.

I, of course, asked, "Dad, don't we need this booklet?"

He'd respond, "I don't need that. How hard can it be to put this together?"

Turns out, it was often harder than it looked.

Do you ever feel this way about your career?

Think back to when you were in college. Do you remember the snazzy collegiate professors handing you the syllabi? They *actually* handed them to me. I'm sure nowadays the students just whip out their iPhones and do a few clicks on the university website.

Syllabi were great because you knew what to study and when to study it. You could be confident you were learning the lessons in the right order. You could take comfort in knowing the person teaching you was knowledgeable or at least had the right credentials. You could have faith in these blueprints for whatever subjects you were learning. What's more, you knew these "credit hours" would contribute to your overall knowledge of a larger curriculum or, at a minimum, check off an elective required to earn your degree.

School is now out of session in the formal sense, but it never really ends. What does end are the syllabi. No matter what era you were born in, whether you're an old fogie like I am or a young gun, the "syllabus of professional skills" has been the same for pretty much all time. It won't be changing any eons soon. The big problem is, I've never seen a neatly packaged one, so I invented my own.

This book in your hands is more than just a book. It's the syllabus for your career with several of the lessons too! Whether you're a middle-school teacher, accountant, salesperson, executive assistant, or chief executive officer, this is a sequenced curriculum you can follow. Whether your highest level of education is a high school diploma, master's degree, or PhD, this curriculum will serve you well.

You, of course, get to take electives not included in this book to build up your specific trade skills. Keep in mind, however, it's my testament your trade-specific skills will take you only so far and yield only so much enjoyment. You will have a greater impact and become more fulfilled with your work and life as you build out the skills I've identified in this book. I know that's a bold statement, but I believe it in my heart. I believe it so much, I took the time to write it all out for you!

Turns out, 133.5 credit hours for that degree
might not have been enough.

While I don't know what your profession is, there's a good chance the beginning of your career started somewhat like mine. I showed up for my first assignment as an information technology consultant. My assignment was to support one of my company's large oil clients.

My supervisor collected me at 8:00 AM. He showed me around a bit. After an hour of getting to know each other, he said, "All good. Now get started writing that software program."

I spent the next handful of months writing software in a language I didn't really understand to handle business functions I certainly didn't understand. While I was doing this, it was apparent to me, to be a success-ful consultant, I'd need to learn a few more skills. I must work effectively with my teammates, listen well, communicate properly, build relationships with my clients, be organized, be efficient, and deliver the programs on time. I apparently forgot to build these skills as I was trying to remember Ohm's Law so I could get my electrical engineering degree so I could get this information technology consulting job so I could help this company build their global purchasing system. *What am I going to do now?*

As a twenty-two-year-old professional, I did what you'd imagine any type-A, eager, rambunctious young person might do. I spent many hours outside the normal business day learning these other skills. It was difficult and painful. To give you an idea of exactly how painful, the year I'm speak-ing of is 1989. Google started in 1998. You don't need my nine semesters of higher math to figure that one out.

Even though I didn't have the world's make-your-life-easy machine to lean on, I considered the time I spent finding the right resources, learning the skills, and practicing them worth every minute. Rather, I considered it time well *invested*, but I don't want it to be painful for you. I also don't want you to waste time working on skills that won't yield the greatest results. That's why I wrote this book for you. The main reason I write books is so, in a matter of hours, people can add all my years of experi-ence to their own.

Three careers, thirty-six years, and a bonus lesson
in fewer than a thousand words....

Since that time as a young professional, I've enjoyed three distinct careers. The first seventeen years, I worked as a management and information technology consultant. During that time, I built consulting organizations and counseled more than 150 different companies across a wide range of industries.

Much like I described earlier in the book, you can only solve so many business process- and system-related issues before you come to the reali-zation there's more to life. While I was good at my job, like the saying goes, "Just because you can, doesn't mean you should."

I like to say, "Don't let what you can do prevent you from doing what you were meant to do."

**Don't let what you can do prevent you from doing
what you were meant to do.**

As much as I enjoyed helping companies solve their business problems, I love helping people grow much more. I decided it was time to seek a new career that enabled me to leverage the skills I'd already built to focus more on helping people.

While I wanted to make a drastic change, I knew I could get on a new track faster if I leveraged the skills and experiences I already gained and applied them to what people needed. I knew how to consult to organizations, sell business services, and had a host of other abilities that would easily transfer to help me build my new career. I also knew how to perform many of the employee roles companies needed to support their businesses because I performed them as a consultant. Naturally, this led me to open an executive recruiting company even though, at that point in my career, I never recruited a single day in my life.

What appeared to be a drastic career change required nothing more than learning a bit about a trade skill—recruiting. After all, I already knew how to market, sell, consult, build relationships, interview, and hire people. As you've probably discovered throughout your career, it's easier to learn the "trade" than the "traits."

To make the marketing of my new company easier, I channeled the sentiment of my previous experience into my new company's name—milewalk®. I have walked a mile in your shoes. This connotation connected well with the client companies I'd support and the job candidates I'd recruit.

My new business and career allowed me to help individuals secure better-suited jobs for themselves. It also allowed me to make a successful, faster transition by leveraging my business skills. It was also the right, next-best step to take on my journey to help more people.

Before we get to the current chapter of my life, I want to pause to share a quick lesson. I offer this lesson to you now because I believe it's not only vital to your long-term career success, but will also serve you well in implementing the principles and tactics in this book.

One of the biggest mistakes I see people make in their careers is thinking short-term. The longer-term you think, the better short-term decisions you'll make. The longer-term you think, the less risk involved in your short-term decision. That is, you'll have a much greater chance of succeeding in any effort the more time you give yourself to reach your goal. Please don't misunderstand my message. I hope you think big and work hard to get there because anything worth having will take a lot of time and hard work.

The biggest issue for most people is they want everything instantaneously. *If I can't get my delivery today, it's bad customer service! Why is my annual salary not $100,000? Why am I not a director yet?*

Thanks to the advancement in technology, we've been able to make great leaps. Thanks to the advancement in technology, we've also been able to airbrush our Instagram-style lives. What you see from your friends, not to mention advertisers, are their highlight reels. These rose-colored lenses not only give you a distorted view of reality, but also cause you to question your own progress in life. Your inside, real-life scenes are no match for public highlight reels.

When you come to the realization short-term pleasure will never beat long-term happiness, you'll be equipped, mentally, to build the right habits that yield long-term results. You are the long-term byproduct of your short-term decisions and acts. Nothing will ever undermine your long-term success more than your need for short-term results.

You are the long-term byproduct of your short-term decisions and acts. Nothing will ever undermine your long-term success more than your need for short-term results.

When I coach people, I teach them not to revisit their long-term plans when they're encountering short-term pain. That's not the time to be changing your goals. That's the moment to keep pushing through. This leads me to my current career and the evolution of it over the past decade.

In 2015, twelve years into my recruitment profession, I decided it was time to augment the milewalk® business to support individuals in their career development. In addition to helping organizations find the best employees, I'd also serve individuals in finding the right jobs and thriving in them.

I knew this new business-to-consumer offering would take time to build because providing premium services to individuals in addition to companies would require a completely different marketing, sales, and support strategy.

Since I started my international, online career coaching business, my team and I have supported more than 100,000 individuals in nearly 200 countries across the world. In addition to supporting these people through my training programs, I also meet one-on-one with and coach approximately 500 people each year.

I share a bit of my story so you know where I've gained experience to enable me to draw the conclusions I used to develop the skill-building approach in this book.

Before you start the car, make sure you know
the fastest and safest route.

As I've evolved in my consulting, recruitment, and coaching careers, I've noticed a common theme among the most successful, happy, and rewarded (by their company) people. Their successes were not solely about how well they knew their specific trade skills or performed their particular jobs. Their successes were much more about how they thought and processed the world.

I also observed there is an array of skillsets that, once learned, will have a more compounding effect over time. If you develop these skills early in your career, they become easier to maintain over time and accelerate your ability to develop higher-level skills.

Additionally, there are foundational skills, which are prerequisites to becoming an effective teacher and manager of others. Turns out, the instruction you get from flight attendants is applicable in other areas of your life. "Put your oxygen mask on first before helping others" isn't just a rule to apply at an altitude of 36,000 feet.

Furthermore, just because you know how to do your job well doesn't mean you'll be able to teach it to others. There are additional processes and communication skills that make a great coach a great coach.

It's unclear to most professionals which skills to develop, when to develop them, how to develop them, and where to get good instruction as they navigate their careers. This issue drove me to design and encapsulate the answers to these questions.

As a result, I simplified this ambiguous developmental issue into a universal, professional learning process which includes an easy-to-follow inventory of skills and systematic approach to building them. That's what my entire skill-building methodology is about—learning the right skills first, practicing them, and widening their use onto your way to making a tremendous, positive impact on people, your company, and this entire world. Your results are also what will lead you to become a standout professional.

My methodology covers five tiers so you can organize your developmental process by identifying the right skills to learn, practice, and track. This framework is intended to provide you with a guideline, not serve as an absolute structure.

You will find, irrespective of your profession or current level of development, the skillsets will, in large part, be applicable to you.

- **Producer: Operating Independently (Tier 1)**: Becoming proficient at managing oneself and delivering outputs of value.
- **Communicator: Interacting with Others (Tier 2)**: Learning behaviors and using communication vehicles to build powerful relationships.
- **Influencer: Inspiring Others. (Tier 3)**: Using communication vehicles to deploy logical and emotional tactics to inspire positive behavior in others.
- **Developer: Leading Teams and Coaching People (Tier 4)**: Motivating and guiding a team or individual to achieve their desired outcomes.
- **Visionary: Creating and Predicting (Tier 5)**: Using expertise to create and implement market-moving ideas and predict trends.

Producer: Operating Independently (Tier 1)

The first tier is about becoming proficient at managing oneself and delivering outputs of value. If you get your own house in order, it will be a lot easier to produce results and help others.

You might think operating independently, being "Tier 1," will be the easiest tier. After all, you simply need to manage you. The good news is building these skills does only require you. That means you can learn, build, and practice them on your own timeline without needing to engage others.

The flipside is the skills required to *effectively* operate independently generally take the longest time to develop, need constant attention, and require the most practice.

While there are a wide range of skills that will help you become proficient at operating independently, the ones I recommend developing here are **focus**, **integrity**, **habits**, **willpower**, **energy**, **confidence**, **planning**, **decision making**, **goal setting**, **productivity**, **patience**, and **self-awareness**.

Within this tier and the others, there will certainly be variations of skills and residual benefits you'll realize once you develop these skills. For example, to me, when you build great habits, you'll also become more disciplined and consistent. You'll also become more reliable, accountable, and credible.

Communicator: Interacting with Others (Tier 2)

The second tier, Communicator, is about learning behaviors and using communication vehicles to build powerful relationships with others. We live in a world of people and that will never change. You need to be effective at interacting with others!

Unlike the Producer tier, building the skills in this tier inherently requires other people. Becoming a great communicator will also involve extensive practice with communicating skills across mediums and situations. This variability among situations means becoming adept will require many trials and errors. By that nature, this tier will require extensive calendar time for you to develop. It's something that will take years rather than weeks or months.

The skillsets I recommend building in this tier are **empathy**, **listening**, **speaking**, **writing**, **storytelling**, **building trust**, **building relationships**, and **reaction**.

Influencer: Inspiring Others (Tier 3)

The third tier, Influencer, is about using communication vehicles to deploy logical and emotional tactics to inspire positive behavior in others. The world doesn't change by itself. You can be the change agent!

Becoming the Communicator, as I outlined in Tier 2, is about communicating with the intent of building strong relationships. The communication required to do that is much simpler than when the goal is to persuade, influence, direct, and inspire others as it is in this tier.

To inspire and influence effectively, you'll need time to develop your subject matter expertise, communication skills, and an understanding of what drives others. This also involves an extensive level of grit, willingness to go against the grain, self-awareness, and authenticity.

The skillsets I recommend building in this tier are **mastering your trade** (your career trade skill), **influence**, **persuasion**, **crafting compelling messages**, **presentation**, **collaboration**, **facilitation**, **negotiation**, **networking**, and **perseverance**.

Being influential requires a great deal of subject matter expertise and credibility related to that knowledge. It's not solely about being persuasive. There are precursors to develop that enable you to be persuasive. Any activities you can perform or skills you can develop in that regard will work to your benefit.

Developer: Leading Teams and Others (Tier 4)

The fourth tier, Developer, is about motivating and guiding a team or individual to achieve a desired outcome. Leaders build more leaders, not more followers.

This tier requires time to observe and interact with many different types of people. You'll also need experience evaluating others' responses and an understanding of human behavior. Organization, planning, and feedback skills are critically important.

The skillsets I recommend building in this tier are **hiring**, **team building**, **managing people**, **delegating**, **motivating people**, **coaching**, **promoting culture**, **managing change**, **resolving conflict**, and **managing risk**.

You're likely getting a sense by now how you're expanding skills you've built in previous tiers to accomplish the goals in the higher tiers. As an example, in this tier, you're augmenting communication skills you developed in the second tier to accomplish a greater purpose of leading.

Visionary: Creating and Predicting (Tier 5)

The fifth tier, Visionary, is about using expertise to create and implement market-moving ideas and predict trends.

This tier requires deep subject matter expertise and experience. You can build creativity over time through observation, critical thinking, and using a structured design to develop innovative ideas. Based on your extensive experience, you'll be able to spot trends, foresee patterns, and predict future results.

The skillsets I recommend building in this tier are **strategy development**, **idea generation**, **creativity**, **forecasting**, and **prediction**.

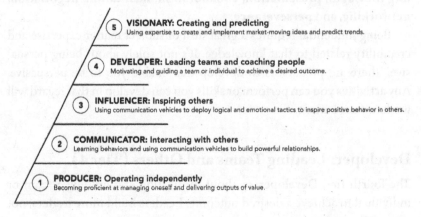

Let's make this a hit and cut it down to 3:05.

If you add up all the skills I suggested across those five tiers, you'll notice there are forty-five! Of course, you and I might have varied interpretations of the skills or add a few here and there. Based on your profession, of course, some skills will be more vital to learn than others.

The skills I cited are ones I feel are necessary and will provide the greatest return for your investment. I also consider them to be universal across professions. For our purposes, I want these example skills to offer context into how you might develop and practice your skill building as you rise up the tiers.

My goal in this book is to offer you a way to organize your career development, build a plan, and make it your own based on your ambitions and goals. You can use my defined tiers and suggested forty-five skills as a career skill-building syllabus for your professional growth. You can pick and choose which "subjects and classes" you want to attend!

As much as I'd love to give you a book that's one giant opus of the forty-five lessons, I'm taking my cue from Billy Joel's song "The Entertainer." In this song, as he sings a satirical take on music fame and pokes fun at the trimming of his 5:40-album version of his song "Piano Man" to the 3:05-version that was played on the radio. Not to mention, but I will, my book publisher who put me on a word count. Kudos to them for being kind enough to let me choose the songs that made this album!

I challenged myself to make this book a hit for you by selecting fifteen lessons I consider most-universally impactful. I chose lessons that offer you the greatest return for the time you invest in learning and building them. If you enjoy these, you can chase me down to get the entire opus, which is in the library of my Leadership Coaching Program. Those additional lessons include videos, workbooks, and implementation challenges!

Reflecting the pyramid shape of the framework, I included five lessons from the Producer Tier, four from the Communicator Tier, three from the Influencer Tier, two from the Developer Tier, and one from the Visionary Tier. These fifteen lessons are some of my favorites and will be applicable to all professionals. Let's start climbing!

Generating Creative Ideas

Coaching and Mentoring
Delegating

Crafting Compelling Messages
Inspiring with Your Personal Story
Mastering Your Trade

Developing Empathy
Building Trust
Networking
Communicating

Focusing
Developing Self-Awareness
Forming Habits
Planning and Running Your Day
Building Confidence

PART THREE

The Producer

CHAPTER 4

Focusing

*Every time my second-grade teacher, Mrs. Jackson, told me to
"focus," I wondered, "Did I miss that lesson?"*

Let's start with the most essential skill you need to build—focus. One
could argue, this is the singular best skill to develop first because you
need it to build any other skill. No matter what else you do, see, think, feel,
or observe, it wouldn't make any difference anyway, because you wouldn't
be able to experience it fully without being able to focus!

Have you ever been taught to focus? Let me guess. You've been *told* to
focus. You've been *told* to concentrate.

Are you a parent? Have you *told* your child to focus? (It's okay to
laugh.) You have? Have you ever taught your child *how* to focus? Why
would you be upset when they fail miserably at your request?

Let's face it, we all have challenges focusing. It starts with not being
taught how to concentrate. It became more difficult over the years as you
accumulated more responsibilities at work and in your life. Managing
more departments and handling more children, while enjoyable, makes
focusing harder. The four dogs I'm trying to calm down as I write these
words make it difficult to meet my daily word quota.

Then, of course, your ability to focus was completely obliterated once
the iPhone and other hand-held computers which we also use to make
phone calls were invented.

Not only do these devices make us more susceptible to interruptions that make it more difficult to focus, they also make it easy for us to practice distraction! I assure you, you will get "better" at whatever you practice. Most people practice distraction all day every day as they glance at the nonstop bubbles, beeps, and vibrations their so-called phones deliver. You're probably an ace at distraction and can write your very own book about it! (Let me know if you want me to introduce you to my publisher.)

How can we overcome this bubble-popping, perpetual-alert-seeking world we've come to "love" so we can actually focus on what matters to us most?

Whether you're fighting the everyday demands of prioritizing your business or trying to avoid that salacious social media or mentally assembling what "really happened" on that media newscast, you need a plan. Because the challenge of focusing is so difficult these days, you need a plan and an entire lifestyle that enables you to work on your plan.

Turning off your phone alerts is a nice tactic, but it's futile if it'll give you anxiety as you maintain the urge to check your social media just to make sure nothing interesting is happening while you're trying to write that email. Furthermore, distractions, and our genuine priorities, come from every direction, not solely our phones or computers.

Imagine you're trying to lose weight. You could take a step in the right direction by eating two or three healthy meals each day. This might help you drop a few pounds over the course of a week, especially if you were previously eating unhealthy foods. To keep the weight off, however, requires an entire approach that includes exercising, grocery shopping, allocating time to cook the meals, and a number of other measures. It takes an entire "lifestyle system" to lose the weight and keep it off.

Focusing requires an analogous lifestyle system. If you want to be present and live in the time zone you're actually standing in as opposed to the past and future time zones most people "live" in, it requires an entirely focused lifestyle.

If you want to be present and live in the time zone you're actually standing in as opposed to the past and future time zones most people "live" in, it requires an entirely focused lifestyle.

Many people I've encountered have set up their lives so they're filled with activities and people and responsibilities that aren't even their highest priorities! Can you imagine how difficult it is to stay focused and enjoy yourself when you're spending much of your time in places you don't want to be, with people you don't want to be with, doing activities you don't want to do, in an environment that doesn't allow you to concentrate?

Pick a letter, any letter, and I'll whip you up a system.

The good news is you can build an entire lifestyle system which enables you to focus. I built my own using what I call the 3Ps: perspective, priorities, and practice. These are the centerpieces upon which all my other mini-systems are built.

I start with the highest priorities in my life first and work my way down to the daily activities that relate to them. This entire structure and the steps I take throughout each day are designed to support my ability to concentrate at any moment, on any activity (alone or with others), in any environment. I've built it so these habits become fully integrated into my life.

While you read this, you might be thinking, *Andy, this is complicated. How do you remember it all?* You'll realize, once you integrate a similar approach into your life, it becomes automatic the more frequently you practice it. The best part is there are checks and reviews embodied within these habits to help keep you on track. Speaking of track....

Another way of thinking about this system is to consider a world-class track athlete. Perhaps she runs the 100-meter dash in the Olympics. This takes her a little more than ten seconds. Imagine the lifestyle system she must have so on race day, in those ten seconds, she can run her fastest. She thinks, eats, sleeps, breathes, and practices every day with these thoughts in mind. Everything in her life literally revolves around preparing her for those ten seconds.

My focused lifestyle system is designed to help me concentrate on whatever it is, whenever it is, wherever it is. You can very easily build a system like this for yourself. Here's how I use each of the 3Ps to focus.

1. Perspective

Let's start at the beginning by taking stock of all the wonderful things in your life. Life can always be better, but it most likely can be much worse.

It's impossible to be grateful and stressed in the same moment.

I've often said it's impossible to be grateful and stressed in the same moment. If you believe me, it would stand to reason, the more frequently you're grateful, the less opportunity there is to be stressed.

As part of my focused lifestyle system, I spend a few moments each morning jotting down those grateful thoughts in my journal. That tiny bit of reflection and thanks pays great dividends because I'm constantly reminding myself of what I have. It's much harder to lose perspective when you're constantly telling yourself how great you have it.

You might think something like taking five minutes each day to write down what you're grateful for is a banal platitude. It's not only a great exercise, but it has a couple of additional benefits.

First, it'll help you intercept your likely-harried thoughts. Most people I know rush through their morning, rush through their shower, rush through their commute, rush through their emails, and so on and so forth until they arrive at work uptight and stressed. Give yourself these few moments to relax.

Second, this exercise offers you a great "warm-up" routine. Routines are the lifeblood of my day. They keep me, my mindset, body, outlook, attitude, and everything else that makes me tick consistent. Consider this opportunity for practicing gratitude a warm-up routine for your entire day. It's practicing before your activities so as you tackle them, you embrace them with grace.

2. Priorities

Priorities determine your focus regardless of whether they're work-related or personal acts. If your priorities aren't in order, that usually means you're focusing on something that isn't truly important to you. This makes it more difficult to remain interested and motivated, which, in turn, makes it more difficult to concentrate and has a way of getting you stressed.

I, like you, want to live a fulfilled life where I'm focusing on the things that matter most. The reasons for this, in general, are obvious, but there are also wonderful extensions to this. When we're engaged in what we want and love, it's much easier to be enthused and enhances our ability to focus.

To help me keep my priorities in order, I continually review what I call my 5Fs and 4-ITYs. These two mini-systems help me keep the main things the main things. My top priorities in life each start with the letter F. I have five of them and I hold onto them for dear life because nothing is more important to me. They are:

1. Family/Friends (Relationships)
2. Fitness (Health)
3. Finances (Money)
4. Faith (Spirit, Soul, Religion)
5. Freedom (Choice)

I don't think my list is overly scientific. You can make your own and call them whatever you want. There are a few important things to remember about priorities. No matter who you are or what you do, your priorities and my priorities probably overlap a bit if not in full. The biggest difference between the happy and successful people versus the ones who are miserable lies in their abilities to keep their priorities in order.

Once you have your priorities in order, they can get out of whack if you don't have a means (i.e., mini-system, getting the hang of this?) to keep them in order. Most everything in your adult life is a choice. I say most everything because I understand circumstances contribute to the path on which you started. For the large part, however, you manage your "yes I wills" and "no I won'ts." Whether it's your job, marriage, dinner with friends, or any other request, invitation, or ambition you have, you control it.

Unfortunately, many people feel like their lives are filled with obligations, not choices. What's worse, you'll become more stressed by the requests or goals you say "yes" to than the ones you simply avoid. I certainly don't want you to say "no" to every opportunity that comes your way. I want you to be fulfilled and happy. That requires inviting and accepting the right people, goals, and commitments into your life. With so many opportunities (eh, demands) available to us, we need a mini-system to regulate the right-for-me versus wrong-for-me or not-right-at-this-moment-for-me ones.

I use a technique with 4-ITYs. It's my quick way to double check whether this is something I should invite into my life.

- Identity (for me): Is it meaningful to me? Will this excite me? Am I passionate about it?
- Community (for us): Will this help me with others? Will this give me a chance to support others?
- Ability (for me): Will this build a skill or help me grow in an area that's really important to me and vital for my success?
- Necessity (for us): Is there a true need for this? Will it serve others and the world?

3. Practice

Once you're living your life in alignment with your highest priorities, it's easier to stay on track. Even so, it does take a lot of practice. Thus far, you've likely been practicing how to be distracted by the incredibly unimportant acts of other people's lives and the beeps on your phone.

It's helpful if you have an approach to help you focus on your priorities. When I say "approach," I mean an all-day, every-day way to go through your day so you can focus, work on what's important to you, and set boundaries for all the areas that generally interrupt your ability to complete whatever deliverable you're working on at any moment.

As an employee and business owner, I've worked in various environments. I've also performed a wide array of activities. When I was an employee, I had meetings, deliverables, presentations, and emails and a similar spectrum like you probably, uh, enjoy.

In my current profession as an international career and leadership coach, I build online training programs and market, sell, and service them. Additionally, I teach lessons via live shows on my YouTube channel, conduct one-to-one coaching sessions, create videos, record podcasts, write emails to build relationships and educate the people in my community, speak at events, and a host of other activities all aimed at running a successful business. With the exception of speaking engagements, I do all of these activities every week! If my days aren't completely dialed in, the work doesn't get done well.

Whether I'm working in a corporate office, my home, or a hotel room, I've noticed there are crucial times throughout each day that provide the best opportunities to ensure my entire day goes well, help avoid unnecessary stress, and ensure I focus on what I'm doing at any moment. Let's run through them and, as always, adjust these based on how you manage your day.

Plan Your Next Day the Night Before

Taking a few minutes at the end of your workday to plan your next day is one of the most important steps you can take to be focused the next day. This enables you to unload your thoughts and ideas so you don't carry them with you into the evening and into your bed.

Our conscious mind is like the RAM of a computer. You can only hold so many thoughts in your short-term memory. The more thoughts you have rattling around, the more you rob yourself of the energy you need to focus and concentrate.

When I plan my next day, I never use a to-do list. I plan all my activities and deliverables according to time. That is, to stay on track, the calendar is your very best friend. A list of activities with no relationship to deadlines (very short-term deadlines that is) is your worst enemy when it comes to production. When you plan your activities and deliverables in your daily timeslots, you'll know what to work on, when to work on it, and what to produce. We'll cover much more related to planning and running an effective day later in the book.

Warm up Before Your Day Starts

If you've ever watched people warm up "before their games," you'll notice them practicing movements in an ideal setting. Whether they're professional golfers on the driving range before their rounds or football players running pass routes on the field, they go through their routines to remind their bodies of ideal movements. This helps them perform better when the competition actually starts. Whenever I start a swimming workout, for example, I use tools such as a snorkel and pull buoy during my first four to eight laps. These aids make it easier for me to keep my body in the proper position. They help remind me of how my body should feel during my workout so I'm practicing effectively.

If warming up properly for sports activities makes sense, wouldn't it stand to reason if you want to focus throughout your day, it would be helpful to practice focusing in an ideal setting before you start "your competition?" After all, you're about to embark on a full day of work, distractions, and demands. It would be nice to remind yourself how to focus by doing it for a few minutes when you're least likely to be distracted.

Each morning, I spend ten minutes practicing my focus. I literally concentrate for ten straight minutes. It makes no difference what you concentrate on. I, for example, focus on moving energy throughout my entire body. I know people who focus only on their breathing or a loved one's face. Just pick something to concentrate on and then try to hold your focus for as long as you can. This might sound easy, but try doing it right now for sixty seconds. I'll bet a dozen different thoughts race through your head during that time. Trim that down to one thought and then move on to try it for two minutes. Remember, practice makes permanent, so keep at it.

Consider Your Perfect and Not-So-Perfect Day

After I practice focusing, I like to think about my entire upcoming day. That is, I like to consider what my ideal day will look and feel like.

Each one of my days is filled with some form of writing or communicating, working with groups of people, and working with individuals. I think about deliverables I need to create and what I want them to look like. I think about the people I'll be interacting with and what they might be going through and what it must feel like to need my help.

We all know not everything goes according to plan. That's why I also spend a few minutes anticipating any bumps that might occur throughout my day. For example, I might not get the deliverable done or someone might interrupt me while I'm working on something. Perhaps I don't get the response I'm hoping for from a client. I don't do this in a self-fulfilling prophecy sort of way. I do it so I can consider how my highest self would handle any curveballs. If you've given some forethought to the possibility something can go wrong, you'll be amazed how much better you handle it when it actually does.

The point here is simply to envision what an ideal day looks like. I spend less than five minutes doing this, but it's my last "warm-up" before go time!

Use Willpower Throughout Your Day

That morning focus practice, which was probably excruciating at first, will be your best chance to build your focus muscles without any distractions. Now, you get to work on focusing throughout your day.

To help you focus "during your game," you'll need willpower. The dictionary definition of willpower is to exert control to do something or restrain impulses. Most of the time, your impulse is to want to look at something else such as your phone. *What was that beep?* You need to control yourself so you don't.

The good news is you can build willpower at any time and place doing anything. There is no shortage of opportunities to practice and build it. Even better, you can build willpower using a very simple-to-understand (yet hard-to-execute) formula. There are three "easy" steps:

- Finish what you start.
- Do it a little better than you expected.
- Do a little more than you initially intended.

As you go through your day, work everything you do from start to finish and overcomplete it if possible. The more frequently you're able to do this, the stronger your willpower and focus will grow. Try to do this for everything at work and at home.

Take Advantage of the Transitions Between Tasks

If your day is anything like mine, you transition between tasks several times. There is the morning commute. Review the emails. Go to the meeting. Get on the telephone for a conference call. Write the white paper. Go to another meeting. Get on yet another Zoom session.

We all accumulate a lot of stress throughout the day, even if we absolutely love what we're doing. Right now, this very moment as I type these words, I'm sitting on my Swiss ball, pecking away at the keyboard, looking at a twenty-seven-inch monitor, and smiling. I love this portion of my day. Even so, I'm accumulating stress in my rump, fingertips, and forearms. In an hour, I'll stop writing and conduct a video coaching session with someone in Saudi Arabia. I love it all!

If I simply stop typing and jump straightaway into the video coaching session, I won't give myself the opportunity to let go of the stress I accumulated in the past hour or refresh myself or my focus for the upcoming coaching session. Now, imagine doing that type of quick transition again and again throughout the day.

I use my transitions as golden opportunities to not only let go of stress, but also set myself up for success in the next task. Here's exactly what I do each time I transition throughout the day:

- Mentally and physically "pack up" what I was just doing and notate where I was in the task so I can quickly restart it next time.
- Take a few deep breaths and perhaps close my eyes, especially if I was staring at the monitor for an extended period of time.
- Let go of the tension in my body by stretching, rolling my neck, or walking up and down the stairs a few times.
- Reflect very quickly to remind myself I just did something valuable.
- Think forward to my next task and what I want to happen.

That might look like a lot, but it only takes five minutes. Isn't it worth five minutes every sixty minutes to keep yourself refreshed and focused throughout the long workday?

Reflect at the End of Your Day

I genuinely believe no matter how successful you are, you'll never feel successful unless you reflect. That's because ambitious people generally look at how much further they need to go instead of how far they've progressed. How else will you know how far you've come if you don't stop for a moment and look back?

We started this process with planning your next day the night before. While you're planning tomorrow, I recommend spending a few minutes reviewing today. Ask yourself a few reflection questions:

- What went well?
- What did I learn?
- Was there anything I did for the very first time?
- What happened today that I'm grateful for?

There are a host of wonderful questions to ask yourself at the end of each day. The most important point is to stop for a few moments, actually ask yourself these questions to appreciate the gift that was this day. Remind yourself of your victories. The purpose of reflection is to make you feel good about yourself and more confident in your ability to grow.

Practice makes permanent, so let's get this right.

At the end of each lesson, I'll include a few thought-provoking statements for you to complete and questions for you to answer. These will help you reflect on your current situation and serve as a starting point to build or improve the skills I outline in each lesson.

After the thought-provokers, you'll find action items, generally in the form of a "challenge," so you can apply the tactics. These challenges are meant to get you heading in the right direction. To truly build and ingrain your skills and benefit from the improvements you're making, you need to keep the momentum going.

As you go through the exercises, I recommend keeping a journal or using whatever tool you prefer to capture your notes. I find it most effective to take the time, consider each question, and write out your thoughts. There is a greater level of connection when you write as opposed to type.

Lastly, it's my hope you'll refer back to these lessons and exercises whenever you need them. I often find myself reviewing my own lessons whenever I feel I'm getting away from my routines and best practices!

FOCUSING EXERCISE

Thought-Provokers

1. The biggest area(s) in my life I need to start giving more attention and focus to is/are...

2. The first thing I can do when I roll out of bed in the morning to practice focusing is...

3. The greatest distraction in my life that prevents me from focusing is...

4. The activities, people, and obligations in my life that prevent me from focusing on the most important areas in my life are...

5. The activities I'll do daily to "slow my life down" so I can focus more on the most important areas in my life are...

Challenge

Week One: Practice focusing on a singular object, image, or thought for five minutes each day. Find a quiet spot in your house, close your eyes, and focus. You'll get distracted and this will feel incredibly difficult at first. That's because you've likely been practicing not focusing for a long time. You won't be perfect in one try. When you get distracted by another thought, don't fight it. Let it pass and move your attention to your breath and then back to your focal point. If you solely want to focus on your breath, that works well too.

Week Two: Continue the week one exercise. Additionally, throughout your day, **select a home-based activity** you can focus on, from beginning to end, without getting distracted. It can be making your bed, doing the dishes, folding the laundry, or anything you do (by yourself) around the house. Regardless of what it is, the challenge is to focus your thoughts only on that household activity while you're doing it.

Week Three: Continue the challenges from weeks one and two. Now, **select a person** you'll focus on each day. This can be a spouse, child, parent, significant other, or coworker. You need to interact directly with the person on the phone, video call, or in person and completely focus on that specific discussion. It's preferable if the discussion is a reasonable length such as ten minutes or longer.

Focusing

Week Four: Continue the challenges from weeks one through three. Now, select a **work activity which takes at least fifteen minutes**. Do that activity with complete focus. This can be the same activity each day or a different one each day. Pay attention to how many times your mind wanders. Try to reduce the number as the days go on.

47

CHAPTER 5

Developing Self-Awareness

When you put on a mask, you're acting, not being.

Self-awareness, according to just about any dictionary, has to do with having conscious knowledge of one's own character and feelings. You might naturally think this cognizance is a state of mindfulness as opposed to a skill that can be developed and practiced.

Self-awareness, however, is a centerpiece to happiness because it feeds your ability to make choices that are congruent with what you like and need. The more congruent your choice with your natural state of being, the happier you'll be. It's that simple.

What complicates this should-be-simple life is the rest of the world doing its level best to throw you off, well, you. The rest-of-the-world can be Mom, Dad, your bestie, your boss, or anyone else you spend a lot or a little time with. That includes, but is not limited to, Instagram and TikTok, two so-called authorities on what's considered desired behavior.

With all these impediments to your most in-sync behavior, it's helpful to get a firm grasp on your essentials in life. These essentials, your most truly desired wants and needs, will help you properly evaluate your life choices. Oddly, this is not something that comes easily for most people primarily because of the ever-present "obstacles" that surround us.

In addition to knowing your essentials, it's helpful to develop a process so you can assess whether your career and life choices will actually fit you versus what you might (incorrectly) think will fit you. You might think you know you and are self-aware, but do you truly know you?

This concept of self-awareness is so complex even the experts, who earned this moniker through their teachings, cannot agree on a singular definition.

Daniel Goleman, who popularized the expression "emotional intelligence" in his book *Emotional Intelligence: Why It Can Matter More Than IQ*, believes it's knowing one's strengths, weaknesses, drives, values, and impact on others.

Experimental social psychologists Shelley Duval and Robert Wicklund, who developed the self-awareness theory in 1972, consider it the ability to focus on yourself and recognizing how your actions, thoughts, or emotions do or don't align with your internal standards.

More recently, Tasha Eurich, author of *Insight: The Surprising Truth About How Others See Us, How We See Ourselves, and Why the Answers Matter More Than We Think*, considers self-awareness to be the will and skill to understand yourself and how others see you.

I think all of these are accurate, but to truly understand self-awareness, become more adept at it, and benefit from it, we need to break it down to its lowest levels.

Is it better to look good or feel good?

First, it's helpful to understand self-awareness comes in different forms. It's not solely about our ability to be mindful, internally, of our actions. All the experts I cited agree, as would I, there are internal and external aspects of self-awareness.

Internally, self-awareness relates to how well we see our own values, virtues, and interests and fit into our environment. Individuals with strong internal self-awareness tend to have high job and relationship satisfaction and are generally happy with low stress levels. That's because these people know what they like and choose careers and personal relationships that truly satisfy their needs.

Externally, self-awareness relates to how accurately we assess how others see us. As you might have guessed, people with strong external self-awareness tend to be high in empathy and perspective. That's because when you have a good handle on how other people think (about you or anything else), it's much easier to be considerate of their thoughts and feelings.

Additionally (according to studies done by Tasha Eurich), you can be internally but not externally self-aware and vice versa.

Let's take a look at how you can develop internal and external self-awareness.

I can even make formulas for touchy-feely stuff.

When it comes to building internal self-awareness, much like we discussed when building your ability to focus, there is an overarching environment and lifestyle you can establish to enable success. It starts with the major aspects of your life and putting them into place so your everyday, walking-around thinking is completely in sync with your behavior.

I consider these six areas vital success factors: 1) Personal protocols, 2) Loves, passions, interests, 3) Goals, 4) Operating environment, 5) Thoughts, and 6) Behaviors.

1. Personal Protocols

If you want to build self-awareness, it's helpful to start with what's important to you and how you will behave toward and care for what's important to you. It's much easier to be happy and perform well when our behavior is congruent with our major wants and needs. I call these major desires, by which I govern my life, personal protocols.

These might go by different names for you, but whether they are written or unwritten, everyone has a list of protocols, values, or tenets they live by.

Corporations have them too. They often call them their cultural values (or traits), guiding principles, or some other moniker of that nature.

Ben Franklin had his famous list of thirteen virtues by which he operated his life. He was so diligent with these, he literally graded himself, on a daily basis, by how well he adhered to them.

Michael Hyatt and Daniel Harkavy in their book *Living Forward: A Proven Plan to Stop Drifting and Get the Life You Want*, used the term "life accounts." They identified nine life accounts and classified them as spiritual, marital, vocational, intellectual, social, financial, physical, parental, and avocational.

People who are explicit about their protocols generally stay in alignment with them. They live more fulfilled lives and tend to manage stress well. They frequently "check in with themselves" to ensure their decisions related to these protocols coincide with their values. Conversely, people who lack internal self-awareness tend to make decisions inconsistent with their protocols. As a career coach, I often hear people say, "The money was so good, I figured I should just take the job." Then, six months into their employment, they wonder why they're unhappy. Ultimately, it comes down to not being thoughtful and congruent with what they needed in a job to make them happy.

Have you ever considered the values by which you want to live your life? Most people I've coached think they know what's important to them, but aren't as explicit as they'd like to be. They also, by their own admission, aren't as diligent in reviewing how they fare in these areas. A major step you can take toward being internally self-aware when it comes to your personal protocols is to take stock of them frequently to make sure they align with where you want them to be!

2. Loves, Passions, Interests

If a large part of being internally self-aware means we are fitting well into our environment, it's important we're spending the bulk of our time in areas we love. After all, it's much easier to enjoy life when we're doing something we love.

While one of your personal protocols might be your vocation, as an example, your love of your career or job (or lack thereof) will contribute greatly to your happiness (or unhappiness).

I'm sure I wouldn't get much argument when I say most people spend the bulk of their lives working, with family, or doing their hobbies. Stripped down, that's where 90 percent of our time is spent. Life gets a lot easier when your interests fit into, if not become a major part of, the areas where you spend the bulk of your time. Conversely, if you spend significant time in areas that are unimportant to you, you'll be stressed out far more frequently than you care to be.

This success factor turns out to be quite a vital aspect of remaining self-aware because, if pursued, it helps us remain congruent in our life by connecting our efforts such as our daily acts and work with our interests, aspirations, and goals.

Alternatively, working in a field you don't love keeps your thoughts and behavior incongruent with your aspirations. What's worse, a person who lacks self-awareness generally spends significant time on aspects of their life they don't truly enjoy—because of how it looks to others! This distracts them from being consistent with who they are and what they want out of life.

3. Goals

I wrote in *Out of Reach but in Sight: Using Goals to Achieve Your Impossible*, "A goal is nothing more than a vehicle to enhance your enjoyment of something you love. The actual attainment of the goal is far less important than the positive impact working toward that goal has on your life." I believe this to my core, which is why I don't waste any time setting goals just to check them off.

Many people establish goals that do nothing but serve as "judges." They now have goals sitting on a list or perhaps their Facebook pages. There it is for all their friends to see. The problem is they constantly look at it or think about it and it has a way of making them feel lousy about the lack of work they're putting in to attain them.

Another way to view a goal is to consider it a facilitator. The pursuit, which facilitates your transformation on your way to achieving a mega goal, will help you grow far more than collecting checkmarks for easily attainable goals.

If you're consistent with setting goals around the things you love, you'll constantly move through life in a congruent manner. This will enable you to be more self-aware and in sync with yourself. This works because people who are internally self-aware know what drives them and tend to choose goals that align to who they are and who they want to become. They have a firm grasp of their capabilities and put themselves in positions to take advantage of their strengths. This is one of the main reasons self-aware people tend to accomplish very high goals.

They have a firm grasp of their capabilities and put themselves in positions to take advantage of their strengths. This is one of the main reasons self-aware people tend to accomplish very high goals.

Conversely, people who are not self-aware tend to put themselves in environments not conducive or aligned to their personal protocols and often don't achieve their goals. These are the situations where people become most at risk for the goal to become a "judge" and cause stress rather than help them with their transformation. This is the exact opposite of self-aware people who focus on the pursuits of their goals (the journey) because their goals support who they are as people.

4. Operating Environment

Putting our personal protocols in order makes it the best first step to keeping our behavior congruent with our values. Establishing the right "operating environment" makes it much easier to be consistent in keeping that behavior congruent.

Your operating environment, in this instance, is a collection of conditions, people, physical spaces, and everything else that goes along with your ability to function. It's the figurative "space" that perpetually surrounds you. It's what determines your ability to fit in and function easily.

If it's not dialed in properly, you might be able to adapt, but typically you're adjusting to behaviors that aren't natural to you. They're not your first inclination and require adaptations that over time will eventually stress you out.

Think for a moment about your relationships, the people you surround yourself with, where you live, the way your house is set up, and your daily routines. Are these essentially all-the-time conditions set up so there is the least amount of resistance and most amount of enjoyment in your life?

Self-aware people are rarely stressed by their daily surroundings. People who lack self-awareness oftentimes finds themselves feeling uneasy in their environments. These environments can range from the big and frequent such as work and home to the small and infrequent such as a dinner party.

5. Thoughts

We have developed automatic thoughts over time thanks to our upbringings, biases, where we've lived, who we surround ourselves with, and anything else that goes along with conditioning the way we think.

When it comes to internal self-awareness and how we think, the question is are the thoughts we have consistent with who we naturally are? Being able to understand how your thoughts are affecting your self-image and relationships is one of the most vital skills in developing self-awareness. I believe our thoughts are a singular success factor and not to be combined with the way we behave because thoughts don't always lead to an associated behavior. People who have a tendency to internalize and ruminate in their thoughts can benefit from becoming mindful of what they're thinking and what triggers them to think that.

I'd also like to add a note of caution to people who internalize extensively. I notice introspective people often ask themselves questions such as, "Why do I do this?" or "Why did this happen?" The act of introspection is good, but this particular approach to introspection doesn't typically lead to the type of answers or transformation people seek. That's because they're asking why they behave the way they do. Looking for the "why" in isolation often doesn't yield the most valuable information which you can act upon and ultimately change.

A more effective way to approach this is to understand what triggers those thoughts in the first place. If you try to detach yourself from the "why" and approach it from the "what" perspective, it helps you become more objective. For instance, instead of asking "Why did this happen?" or "Why am I this way?" you can shift it to "What causes me to feel that way?" or "What is common among those jobs I didn't like?" This will help you get external, more objective, and cite the triggers and environments that cause those thoughts.

Over the years, I've used a simple three-step formula to help me become more aware of my thoughts. I also use this same technique to help me build my empathy, which I'll cover later in the book. This technique essentially puts checkpoints in place to help examine your thinking. It slows down the speed of your thoughts to help you become more mindful, which is necessary because we tend to forget what it's like not to know what we know or believe what we believe.

The three-step formula is simply to anticipate, practice, and reflect on your interactions with others. Previously, in the Technical Set chapter, I shared my routine before I start my weekly live coaching sessions. Before I head into any session, I remind myself the people who are attending need my help. It might sound obvious, but do you think most people actually pause to remind themselves?

I put myself on alert to be gentle and empathetic because they don't know what I know. This is the *anticipating* part. I'm likely going to get similar questions every week. I constantly remind myself that the people who are asking the questions may have recently discovered me. They needed me today. They didn't need me yesterday. I even pause for a quick second during the show before I answer each question. It only takes a few seconds and no one notices but me.

During the interactions, when I'm answering their questions, I focus on *practicing* these same thoughts. It's much easier to do when you've prepared yourself in advance. Then, when the live show is over, I watch it and evaluate, that is *reflect* on, how I performed as it relates to my thoughts, gentleness, and compassion. I think *What would that person think of me, my instruction, and behavior?* I do this not to obsess over the need for someone to like me, but to evaluate what I could control in my teaching and coaching.

The more frequently you practice a routine like this, the more you'll train yourself to become automatic in a positive manner rather than automatic in a biased manner.

6. Behaviors

While I consider thoughts more of an internal factor, I think behavior coincides with what you show the rest of the world. Thoughts are, of course, the thinking part. Behaviors are the doing or saying part.

I often say, "Think. Say. Do. You will never be more at peace than when those three are the same." It's true!

Think. Say. Do. You will never be more at peace than when those three are the same.

When it comes to the doing part, the two most important aspects are whether your behavior is in alignment with your personal protocols and how your behavior affects others.

The first part is a self-evaluation. The second part requires great effort and practice over a lengthy period of time to gain the proper perspective.

With behaviors, much like thoughts, internally self-aware people will use the checkpoints technique to examine their behaviors. Much like I watch my live coaching shows to see how I behaved, self-aware people will take the time to examine their behavior. Those who lack self-awareness typically fly by the seat of their pants.

In addition to the checkpoints technique, you can use a journal to capture your behaviors. The most important "data" to capture, in addition to your behavior, is not how you felt, but the circumstances or events surrounding the behavior. That is, notice what causes you to behave in a particular manner. This is much more like a food diary than a "feelings" diary (e.g., I ate this and this is how my body reacted).

> *It doesn't matter what you think of me.*
> *It matters what I think you think of me.*

We can do a lot to improve our internal self-awareness because we can control the steps. It's entirely up to us. When it comes to improving external self-awareness, however, we'll need a little help from our friends!

External self-awareness relates to how accurately we assess how others see us. The only way we'll know whether we have an accurate picture is to ask them. There are a few problems with asking people their opinions. First, they might not tell us the truth. Second, they might not be accurate. Even so, it's helpful to make the effort.

I recommend starting with people you trust. You can speak with colleagues, friends, and family. If you're lucky, your company might even have a 360-degree feedback process in place. If not, there are various multi-source feedback assessments you can find online.

When you ask for feedback, it's important you ask questions that will yield helpful insight. Here are five of my favorite questions to ask:

- How do I make you feel—about yourself? (Not how do you feel about me.)

- On a scale of one to ten, how consistent am I between my communication and behavior?
- What have I taught you?
- What behavior of mine do you want to build in yourself?
- What behavior have you observed in me you don't want for yourself?

If you love the idea of getting more insight to help develop your external self-awareness, especially as it relates to growing in your career, there are plenty of strength-weakness and alignment-to-corporate-values types of resources. A few I recommend based on my research are Career Assessment Site, Holland RIASEC Model: The Holland Occupational Themes, Personality Pad, and SelfStir.

DEVELOPING SELF-AWARENESS EXERCISE

Thought-Provokers

1. My current, single greatest area of stress in my life is...

2. The three best steps I can take to improve that area of stress are...

3A. The goals I have that are truly worth keeping are...

3B. The goals I have that are unnecessarily stressful are...

4A. The one physical space (room in my house, office, etc.) that causes me the most stress is...

4B. The one step I can take related to that space to lower my stress level would be...

5A. An activity I perform frequently to interact with someone else is...

5B. A few reminders I can use before those interactions to help me become more empathetic are...

Challenge

Week One: Spend time thinking about and getting clear on your **success factors**. Literally write them down. Take the entire first week to get this in order. Life has ups and downs and it's easy for our priorities and behaviors to get a bit out of whack. You can consider the ones I shared such as personal protocols, loves/interests/goals, operating environment (work, social, home), thoughts, and behaviors as a starting point, but make this list your own!

Week Two: Evaluate yourself for each success factor area and build your plan. Now that you have your success factors in order, take stock of how effective and congruent you are in each area. I'll leave the scale to you. You could use a number (one to ten) or qualitative scale (great, okay, not-so-good). The most important step is to determine which areas of your life need the most work to get you in sync with who you want to be.

Week Three: Practice building **internal self-awareness**. As much as I'd love to say, "Just do it better," I know that's impractical when changing any behavior. In this lesson, I highlighted practicing being present and reflecting. From a challenge perspective, I'd like you to focus as much as possible on reflecting each day. Perhaps take a few moments at the end of each workday. Ask yourself, "Was I mindful? Did I focus on the 'whats' versus the 'whys'? Did I reshape the way I looked at situations?"

Week Four: Practice building **external self-awareness**. Get feedback from people you interact with frequently. I'd try to get one person each day. Ask them to provide you with feedback. You can ask the questions I cited in the lesson on practicing external self-awareness, identify your own, or use ones that are part of your corporate evaluation process. The most important factor here is to get the feedback so you can become more conscious of how you're affecting others.

CHAPTER 6

Forming Habits

Success is not a single event, but a great habit developed through the perfect combination of commitment and time.

We need habits to operate our lives. Some people seem to effortlessly create good ones, while others struggle. Don't worry if you're in the latter group. Anyone can build solid, positive habits with the proper formula and effort.

You might be wondering why you need habits in the first place. There are a lot of ways to consider this question, but it's really pretty simple—we are our habits in every sense. Consider yourself for a moment. You are a byproduct of the habits you have and the acts you do every single day. The outcomes of our lives are nothing more than lagging measures of the habits we employ.

The outcomes of our lives are nothing more than lagging measures of the habits we employ.

Habits benefit us not just in a get-things-done or stay-on-track sort of way. Our brains want that automation that comes with habits. If our brains are not on automatic pilot, we get tired. Do you ever get tired when you're traveling? It's not because you're traveling. It's because you're constantly taxing your brain! You're in a hotel room and don't know where the light switch is or how to open the curtains. You need to consciously look for these. You're driving a rental car and you don't know how to turn on the windshield wipers. You're eating in a restaurant you've never eaten before and it seems to have page after page of entrées on the menu. You feel the need to scan every one of them. Your brain is running constantly. Contrast these scenarios with when you're at home. You could probably close your eyes and find your way around because you've developed habits!

Sometimes we want to challenge our brains. Other times we don't. The goal is to design your life with a balance that includes the challenges you want for growth and enjoyment as well as the mini-habits (e.g., car keys in the tray so I don't need to look for them) and major-habits (e.g., diet, exercise regimen) to help you enjoy the process. If this sounds complicated, let's make it simple by starting in the right place.

Start with who, not why.

The best place to start with habits is to choose the ones that most fit the lifestyle you want. It's about who you want to be. Everything we do in our lives feeds our self-image, including our habits. That's why whatever habit we create or goal we set best serves us when it supports *who* we want to be.

Everything we do in our lives feeds our self-image, including our habits. That's why whatever habit we create or goal we set best serves us when it supports *who* we want to be.

This is just like the congruency element we addressed when developing our self-awareness. The more in alignment our habits are with who we want to be, the happier and more fulfilled our lives will be. For example, if who you are is a healthy person, the habits you might imagine setting would center on diet, exercise, sleep, and other aspects that support a healthy lifestyle. You might have a routine where you shop at the grocery store on Wednesdays and Saturdays. If you want to be an organized person, your house is likely clean with a place for everything and everything in its place. I'm sure you get the idea.

Is that a habit, routine, or lifestyle system?

Before we dive into the "here's how" of building great habits, let's talk nomenclature. There are habits, routines, lifestyle systems, practices, and another dozen or so words or expressions people use interchangeably.

61

Technically, there are specific definitions and variations of each of these. Some gurus will argue a habit (car keys on the tray next to the front door) is a mindless, automatic act whereas a routine requires more intention and effort (your daily run or bi-weekly trips to the supermarket). All this is true, and I can spend the next thousand words explaining the differences and nuances, but that would matter little for the purpose of this lesson. To save you the time and me the typing, the crux of my message is I simply want you to develop regimens, automations, and good practices so you can build an enjoyable life. Call these whatever you want as long as you're happy.

Let me introduce you to Habit's best friends.
Here are When, Where, and How-Many.

Before we get to my actual formula for building a habit, it's important to note there are three critical enablers that'll make it much easier: 1) Intention, 2) Frequency and Consistency, and 3) Environment. If you use these enablers to your advantage, the level of effort (or willpower) you'll need to exert to follow through and build your habit drops significantly.

It's also important to note, these three enablers work in conjunction with each other. They are, essentially, all required for the best habit-building results. It's great, for example, if you intend to run at 5:30 PM today, but intention alone might not be enough when 5:30 PM rolls around and you're tired after a long day of work. You might also be transitioning from your office at that time. That means your current environment, which includes your computer with the email inbox open and other distracting work-related cues, could trigger a different behavior.

Consider these three factors the ingredients you need to prepare a high-quality meal. Your cooking technique matters, of course, but what goes into the dish matters equally as much. If you're missing any of the ingredients, the dish doesn't usually turn out as well. Let's look at how these enablers work together to help you build your habits.

Intention

Have you heard the expression, "Name the time and place?" Turns out, that expression is a pretty good one when it comes to building a habit because your intention to do something can help when your motivation to do something wanes. This would stand to reason because anything we do that requires effort starts with our intention to do it.

Peter Gollwitzer, a German professor of psychology at New York University has performed studies regarding the role intention plays in goal attainment. Of course, a habit we want to build or break is effectively a goal we want to achieve. He posits the more intentional we are about doing something, the greater the likelihood we'll actually perform it.

I believe this to be true whether it's a daily habit, few-times-each-week act, or one-time event. I've noticed the most important factors in my success when setting intention are when (time) and where (place). If you want to be a master of intention, you'll take the penultimate step and write it down (see what I did there?).

Gollwitzer distinguishes intentions as they relate to achieving a goal and the implementation of the goal. That is, a goal-based intention is the "what." This is something such as, "I intend to go for a run," or "I intend to run a marathon." An implementation intention is the "where," "when," and/or "how" you'll achieve the goal in the form of a conditional step such as, "When I wake up tomorrow morning, I'll go for my run."

Here's why this works and how it helps when our motivation wanes. I, in fact, do love to run. It's like brushing my teeth, except I do it three times each week for my triathlon training instead of three times each day. Sometimes, I run first thing in the morning. Other times, I run before lunch or dinner. You can imagine I might be tired after a long day of work or even when I wake up in the morning. My motivation isn't always dialed up when my calendar says, "Run at 10:30 AM on the Des Plaines River Trail."

Even so, the commitment to run is triggered by the date I set with myself and where I'm supposed to be. The more specific you are about your intention, the greater the trigger and boost to get you going. As an example, "I will meditate every day at 5 AM" is a good start. "I will meditate every day at 5 AM in my sunroom after I have my cup of Café Du Monde Coffee and Chicory" is the stuff legends are made of.

Frequency and Consistency

In addition to intention, frequency and consistency are equally as important in creating great habits. Frequency is the number of times each day or week you perform the habit. Consistency is the "when" you do it.

As I've worked through my professional and personal habits, I've determined, for me, regularity facilitates the consistency and ease with which I can do something. For example, meditating at 5:00 AM every day will be easier to keep the habit than if I meditated 5:00 AM on Tuesday, 4:00 PM on Wednesday, and so on. When I operate my workday, it's more effective for me to write at 6:00 AM every day than it is to write in the mornings on some days and the afternoons on other days.

Sometimes, especially if you're not performing the habit first thing in the morning, life interrupts your ability to be consistent. What happens if your scheduled 10:30 AM run gets interrupted because your boss decides to have an impromptu meeting? In these cases, at the end of my workday when I plan my schedule for the next day, I use an "if/then" concept for anything I feel is really important to me. This provides me with a backup plan in the event something sidetracks my habit or schedule in any way. For example, if I can't run at 10:30 AM, then I'll move it to 4:00 PM and move my 4:00 PM to the following day. I realize this might not always be possible, but if something is important to you, it's worth spending a few minutes to figure out your contingency plan.

Environment

When building a habit, your environment matters. You need to cue it for what you want; otherwise, it will cue you based on what you're used to. That's because we tend to see our habits in the environment they occur. For example, we become comfortable with the fact we drink in bars with cool lights, music, and football games on the television. Causal smokers tend to want to light up when they're partying with their friends as opposed to when sitting home alone.

When building a habit, your environment matters. You need to cue it for what you want; otherwise, it will cue you based on what you're used to.

If you alter your environment, you can remove the behavioral biases associated with the bad habits or introduce positive ones with the good habits. Changing your environment doesn't mean remodeling your house or office. Your "new" or "cued" environment can be as simple as not putting your cell phone on your nightstand when you sleep. It can mean avoiding the potato chip aisle (my Kryptonite) when you're at the grocery store so the family-size bag doesn't make its way into the cupboard and eventually into your mouth.

The benefit of planning your environment is not limited to what you do or don't do at any given moment. You can set up your environment to cue what you want to happen next. For example, at the end of my workday, I make sure my office desk is set up for the next morning so I can get started quickly. Perhaps you put your running outfit on the chair next to your bed to cue your morning workout. Much like with intention, your environment will help you when your motivation wanes.

Let's get on with a little neuroplasticity!

What's the formula to make your habit stick? It needs to be part of who you are or who you greatly desire to become. Make no mistake, even if it is part of who you are, you're making a change. Any change in your life, especially a drastic one, will require you to rewire your brain. You are ultimately reshaping the way you look at yourself. This is no easy task, but you can do it if you're thoughtful, repetitive, and reflective.

The formula I've used with great success takes four steps:

1. Cue environment: Establish the setup, room, place, or wherever you perform the habit.
2. Do the task: Simply perform it.
3. Reflect: Consider what you did, track it, and think about the positive ripples.
4. Reward yourself: Offer yourself some form of positive reinforcement.

If you follow through with these four steps, and do them repetitively and consistently, you'll be able to build any habit you desire. I do, however, have a word of caution on cutting corners. My guess is you can relate to setting up the proper environment and doing the habit, but I've noticed many people I coach have a tendency to skip the reflecting and rewarding steps. The habit, and, in turn, your new view of you, won't stick without executing those last two steps.

This happens for a few reasons. First, no matter what you've accomplished, you will never feel successful if you don't take the time to reflect. People who are ambitious tend to look forward and dwell on where they are *not* as opposed to how far they've come. They tend to think about the gap between where they are today and where they want to be.

Your growth, in any form, will have more to do with where you place your attention than your ability. If you keep focusing on the gap, you'll continue to see a gap. If you take a few moments to reflect on what you've accomplished, you'll likely accomplish even more. This self-reflection helps you build confidence, reshapes the way to look at yourself, and serves as fuel to keep you going.

A very simple way to supplement your reflection is to use a paper-based or application-based habit tracker. When I'm building a new habit or want to become more diligent at one I already perform, I track it on my large calendar desk pad by placing a checkmark to show myself I'm consistently doing what I intended. Whatever you do, I recommend you keep it visible so you can actually see what you've accomplished.

When it comes to rewarding myself, I use a couple of different tactics. Occasionally, there's a great reward such as "After I meditate for sixty straight days, I'm booking a weekend at a spa!" Most of the time, it's not that luxurious. More importantly, I want to reward myself frequently, not to mention I'd go broke if I kept booking spa vacations.

So that I can reward myself daily, I use a different version of the "if/then" concept I mentioned when addressing consistency. To help with consistency, the "if/then" concept served to note my backup plan. When it comes to rewards, I use the "if/then" concept to cite the actual reward. For example, "After I write 1,000 words for my book, I'll eat breakfast."

I gotta be somewhere. Will this take long?

I often get asked how long it takes to build a habit. I've done extensive research, read many books on the subject, and performed several trials in my own life. I've seen "experts" tout the number of days such as twenty-one, thirty, or sixty-seven. Based on my experience, I don't believe any of them because I've built some of my habits in three days while others took three months.

Let me offer this when it comes to how long it might take you to build your habits. I think every person is unique and the time it takes will vary. We have different upbringings and environments that help or hurt our abilities. Regardless of your situation, however, I think the speed at which you can build the habit depends on two factors. First, consider what the habit is you're trying to build. Second, evaluate how effectively you're implementing and practicing the tactics I've shared. If you set your environment properly, keep your schedule in doing the habit, reflecting, and rewarding yourself, you can retrain yourself quickly.

I also think you need to consider the number of repetitions you perform as opposed to the number of days it takes. You can build a habit a lot faster when you have more attempts.

FORMING HABITS EXERCISE

Thought-Provokers

1. Areas of my life where I want to develop better habits are...

2. Areas of my life I should start avoiding because I'm slipping into bad habits are...

3. Times on my calendar (morning, coffee breaks, lunch, etc.) I should open up to develop better habits are...

4. General "environments" in my life I can clean up to facilitate my most important habits are...

5. Current bad habits I should stop are...

Challenge

Week One: Break a bad habit. Identify what you consider to be your worst habit. Give yourself a running start for avoidance and plan to eradicate it. On a Monday, start to break it—COLD. Make it five days and you will be shocked how wonderful you feel!

Week Two: Get **more consistent** with an existing habit. Continue the week one challenge to keep your bad habit away. Now, find something you have already tried to make a habit, but need to do more consistently to ingrain it. Perhaps you plan your workday twice each week, but want to go five for five. Give it a go!

Week Three: Start a **new, wonderful habit**. Continue the week one and two challenges. Now, start that new habit you've been waiting to try. Want to meditate? Want to exercise? Want to rid your diet of dairy? This is a great time to get started!

Week Four: Start a habit **combo**. For week four, keep the three previous weeks' challenges going. Now, try to start combining your habits so they run serially. Perhaps it's the exercise-then-eat-healthy combination or reflect-then-plan-your-next-workday. You'll love the momentum and power you'll feel!

CHAPTER 7

Planning and Running Your Day

The first time I ever heard of a "to-do" list was from Paulo,
my Brazilian instructor....

It was Monday, February 13th, 1989 at exactly 9:45 PM CST. I know it was that time because I had just looked at my watch. I was twenty-two years old. I had recently finished a four-week, local office-based training grind with a large consulting firm who shall remain nameless (okay, Andersen Consulting, now known as Accenture).

This particular Monday began a three-week, centralized (that is, worldwide) training regimen designed to prepare you for the long hours you were about to embark on as a consultant. Apparently, this program was so effective that a good portion of the thousands of new employees quit. "Weed 'em out," I think the expression goes.

After working from 8:00 AM to 12:00 PM and then again from 1:00 PM to 5:00 PM and then yet again from 7:00 PM until this moment at 9:45 PM, I was starting to question my choice of employers. This was day number one of nineteen straight days of this. That includes weekends, so I did truly mean straight.

Technically, day one was just about over, but I still had time to squeeze in one more life lesson before I dashed to the Moose Lodge for an adult beverage.

This entire day, I had been sitting at a rectangular table with five other newbies. While evenly balanced at three men and three women, this table and entire program was as eclectic as you can get. This sixsome of recent graduates held an array of next-to-useless degrees. As eighteen-year-olds entering college, we evidently thought we were going to be a mechanical engineer, general businessperson (not sure what you are when you have a general business degree), economist, liberal arts person (again, don't know), theologian, and electrical engineer (me).

We were an assorted group to say the least. How we got together at this very table on this very day in this very town was anybody's guess. I'm sure it was fate.

The last character, and I do mean character, in this story is our instructor, Paulo, from Brazil. Paulo, at precisely 9:45 PM, started our instruction to wrap up the day (uh, night). He said, "Every night between 9:50 and 10:00 PM I'd like you to create a to-do list for your next day's activities before you tidy up your 'desk.'"

Like a good student I wrote out my list quickly. (I was still in the habit of listening to the instructors as I'd only been out of school a month or so.)

Paulo did not like the way I performed this task. He informed me that it needed to be "in a list format." It should include my prioritized tasks for the next day.

I informed him this was not the most effective way (in my humble opinion) to ensure I got everything done nor would it ensure I got everything done as quickly as I could.

He seemed puzzled because my "to-dos" and "deliverables" were in a calendar format with timeslots during the eleven hours I would perform and complete them.

I made the futile attempt to explain to him that a calendar format would keep me focused and mindful of the clock, help me avoid distractions, and benefit me in other ways which made total sense to apparently only me. I decided no good could come of this disagreement and made a list like he wanted. I kept my calendar thingy too as a precaution.

The next day, I felt like the odd duckling because I was the only one who actually finished all the tasks set to be completed that day. I assure you this had absolutely nothing to do with my smarts or skills. I'm certain of this because we were developing software on that Tuesday and in my entire collegiate life, I never finished a software program without massive help from my smartest buddies.

I attribute it to my time-based, deliverable-based method I've been using for over thirty-five years to run my projects, weeks, and days.

I have long thought, probably since I heard someone once say it, that "to-do lists are graveyards where important, but not urgent, tasks go to die."

The calendar gives you control. The calendar can be proactively planned in advance with care given to high-value activities that transform you, your team, and your business. "Daily" to-do lists with no relationship to the clock practically say, "Please interrupt me!"

The calendar gives you control. The calendar can be proactively planned in advance with care given to high-value activities that transform you, your team, and your business.

"Daily" to-do lists with no relationship to the clock practically say, "Please interrupt me!" They make you want to scratch things off rather than think.

You are in the thinking and doing business so let's cover how to do both!

If I don't have a list, how will I know what to do?

Notwithstanding my little disagreement with Paulo, I love lists! Lists are incredibly important to run your life, company, projects, teams, and other large- and small-scale efforts. The most important factors to consider regarding lists are what types of lists to have and what goes on them.

I developed a strategy to determine what goes on my lists. That strategy has two parts to it. First, my corporate strategy outlines who we'll be as a company, what types of products and services we'll offer the world, and other high-level, very-important directives. This strategy serves as a guidepost to keep us dialed in and focused while avoiding distractions from outside influences who want us to be something we're not. The second part relates to how I prioritize what's important. The sequence of projects related to serving our customers, building new products, marketing, selling, writing books, and so on must be deliberate.

While I won't go into the details of the ins and outs of my strategies and techniques as they relate to which projects we implement, the important aspect for you is to make sure you align your projects with who you are as a company and employee. I realize as an employee, your projects and deliverables could be a function of your team's goals or as simple as whatever your boss tells you to do. I'm good with all that as long as you're able to manage and run your day in an organized, efficient manner.

It all comes down to what you do at any moment on any given day. What I do is a function of four lists I manage as well as specific project plans for our efforts. Regardless of your professional function, you will have a similar structure to what you're doing on any given day. My four lists are:

Master: The master list is a very high-level list of major projects and initiatives I'd like to accomplish. It's the "kitchen sink," and includes no detail other than the project names. Although it's my "everything list," I primarily focus on projects we'd like to accomplish in the current year. I place each project in a designated month I'd like to complete it. This list will include projects such as complete book manuscript, conduct leadership workshop, and launch new online training program. The nature of this list is to include projects with some level of "finality" or completion. That is, I complete the workshop and it's done. I might perform that workshop again as a second version, but the project itself is complete for the time being. The purpose of this list is to give me a birds-eye view of major efforts we perform as a company.

Quarterly: From projects on the master list, I select ones I'd like to accomplish within the current three-month period. This serves as my quarterly list and I consider it a "ninety-day cycle." It allows me to get a view of my projects and plan our company schedule for that three-month period in more detail. While still at a high-level, I'll plan the priorities, deliverables, and target dates for the thirteen weeks within the quarter. This enables the entire team to see what we're doing during any given week and what's expected of them to support these efforts.

Monthly: For the current month, I start to get more granular. I call these periods "thirty-day pushes." During the month, I review activities and deliverables cited on our various project-specific plans. For example, we might be conducting a workshop during a particular week within that month. This workshop will require dozens of major activities we need to perform. The workshop project plan will include a complete list of activities, deliverables, due dates, and person responsible to complete the deliverables. Some of the specific activities might include developing communications to announce the workshop, preparing and distributing social media messages, building the presentations I'll use to deliver the workshop, and a host of other deliverables. I'll collect these activities and deliverables from not only this particular workshop, but also any other project we're working on for the current month. This aggregation becomes my monthly list. If any projects span multiple months, I'll simply pull the deliverables due during the current month to make sure I've accounted for them.

Weekly: I consider each week a "five-days-of-delivery" effort. Much like collecting activities and deliverables from the project plans to build my monthly list, I now transfer deliverables to this particular week. Technically, my weekly list isn't actually in a list format. The reason I don't make one simple list is because I'll perform several activities, some of which are due that week while others will be due in the future. It's important you have this level of visibility to your different types of activities so you can plan an effective week filled with short-term, mid-term, and long-term projects.

What gets scheduled gets done. What gets scheduled at your ideal times gets done better and faster.

Running a productive day and being able to focus on any given task at any moment in time starts with planning an effective week. As I mentioned, I consider each week a five-days-of-delivery effort. I've found a Monday-through-Friday period of time to be a reasonable span for most people to track easily. Sometimes, it's more difficult to see exactly where we are when we're in the middle of a nine-month project. It's helpful to breakdown the activities into more manageable pieces.

Another benefit of managing our efforts in terms of weeks is it provides some contingency to recover from unplanned interruptions. That is, it'll be easier to plan your deliverables and complete them within a week versus a singular day. If you get sidetracked on a four-hour issue you didn't plan, it'll be difficult to get everything you intended to get done on the day that issue arose.

To help me keep my entire week in order, I perform three vital steps to ensure I effectively manage, perform, and complete short-term and long-term, high-value activities:

1. Categorize activities (and deliverables) based on their type and due date.
2. Organize them into a workable format.
3. Schedule them during the week.

1. Categorize Based on Type and Due Date

First, I consider the types of activities and deliverables I want to accomplish each and every week. I ask myself:

- What projects and deliverables are due this week? These can be a sales meeting, white paper, presentation, system conversion, or anything with some level of finality.
- What projects and deliverables are important to move along (within our thirty-day push) but do not need to be finalized this week? These can be research activities, writing portions of a large document, or anything that spans multiple weeks.
- Which areas are really important for me to spend time on even though there is no deadline? These can be activities such as building your skills or learning new tools.
- What one-time or ongoing events are scheduled for this week? These generally include appointments, standing meetings, conferences, doctor visits and other unique, one-off, or recurring acts.

2. Organize into Workable Format

Once I have a complete inventory of my projects, activities, deliverables, and meetings, I organize them into an easily workable format. I want to have visibility to them so it's easy to move them into the time slots I want to perform them. To keep it simple, I lay out my activities and deliverables for the week into three columns. You can consider each column a list:

Column One (deliverables due this week): In the first column, I list the projects and deliverables due that week. These are the official, to-be-completed, check-them-off items.

Column Two (move these along): The second column is for activities I need to perform to make progress during this five-day period, but aren't due to be finalized. For example, this column might include activities related to a book project such as write 10,000 words or complete chapters seven, eight, and nine. These, in and of themselves, are intermediary deliverables to ensure I can complete the book project on time when its due two months from now.

Column Three (ongoing activities, recurring deliverables, skill building): I reserve the third column for activities I perform every week, but the specificity of the activity for that week is unique. For example, I perform ten individual coaching sessions each week, but the people I conduct them with are different each week. This column helps me organize and keep track of them. I also release an email digest every Tuesday morning that includes a new video on my YouTube channel, but the contents of the digest every week are different. While these are recurring tasks and deliverables, they are unique final products. You might have a standing meeting every Monday at a set time. This is also a great spot to include your skill-building activities.

The chart on page 76 is an illustration of how I use two freeform, open pages in my planner to create my "weekly list" of activities and deliverables for that five-day period.

3. Schedule the Week

Now, I can see what's due now and soon. This enables me to easily transfer the activities and deliverables into the appropriate time slots throughout the week. While all three of these steps are vital, placing the activities and their corresponding deliverables into your calendar is ultimately what ensures they actually get done. What gets scheduled gets done. What gets scheduled at your ideal times gets done better and faster.

Before we get into how I transfer my activities into their scheduled time slots, I want to share how I plan when I want to perform certain activities.

Weekly Inventory of Deliverables

Immediate	Near-Term	Ongoing
Leadership Program	**Productivity Event**	**Tips Digest**
☐ Complete talk	☐ Plan workshop	☐ Confirm content
☐ Complete workbook	☐ Draft challenge emails	☐ Complete video
☐ Send RSVP email	☐ Update lesson plan	☐ Draft social media
☐ Develop product post		
☐ Conduct session	**Book Marketing**	**Live Office Hours**
☐ Load video	☐ Confirm workplan	☐ Talk points
☐ Send replay email	☐ Draft announcement	☐ Write digest
		☐ Deliver talk
Job Search Program	☐ Ambassador Meeting	**Review Resumes**
☐ Finalize lesson plan		☐ John J.
☐ Send RSVP email	**Community**	☐ Sunny B.
☐ Develop product post	☐ Plan event	☐ Tammy F.
☐ Conduct session	☐ Email save-the-date	☐ William J.
☐ Load video		
☐ Send replay email		**1:1 Coaching**
		☐ Cathy T.
		☐ Bob H.
		☐ Steve S.
		☐ Sara M.
		☐ Connie V.
		☐ Tom C.
		☐ Michele H.

Weekly Tentative Breakdown by Day

MITS and Additional Activities

MONDAY
- ☐ Complete leadership talk
- ☐ Send leader RSVP email
- ☐ Confirm "Tips" content, video
- ☐ Team planning
- ☐ Team status
- ☐ Sunny B. Resume
- ☐ John J. Resume

TUESDAY
- ☐ Complete leadership workbook
- ☐ Run through job search lesson
- ☐ Send job search RSVP
- ☐ Cathy T. 1:1
- ☐ Bob H 1:1
- ☐ Tammy F. Resume
- ☐ William J. Resume

WEDNESDAY
- ☐ Job Search Coaching Session
- ☐ Load video, update product
- ☐ Send email to members
- ☐ Steve S. 1:1
- ☐ Sara M. 1:1

THURSDAY
- ☐ Live Office Hours
- ☐ Review Live Office Hours replay
- ☐ Run through leadership lesson
- ☐ Connie V. 1:1
- ☐ Tom C. 1:1

FRIDAY
- ☐ Leadership session
- ☐ Load video, update product
- ☐ Send email to members
- ☐ Michele H. 1:1
- ☐ Doctor appt

I consider everything I do including writing, creating training products, teaching during live shows, conducting coaching sessions, building my skills, running the team status meeting, balancing the corporate accounting books, and a variety of other acts. I know whether the activity gives me energy, takes it away, or leaves me indifferent.

Based on how it makes me feel and what's required of me, I attempt, where possible, to schedule the activities in the time slots that best align to my energy level. For example, I know that writing a book such as this will give me energy and also require a lot of creativity. I'm the most energetic and creative in the morning, so I schedule my writing sessions very early in the day.

I also know that performing one-to-one coaching sessions will boost my energy. I get charged when I engage directly with people to help them. That's why I prefer to conduct my individual coaching sessions in the afternoon. As my energy tends to wane later in the day, I'd rather not do my solitary, creative work at that time. These are just a few examples, but aligning your activities to coincide with your energy levels can tremendously boost your productivity. Of course, I realize you might not always be able to choose when you get to do your activities, but, where possible, consider this an extra aid to raise your output levels.

Over the years, I've tinkered with when I perform which activities based on how effective I am at various times throughout the day. Based on my tinkering, I've discovered something about myself. Sixty minutes will equal sixty minutes elapsed time for everyone, but, when it comes to my personal production, one hour before 8:00 AM is worth two hours after noon. Recognizing this, I designed a "weekly starter template" of my preferred schedule to expedite my planning.

Sixty minutes will equal sixty minutes elapsed time for everyone, but, when it comes to my personal production, one hour before 8:00 AM is worth two hours after noon.

I take the activities and deliverables I've already inventoried in my three-column format and quickly load them into the designated spots in my preferred weekly schedule. While each week is slightly different depending on our events, the following figure illustrates how I generally schedule my time.

My Weekly "Preferred" Schedule

	MONDAY	TUESDAY	WEDNESDAY	THURSDAY	FRIDAY
4 AM	MEDITATE	MEDITATE	MEDITATE	MEDITATE	MEDITATE
5 AM	EXCELLENCE PLAN	EXCELLENCE PLAN	EXCELLENCE PLAN	EXCELLENCE PLAN	EXCELLENCE PLAN
6 AM	CONTENT CREATION	CONTENT CREATION	CONTENT CREATION	WORKOUT	WORKOUT
7 AM	CONTENT CREATION	CONTENT CREATION	CONTENT CREATION	WORKOUT	WORKOUT
8 AM	CONTENT CREATION	CONTENT CREATION	CONTENT CREATION	CONTENT CREATION	COACH PREP
9 AM	CONTENT CREATION	CONTENT CREATION	CONTENT CREATION	CONTENT CREATION	COACH PREP
10 AM	WORKOUT	WORKOUT	WORKOUT	SETUP LIVE SHOW	BRUNCH
11 AM	WORKOUT	WORKOUT	WORKOUT	LIVE OFFICE HOURS	GROUP COACHING
12 AM	LUNCH	LUNCH	LUNCH	LIVE OFFICE HOURS	GROUP COACHING
1 PM	TEAM PLANNING	CONTENT CREATION	CONTENT CREATION	LUNCH	POST UPDATES
2 PM	TEAM STATUS	CONTENT CREATION	CONTENT CREATION	CONTENT CREATION	WEEKLY REFLECT
3 PM	1:1 COACHING	1:1 COACHING	1:1 COACHING	1:1 COACHING	WEEKLY REFLECT
4 PM	OR SKILL BUILDING	OR SKILL BUILDING	OR SKILL BUILDING	OR SKILL BUILDING	RELAX
5 PM	1:1 COACHING	1:1 COACHING	1:1 COACHING	1:1 COACHING	RELAX
6 PM	PLAN/REFLECT	PLAN/REFLECT	PLAN/REFLECT	PLAN/REFLECT	RELAX
7 PM	DINNER	DINNER	DINNER	DINNER	DINNER

Once you have a plan of your own, you can use a simple five-step process to transfer your inventory of activities and deliverables into a time-based plan for your upcoming week:

1. **Start with your template:** Begin scheduling your "usual" and preferred dates and times for activities based on your energy levels.
2. **Preload your appointments:** Populate those already-scheduled activities, meetings, and commitments.
3. **Plan your due dates:** Determine your work times for projects with deadlines and deliverables.
4. **"Pay" yourself first:** Plan your personal and professional development time.
5. **Fill in the rest:** Identify activities and deliverables for whatever is remaining.

Keep in mind, at this point, you're getting ready for the week using forethought to get all your activities and deliverables in your most-preferred time slots. Each evening, before your next day, you'll have a chance to finalize the next day's schedule. Even so, imagine how great you'll feel when you have a complete handle on your week before it even starts!

Why do we think we can accomplish so much in one day
but so little over the course of our lifetime?

Now that you have a great plan for the week, we need to execute it on a daily basis. All the planning in the world doesn't mean much if you don't actually do the work you planned to do. It's also not solely getting done what you planned to do because you could be planning the wrong activities. I find there are generally two issues when it comes to achieving daily and lifelong accomplishments.

First, most people don't protect their schedules and what they have planned. They allow any intrusion, even by their own doing, to interrupt them. This constant lack of focus and unconscious desire to be sidetracked will kill your productivity.

The second issue is much worse. I've noticed a common issue among people I coach. They think they can accomplish a lot in one day. Their to-do lists is a mile long with a bunch of low-priority, busy-work type of activities. There are far fewer, if any, long-term, high-value activities.

Why do you think you can accomplish so much in one day, but so little over the course of your lifetime?

Before we go further, I'd like you to pause for a minute and ponder this question. Why do you think you can accomplish so much in one day, but so little over the course of your lifetime? Most people I've met think writing a book, or creating a television show, or climbing (their literal or figurative) Mount Everest are wholly unattainable.

What if you carved out an hour each day and your activity was to write and your deliverable was 1,000 words. In one month, you'd have a 30,000-word book. Most books you read don't even have that many words. It's an analogy and I'm sure you get the idea. You need forethought, discipline, and simply to follow through!

Accomplishing major goals like these are about balancing your day. If you want to reach great heights, each day will need to be filled with short-term, mid-term, and long-term activities and deliverables. You'll need to plan well and stick to it and not let yourself fall victim to the short-term, "urgent" fires that seem to rule the day. Let's cover how to make this happen.

What does success look like?

I've helped hundreds of thousands of people with their job searches. One question I ask them to answer before they take a new job or a new position is, "What does success look like?" I want them to ask this question of themselves and their potential employers. This could be success in six months or one year or three years. If you take on a new role or project without knowing your success criteria, you're in trouble. At a minimum, you won't know if your boss is happy or whether you'll still have a job whenever you reach the "deadline."

Have you ever thought about what a successful day looks like? I'm not speaking about whether you checked off all your to-do list items. First of all, I don't even want you to have a daily to-do list. Second, have you defined success?

Whenever I plan and execute my days, I have a list of success criteria I use to ensure I'm in order. When I strip out all the noise, there are only four aspects of my day that matter to me. Everything else is far less important if not completely irrelevant. When these are dialed in, you'll be amazed how great you feel and how much you accomplish:

1. **Happiness:** Do you enjoy what you're doing? Are you working for the right company? Are you in the right career? Should you build your own company? Are you living "your gift?" Does what you're doing matter to you?

2. **Outputs:** What are you producing? Do your deliverables matter or improve anything?

3. **Speed:** How quickly are you producing those outputs? Faster mini-deliverables leads to faster major deliverables.

4. **Value:** What happened as a result of you creating your outputs? Did a person, group, or company benefit?

I realize you might have only so much control over your activities each day, but it's worth spending some time considering this success criteria or developing some of your own. You want to make sure you are enjoying yourself. If what you do day in and day out isn't aligning to what makes you happy, it's time to rethink your life.

Planning your day is a standing, daily meeting with yourself!

As odd as it sounds, your plan for the next day should be a daily deliverable every day! You have your weekly plan, but we need to drill down to each day and ensure you're focused on executing each moment. On my calendar, for example, somewhere between 5:00 PM and 7:00 PM, I'll have an activity to reflect on the current day and plan for the next day.

Planning for the next day means confirming my entire schedule and deliverables for tomorrow. In my weekly plan, I might have already identified a coaching session for Tuesday at 3:00 PM. On Monday, at the end of my workday, I want to ensure I have that person's information, I've reviewed it, and I know what our goals are for the coaching session. I'd prefer not to be scrambling at 2:55 PM nor do I want to take up valuable time on Tuesday organizing this material. The same would go for any project or meeting I was conducting.

There is another not-so-little benefit of planning your next day the night before. When you've reviewed and organized everything for tomorrow, your brain knows this. You won't need to expend any short-term memory, specifically your "working memory," holding onto reminders or random thoughts related to your next day. You'll actually sleep better because your mind isn't racing or expending extra energy.

Planning your day comes down to two factors—creating a plan and filling it in with the right priorities. The first act, simply creating a plan, will help you with your speed to produce the outputs. The second act helps you with creating higher value as a result of your outputs.

To execute good practices, the first step is to get into the habit of planning. Simply sitting down with the intent of planning is a great start. (Sounds like you're building a habit with intention!) The following questions will help you not only streamline your planning, but also make sure you're focusing on my valuable acts:

- **Do I have my weekly plan to jumpstart my daily plans for that week?** This will reduce the amount of time you need to spend planning each day.
- **Do I have a regularly scheduled time slot to plan?** The end of each day is a great time to plan because you can assess what you completed, evaluate unexpected items that arose, and consider anything that wasn't completed to determine if you need to roll items to the next day or throughout the week.
- **Have I identified my most important tasks (MITs)?** Not all activities you'll perform on a given day are of equal importance. If you could only complete one task, what would that be? If you could only complete one more, what would that be? How about a third?
- **Have I considered my activities in relation to my energy levels and attempted to schedule them according to my energy?** Where possible, give yourself every advantage to completing your activities the fastest with the highest level of quality.
- **Have I filled in all my time slots?** It's best to account for every single minute. The devil waits to steal your idle time. If you have a little fifteen-minute gap in between meetings, it's better to block it out with "recovery time" or "check email" than not have anything.

The fact you've considered this gap will often lead you to identify something productive or effectively recover from an interruption.

- **Have I considered which activities could be moved to a different day in the event of an unplanned interruption?** Occasionally, you'll get sidetracked or interrupted. It's very effective to know which activities you could rearrange. If you've considered your most important tasks already, you have a great start on knowing which need to be completed. Everything else, by default, is negotiable on whether it gets completed that day.

- **What are the consequences of not getting something done?** As you plan your day, including your MITs and additional activities, it's a good idea to note the consequence of not getting a deliverable done. If you encounter a situation where you need to shift something, you'll know how dire it is. If the paper you're working on today isn't due for two days, you could finish it tomorrow and still have it ready by its due date.

Your planning will help you complete your deliverables, but you also want to make sure you're working on the highest priorities and creating the most value. These priorities and their corresponding value are confirmed by aligning them to your corporation's overall strategy, your team's goals, and a host of other factors. While you might not have a clear understanding of some of this information, that doesn't mean you shouldn't make an attempt to evaluate your activities and value. Start by focusing on what you can control. For example, each evening when I plan the next day, I ask myself:

- **What are my *highest value* activities?** My highest value activities are not necessarily my MITs for that day. A higher-value act might be to reshape an internal system used to operate my business, but a MIT for that day might be to complete a newsletter digest that needs to be emailed the next day. That digest is something I promise to my community every Tuesday, so, to me, it's a non-negotiable deliverable that must be complete on that particular day.

- **What can I and *only I do* that, if done well, will make a real difference?** Whether you're running a business or team or trying to operate solo more effectively, it's best to assign activities to the people who are best suited to handle them. Usually, there will be a relationship between the cost of those employees and the value they contribute. After all, you don't want an expensive resource who can perform very-complicated, high-value tasks to be working on something a more cost-effective resource can handle. It helps if you're continually evaluating this. If you're operating your own business or team, take note of where there exist opportunities to delegate or outsource activities.
- **What is the most *valuable* use of my time *right now*?** Try to focus on the projects and activities that provide the most value. This might require you to resist the easily completed projects for the ones that are more impactful.
- **What can I *learn* tomorrow that will make the greatest impact on my professional growth?** Hopefully, you've allocated some learning time on your calendar for the next day. You might already have a skill-building activity in mind, but always check to make sure you're focusing on the skills that provide you with the most return for your invested time.

Lastly, as I review my daily plan for the next day, I try to review it for balance, variety, and frequency of the activities and deliverables.

By **balance**, I mean working on short-term, mid-term, and long-term projects. For example, my MITs will, by definition of needing to be done that day, be short-term deliverables. I'll make sure to move along the mid-term and long-term projects so when they turn into short-term MITs in the upcoming weeks, it's not an overwhelming burden.

By **variety**, I mean performing different functions. Mixing it up is fun and will keep you sharp, not slow you down. As a business owner, I build products and services, perform customer service, and generate revenue by increasing brand awareness and selling. I improve my ability to perform service and sell through data analysis. I find it's more effective for the business, and me personally, to do a little bit of each every day. It's like a well-balanced diet for business and personal success.

By **frequency**, I mean how often I "touch" something. Some experts claim it's better to bulk your activities for efficiency. In some cases, this is true. You can gain great economies of scale, but you need to recognize what type of activity it is. In my line of work, for instance, much of what I do is practice a skill to get better and better. The more practice, the better and faster I get. Writing this book is a great example. I write each day for a few hours. If I bulked up my writing and did ten hours on Saturday and then didn't return to it until next Saturday, it would be inefficient because I'd require more start up time. The other aspect is writing is a skill that needs to be practiced. It's just like playing a musical instrument. There is a reason your piano teacher wants you to play for thirty minutes each day as opposed to four straight hours each Saturday. You get better at it the more frequently you practice it.

> *"Everyone has a plan 'til they get punched in the mouth."*
> —MIKE TYSON

As Sun Tzu wrote in *The Art of War*, "Every battle is won or lost before it is ever fought." With this in mind, you might be feeling pretty good about the plans you've put together for your week and the day you're about to live.

I'm guessing Sun Tzu never met Mike Tyson, former world heavyweight boxing champion and owner of the nickname "Iron Mike." I tend to agree with Iron Mike on how he viewed his opponent's plan.

Maybe you feel the same way when you're all set to go, suit pressed and hanging on the doorknob, car filled with gas for your morning commute, and your office desk clean and organized. You're ready! Then, you spill coffee on your shirt, change it, and think forward to your day as you sit in traffic you didn't expect thanks to the three-car pile-up you had nothing to do with. When you get to work, you check your now-full email inbox you completely cleaned out yesterday. Some client wants to have an urgent call with you in an hour. You're wondering, *What happened to my nicely planned day?*

Most days aren't like this. In fact, most of the time, we inflict our own time-management and productivity wounds simply because we aren't disciplined in the way we run our day. Your plan is a great start. If you designed it as best you can with the highest value activities and priorities and adhere to your schedule, you'll accomplish great things day in and day out.

The problem is sticking to the plan requires discipline, willpower, savvy issue management, protecting your time, avoiding stress that naturally accumulates as the day goes on, and a host of other in-game maneuvers. Planning your day is akin to the textbook stuff you learned in college. You have perfect field conditions and no issues. Running your day is more like the real-life career you've grown accustomed to which has no resemblance to the topics you studied in school.

You've already worked the time-management best-practices into your plan. To run a high-output day now, however, requires you to tap into your focus and willpower skills.

Run your day like clockwork.

Each day, I use a handful of habits I've built, skills I constantly practice, and a host of techniques that helps me not only be productive, but, more importantly, enjoy what I'm doing at any moment. Being present and actually experiencing and benefiting from that experience is the greatest gift you can ever give yourself. Here are some of my favorite tips, tricks, dos, and don'ts as I run my day.

Consider the Day

I spend five minutes, immediately before I start my "official" workday, considering what the perfect day looks like. I review my schedule, all the activities, my expected deliverables, the people I'll be coaching, and everything else on my calendar. I'm imagining success at this point.

As importantly, I also take a quick moment to imagine how my highest self will handle any interruptions, unexpected issues, or expected activities without designated times. For example, a few years back, my executive recruitment company, milewalk, was performing a search for a consulting firm. We were tasked with recruiting a very senior-level executive for this organization. I was working directly with the Chief Executive Officer.

A few days prior, we had our top candidate accept a job offer with another organization. The CEO was very disappointed. I called him on a Tuesday to discuss this in more detail. He was traveling and didn't return my voicemail message that day, but did send me an email late that evening indicating he would call me tomorrow while he was driving to the airport.

As I planned my Wednesday, I didn't know when he would call me and I already had a completely full schedule. That meant, if I wanted to speak to him, I'd need to answer the phone whenever he called regardless of what I was doing at that moment.

As I considered my day that morning, I reminded myself he'd likely be upset when he called, I should be empathetic, and direct the discussion toward overcoming this setback. He didn't call during the morning. After I finished my lunchbreak, I spent a few moments considering my afternoon and the possibility he'd call. Again, I reminded myself how to handle the call.

When he called me at 2:55 PM, I noticed his number on the caller ID, took a quick breath, and thought back to my reminders of how my highest self would act. I picked up the phone in the best possible frame of mind because I already prepared myself for this occurrence. He was upset, as I expected, but we had a tremendously productive call.

Think about your day. Are there times you don't handle interruptions or setbacks well? This generally occurs for two reasons. First, you haven't thought about how to handle these issues in advance. Second, that lack of forethought is exacerbated by the likelihood you've accumulated stress throughout the day. (More on how to alleviate this in an upcoming tip.) When these issues occur, you're practically ready to snap!

Taking a few moments in the morning to think through your day not only helps you make sure things go right, but also helps you handle them effectively when they don't.

Forget the Frog

Mark Twain once said that if you have to eat a live frog—that is, do an unpleasant task that day—do it first thing in the morning and nothing worse will happen to you for the rest of the day. Many productivity experts tout this eat-the-frog strategy so you can get over the hump right away and make the rest of the day feel like you're moving downhill.

I'm not exactly sure why anyone would want to do this. I want to enjoy everything I do, especially the challenging tasks. I also want to align that froggy thing when it coincides with my energy level. More importantly, I want to "stack wins," which helps me feel like I'm getting out of the gate quickly and feeds my self-esteem and confidence.

I literally think of everything I do, once I wake up, as a victory. I woke up. That's victory number one! I open the blinds in the bedroom. I know it's jet-black outside. I still open them. That's another victory. I walk down the stairs. As long as I don't fall, that's another victory. I feed the dogs before their barking wakes up the neighbors. I check to make sure all four of them eat and don't steal each other's food. If I can manage that difficult task, I get another checkmark and a bonus victory. This goes on until I make it into my meditation session. Then, I journal. Then, I transition into my idea-generation session (more on this later in the book). That's three more victories. The ideas I've jotted down related to new projects and improvements for my business gets me excited and charged and helps me keep an upbeat perspective regarding what's possible. All of this is feeding my mindset in a positive manner.

As importantly, I make sure that I'm doing activities that are 100 percent in my control. There is such a low likelihood of anything going wrong. I now have momentum as I transition into my next activities, which are generally creation-based such as writing a book or preparing a lesson or building a training product.

Cue the Environment

When I discussed building great habits, I covered why cueing your environment is so important. It helps you get a fast start and get in the mood for whatever you're about to do. When it comes to running your day, your actual physical environment helps with that too.

I clean my desk the night before and set up the material, book, journal, or anything I need for the first act I'll do at my desk in the morning. The clutter-free office helps with your organization and ability to find what you need when you need it. Readying your desk for the first act helps you eliminate any wasted motion when you get started.

Work the Calendar

During the day, work your calendar not a to-do list. Lay out your calendar so you know which activities you'll do or meetings you'll have in the respective timeslots. Most people naturally do this for meetings, especially thanks to electronic "calendar invites." Rare few do it for non-meeting activities. Rarer still is someone who'll cite the deliverable to be completed within that time period.

If between 10:00-11:00 AM, you're working on writing a white paper, be specific about what the final product should be at 11:00 AM. Enter it into the calendar, not solely on your list for the day. Will the entire white paper be completed? Are there specific portions of the white paper you'll complete?

The most important thing is you've identified a relationship between time and output. The reason you let yourself get interrupted or dilly dally your way to an unfinished product is because you haven't associated the deliverable with the timeframe in which it needs to be done.

> **The most important thing is you've identified a relationship between time and output. The reason you let yourself get interrupted or dilly dally your way to an unfinished product is because you haven't associated the deliverable with the timeframe in which it needs to be done.**

This is yet another reason why it's helpful to account for and plan every minute of your day. If you're not sure what you'll be doing between 2:00-3:00 PM, figure that out and put something on your calendar based on your projects and priorities. If you're not sure what you'll be doing (that's scary), it's more effective to make an appointment with yourself such as "recover from morning issues" or "coffee break" or some placeholder that shows you where the opportunities are throughout your day to take a break or address unplanned interruptions.

Recharge and Reset

My entire morning routine each day is designed to help me focus throughout the day and get charged and excited about the day I'm about to live. That only lasts so long because you'll accumulate stress and tension throughout the day. I'm not speaking about getting tense. Even if we love every activity we're doing throughout the entire day, we'll still accumulate tension in our heads, backs, and arms.

At this very moment, I'm typing these words and have been writing this section for approximately one hour. While I've smiled the entire time, I'm still accumulating tension in my forearms from typing. I've also been staring at my large twenty-seven-inch monitor. Even though my environment is ergonomically designed, I'll still realize some tension in my neck and back and eyes.

Approximately every fifty minutes during the day, I take a quick break to help release this tension. If I'm continuing with the same activity when I return from the break, I'll simply use my break time to stretch, walk the dogs, or look out my window. I'll do anything to move around.

If I'm transitioning from one activity to another, I use my break to stretch and mentally and physically complete what I just finished and think forward to what I'm about to do next. This helps release accumulated tension, but also ensures I'm not taxing my short-term memory to hang onto anything unnecessarily. I want to think about what I just accomplished and put it back in its mental or physical place so I know where to find it when I need it next time.

Here's a great example. Each morning, I write for an hour or two so I can complete this book. I have a specific block of time allocated to write the book. I don't have a to-do that says, "Write chapter three." I know, before I start, I'll be writing chapter three. My goal is to write 1,000 words within that hour. When the hour is over, I check to see how many words I wrote. I also label where I left off so I know where to begin tomorrow.

Before I move onto the next activity, I make notes in my writing logbook. I enter the section I wrote, how many words I wrote, and make a few other notations. This gives me a few seconds to pack up what I did, make sure I know where to start next time, and also reflect on what I just completed. No matter what I just accomplished, I'll provide myself some words of positive encouragement such as, "You wrote 1,000 words!" Now, I'm feeling good about what I did even if it was a tough writing session. I give myself immediate feedback so I recognize I put in the work. That, in and of itself, is a victory.

Next, I think forward to what my goals are for the next activity. What is it I need to accomplish in the next hour? What does success look like at the end of the next hour? I confirm what's in my calendar. Success was notated with the associated deliverable the night before when I planned this, but I want to confirm and re-register it right before I start. By giving yourself a few moments to think forward and really consider what you're about to do, you put yourself in a great position to have a productive hour.

I do this during each and every break when I transition between activities. What happens when you don't do something like this? You race from one activity to the next and your stress and tension levels build up. You go from meeting to meeting or call to call and don't get a chance to consider your agenda, goals, and how the others are feeling. Stress accumulates throughout the day if you don't let it go.

Think about a customer service agent who answers one phone call after another. People are calling the support line because they have problems. That means everyone who calls is bummed out! If the agent keeps clicking from one phone call to the next and doesn't take a few seconds to consider the person who needs help, there will be no chance of remaining empathetic and doing the job effectively. Of course, there's also no opportunity to take a breather and let go of the stress from the previous phone call. These recharge-and-reset breaks are vital to keeping your energy levels high and stress levels low.

Reflect

No matter how successful you are, you'll never feel successful unless you reflect. Nowadays, our days are blurry, our weeks are foggier, and we can't even remember what we ate for lunch yesterday. If you identify with that statement, how on Earth are you going to register what you've done, accomplished, and need to re-do if you don't stop for a few minutes to think about it?

**No matter how successful you are,
you'll never feel successful unless you reflect.**

This means consciously taking a step back to assess what's actually happening. What worked? What didn't?

Here's a little story about this tip in action. On Wednesday, January 11th, 2023, I performed my morning writing session for this book. I won't forget this particular session for a few reasons. (I know you're wondering, so it's January 18th, 2023 as I type these words.) The first reason I won't forget this day is because I struggled mightily with that particular section of the book. It's the lesson on Networking, which if you're reading this book in order, you haven't gotten to yet.

I rarely struggle when I write because my goal for the first draft is to simply produce the words. I don't judge them. I'm not happy with them. I'm not sad with them. I don't even think about them. The only goal is to generate a particular number of words. I know I'll edit all the words later. If I produce the words, I achieved the goal. That's the end of it. I record the victory and move onto my next task.

On that particular January 11th, however, I really struggled with the organization of what I wanted to write. That meant I was producing the words at a slower rate than I usually do. I finished the one-hour session. I felt beaten up. It was as if my words decided to give me a whipping.

Next, I did what I always do after a book-writing session. I opened my writing logbook and entered the word count, topic, section, and a few notes. I wrote 1,440 words that morning. In an instant, I went from feeling bruised to completely reenergized. I had accomplished my mission even though I wasn't at my best. I said to myself, "Good job. Don't forget this session. You'll need this memory next time you struggle with writing." I parked what I was doing and "recharged and reset" a la the previous tip I shared. I was then off to write an email to my community.

That act of reflecting took a mere twenty seconds, but it changed my attitude and prevented me from feeling bad as I went into my next activity. In fact, it helped me avoid feeling frustrated for the entire twenty-four hours before my next book writing session. Even though I was struggling during the session, there was technically nothing to be frustrated about. In fact, it's days like this you'll need to draw upon when you need to dig deeply to keep going to accomplish your long-term goal. Instead of moving into the next hour, carrying stress that could have accumulated until the next day, I took stock of what actually happened. I accomplished my goal. I looked for the good in what I did, rather than dwelling on how I was feeling temporarily.

Reflection, the act of intercepting your automated thoughts and feelings in this case, is a vital tool in allowing you to attach proper meaning to your experiences. Remember my saying, "Your experience is not what happened to you. It's the meaning you attach to what happened to you." A bit of reflection sprinkled throughout your day, especially when you transition tasks is a key weapon to keeping upbeat and remaining stress-free.

The end of the day—before you plan your next day—is THE best time to reflect on your entire day. At the beginning of my planning session for the next day, I reflect by asking myself these questions:

- What did I accomplish?
- What went well?
- What went poorly?
- What do I need to roll to tomorrow?
- What should I stop doing?
- What is one limiting factor, internal or external, that prohibits speed when accomplishing my tasks and goals?

There are many techniques for winding down your day as it relates to reflection. Play around with this to see what works for you. The most important aspect is that you slow down and do it!

"My day went just as I planned!" said no one ever!

You have your plan and everyone else seems to have a plan to interrupt your plan. It might feel like that, but we know most people have no ill intent. Whether that's a bored coworker, a colleague who needs help, or your boss who just can't seem to get anything done without pestering you, there are lots of intrusions.

Let's take my family for example. When I was an executive recruiter, I was on the phone approximately six hours every day. I needed to call prospective companies, speak with clients, and recruit and interview job candidates. Of course, I needed to do research and other desk-work activities to run my company too. To build a thriving business, I needed a very structured schedule as you might imagine, so I developed one based on the productivity principles I've shared with you in this lesson.

Part of that schedule included "The Sacred Six." I didn't just call this part of my schedule The Sacred Six for me. I used that term to explain to my mom and siblings when I would be absolutely unreachable. (Dad had his high-powered job so he wasn't likely to need me at these times.) During the hours of 8:30-11:30 AM and 1:30-4:30 PM, I was on the phone working my day. These hours were off limits to interruption. If I received a phone call or text or email or any form of communication during those times, it would simply need to wait.

Since there's an abundance of love in my family, I took a lot of ribbing, but that's what it takes if you want to stay on track and remain focused on achieving your goals. You must set boundaries with your coworkers, friends, family, and whoever else could innocently interrupt your day.

Let's run through some of the most common derailers of your time and activities and how to avoid them.

Self-Inflicted Wounds

Most of your interruptions will be self-inflicted. This is statistically inarguable. If you don't believe me, spend two entire days tracking everything you do every time you do it. How many times did you peek (unnecessarily) at your email inbox? How many times did you glance at your phone because it vibrated or beeped? How many times did you check social media? How many times did you pick up the phone when you received an unexpected call of any kind?

I'll cut you a break here and we won't even consider the number of times you're focusing on busy-work or procrastinating because you don't want to do the deep work that creates high-value outputs.

If your husband is in the hospital or your wife is pregnant or one of your parents or children are sick, of course, you need to be accessible and immediately available. By all means, remain on high alert. (I'm not a monster!) Most of the time, however, this is not the case.

Set times to check email and turn off your computer and cell phones. Watch what happens. You're welcome.

Changing Priorities

Occasionally, maybe oftentimes, if you work for a company that plans poorly, your priorities will change. Sometimes, priorities change throughout the day because your boss is shuffling your tasks. Other times, priorities can change at a grander level. Let's address how you can handle both of these.

For the situations where you're working on one activity and your boss asks you to stop so you can focus on another, simply stop and breathe. These issues happen from time to time.

As I mentioned earlier (and also as part of the Focusing lesson), it helps to "consider your day" in the morning. When you recognize not everything goes according to plan and spend a few minutes considering how you'll react in the event something doesn't, you'll be amazed how much better you handle it when this occurs. If you've done the "recharge and reset" before this hour when the shift in priorities occurred, you have an extra layer of protection from getting bent out of shape. You can quickly recognize, *This has happened.*

Most of our stress comes from our expectations about the way we think things ought to be. In this case, you expected no interruption or change in priority. Just roll with it.

What happens when there is a more significant shift in priorities? We can easily manage shuffling tasks on a given day, but what happens when we encounter a situation that affects our activities in the upcoming days, weeks, and months? From an immediate-reaction standpoint, stopping and catching your breath is still a great idea. Something of this magnitude, however, will require a more-evolved outlook. I like to say, "Life happens for you, not to you." Everything that happens in your life is meant to help you thrive. That's true. I'm not speaking of suffering related to a family member's death. I'm speaking about your career. How you look at these changes will affect how you feel and perform.

Here's a little story. In March 2020, the United States was experiencing its first major wave of the COVID-19 pandemic. While cases of people being infected had been occurring for months in my country, it wasn't being recognized nationally or substantially addressed until this point.

As I mentioned, I offer weekly videos, podcasts, and newsletter digests to keep my community and customers informed and educated on the latest and greatest job searching and leadership development concepts. I conduct a weekly Live Office Hours show on my YouTube channel, hold special public workshops, and offer premium training programs related to supporting your career. Much of the content I develop, distribute, and discuss on these platforms are prepared and scheduled weeks or months in advance.

On a Friday in mid-March, our state was notified we'd be going into a "shelter-in-place" mode. This meant restaurants, health clubs, office buildings, and many other places would shut down until further notice. I knew this would have tremendous ripple effects on how we'd live in the short- and mid-terms (if not the long-term). It would greatly impact people's jobs.

All of the content I'd already scheduled for the next month wouldn't be the most needed, let alone the most empathetic and supportive. My next newsletter digest, video, and podcast was scheduled to be released in a couple of days. I needed to scrap it all for weeks to come and create new, more-relevant content.

I could have been upset, as if I could have controlled any of this. I immediately thought about my community. I thought, *This is a golden opportunity to serve them when they'll need it the most.* They need to be informed on what's likely to happen and what they can do about it to best position themselves. The people who are job searching need to know which companies will thrive and need more employees. The employed people will need to know how to work from home more effectively. I started to build lessons on these topics and techniques.

This terrible situation was a chance for me to be there for them and educate them on something that's confusing and scary. It was an opportunity to show them I care about their well-being. I looked for the good in this awful situation. This change in priorities was more important. Sometimes life and business throw you curve balls. You can learn how to hit them if you have the right outlook.

Unknown Outcomes

There are situations when you might not be able to accurately estimate the amount of time an activity or deliverable will take. Perhaps you're developing a product for the very first time. You might be a salesperson who is spending the hour making outbound sales calls. You're not quite sure how long you'll spend on the phone with a prospect.

I, for example, often have a stack of phone calls to return each day. If there are ten people whose calls I need to return and I have one slot between 2:30-3:00 PM to do that, I start calling based on priority and urgency. Let's say I get the person's voicemail on my first call. On the second call, the person picks up. We talk for five minutes. For these varying activities, the important aspect is to have your calls prioritized much like you would your MITs. Which calls must I return today? Which calls are nice to return? Which are very nice to return? Think in terms of consequences if the call is not made. That is often helpful.

Now that you've learned some of my most effective planning and organizing techniques to live a great day, it's your turn to implement the ones you like. Focus on adjusting my tactics based on your company, position, and goals. Head to the exercise to get started!

PLANNING AND RUNNING YOUR DAY EXERCISE

Thought-Provokers

1A. My highest value activities are...

1B. The one step I can take to prioritize each of these high-value outputs is...

2A. The one skill I can allocate time to developing that will significantly increase my job performance is...

2B. I can create two hours on my calendar this week to develop this skill by scheduling time on these days/times...

3. When I consider my day each morning, the questions I'll ask myself are...

4. When I reflect at the end of each workday, the questions I'll ask myself are...

5A. The three most-frequent, self-inflicted interruptions are...

5B. The steps I can take to stop these interruptions are...

Challenge

Week One: Perform next-day planning for five straight days. During the first week, set time aside at the end of your workday to plan the next day and reflect on the current day. Of course, you want to be effective in the planning step, but success in this first week is getting comfortable with making and keeping this appointment with yourself! Continue this step throughout the entire challenge.

Week Two: Evaluate how effectively you **adhere to your daily schedule** and outputs. You can use whatever grading scale you want (e.g., scale of 1–10, the number of interruptions, the percentage of MITs completed) as long as you perform an honest assessment. If you take a few moments at the end of each day to think about what happened, what worked, and what pulled you off track, you'll notice the trends. Evaluate yourself for the next fifteen workdays.

Week Three: Schedule and take your breaks plus **perform your recharge-and-reset** transitions. As you plan your next day, look for the spots to actually schedule your breaks and transitions throughout the day. Use these times to mentally complete what you just performed and confirm your goals for what you're about to do. Start this in week three and continue for the next two weeks. (You can start this on the first day of the challenge, but it'll be much harder than your think.)

Week Four: Capture your **interruptions and grade your reactions** to them. You have a plan and people will unintentionally interrupt it. During the last week of the challenge, pay particular attention to how you react to those interruptions (even when you interrupt yourself). Can you politely swat them away? Is it a high priority that requires you to stop what you're doing? Did you anticipate this possible interruption? The most important part of this exercise is to become conscious of how you're reacting so you can ultimately improve your reactions.

CHAPTER 8

Building Confidence

You were born fearless. What happened?

Fear is learned. For proof, look at a child. Children don't know to be afraid. Adults teach them to be.

When I was not quite a teenager, I spent time at Rehm Park in Oak Park, IL. It was a community pool that also had a large, three-level diving platform. The first platform was ten meters high.

As a twelve-year-old boy, I looked at that platform and thought that simply wouldn't be reckless enough, so I marched to the top platform which rose twenty-five meters above the pool.

At this age, I didn't know my one-hundred-pound body would be traveling at 22.14 meters/second and it would only take a mere 2.26 seconds to hit the water. All I knew was, when I jumped off, I was moving toward the water so fast my heart felt like it was pushing at the top of my head.

It wasn't until I was in college and took advanced physics as an electrical engineering student where I learned these petrifying numbers based on velocity and energy at impact and a bunch of other stuff I've thankfully forgotten.

Twelve-year-old Andy said, "Let's do it again! Let's do it again!"

Nineteen-year-old Andy asked, "Whoa. I was going how fast? Is that even safe?"

Fifty-eight-year-old Andy wondered, *Was I out of my mind? I'll never do something that stupid again!*

I needed to learn to be afraid of the high dive. I didn't know I was supposed to be afraid. It wasn't until I matured that I learned what might have happened to my body if I contorted it in the wrong direction.

How does my adolescent story relate to a well-adjusted adult like yourself?

Fear is learned. Imposter syndrome is learned. Any question you have about your ability to be confident in anything is learned. These feelings certainly can be partly genetic, but more are born from our environment, experiences, and conditioning. They are further exacerbated by a host of other factors such as anxiety or a distortion of reality that comes with hawking your friend's Instagram-airbrushed highlight reel.

The most oxymoronic thing about being confident is the thing that most-frequently erodes our confidence—failure—is actually the primary element that builds it.

Confidence and success are not found in the quality of your talent, but in the quality of your thoughts.

Confidence has more to do with your relationship with failure than success. When all goes well and we win, it's easy to believe in ourselves. Failures, on the other hand, can negatively impact our confidence levels if we don't interpret them properly.

Confidence has more to do with your relationship with failure than success. When all goes well and we win, it's easy to believe in ourselves. Failures, on the other hand, can negatively impact our confidence levels if we don't interpret them properly.

Some people register failures as a final event. This causes them to doubt their abilities and lose confidence in themselves. This can be especially damaging if they view the failures as significant.

Other people consider failures as part of the growth process. While no one desires failures, these people expect them in a positive way. These failures, part of their everyday lives, are nothing more than opportunities to learn and grow. This viewpoint, in turn, builds their confidence because they're constantly practicing, gaining knowledge, and experience. They perceive this as progress!

A failure does not make you a failure...failure is not an event. It's a mindset.

I often say, "A failure does not make you a failure." That is, a singular failure does not make you a complete failure. To me, failure is not an event. It's a mindset. Failure doesn't prevent success. It enables it. Therefore, failures will lead to success and repeated success will lead to confidence.

There is a trick to this delicate balancing act between failures, successes, and building confidence in yourself. It's to design how and when your failures occur so you can interpret them properly and have a healthy relationship with them.

Wouldn't designing failure into the process be defeating the purpose of life? In fact, it's exactly the opposite.

I'm sure this sounds odd. Wouldn't designing failure into the process be defeating the purpose of life? In fact, it's exactly the opposite. It's actually more effective to design your efforts and skill-building activities to perpetually increase your level of difficulty so failures are the prerequisites to success. You recognize you will stumble a bit before you reach the next levels of success in anything you do.

I refer to this technique of growth as progressive mastery and we'll be covering it in more detail later in the book. For now, recognizing virtually any area you want to grow in your life and become more confident in your ability, requires multiple (maybe many) attempts to overcome hurdles to reach the next level. When you have a built-in understanding and expectation your missteps are part of the process, you'll see them as steppingstones to growth rather than failures.

Remember this tidbit. I chuckle when I hear people say, "Failure is not an option." If failure is not an option, then neither is success. Failure should not just be an option; initially, at least, it should be your most-probable outcome! That is true at any level of your development. Even when you become a master of your trade, you'll still experience these failures as you attempt to progress to the next level. If you're not encountering failures, you've stopped growing. The major difference between incredibly successful, confident people and others is that successful people design their lives to fail often instead of just once.

The major difference between incredibly successful, confident people and others is that successful people design their lives to fail often instead of just once.

These confident people also understand confidence is not something that can be given to you. It's also not something you can give to someone else. Confidence must be built. When self-confidence is built properly, it affects other aspects of your life. It builds your self-efficacy, improving your view of your ability to influence the events in your life. It also builds self-esteem, improving your view of your self-worth.

What does a life designed to "fail" look like exactly?

How do we build our lives so we develop confidence? First, we need to understand the types of situations which call for us to be confident in our abilities. Of course, these situations are endless. Through coaching thousands of individuals, however, I've found people are most susceptible to lack or lose confidence in three types of scenarios:

- Executing a task they're either unsure how to do or reluctant to do.
- Taking on a big project that appears daunting.
- "Looking badly" when performing an activity.

Of course, we'll all encounter variations of these three situations throughout everyday life. The most important thing to realize is you build and keep your confidence by following a formula similar to the one I recommended for forming a habit. There is an element of cueing your environment, doing the task, reflecting, and rewarding yourself. Remember, if you want to change your mindset and thoughts about anything, you need to "do" your way into this new mindset. Let's cover each of these scenarios and the formulas you can use to build your confidence.

Executing a Task

Sometimes in our lives, we're required to do a task or activity and we simply don't have the confidence to do it. This can be an activity that's part of our job or something we're doing as a hobby. It could be some act that's thrust in front of us out of necessity such as finding a new job.

You might need to make cold calls to prospects you'd like to turn into clients. It could be an entire dance routine where you're having trouble with one on the particular steps. Whatever it is, building confidence in these situations is about putting in the repetitions.

You do it. Evaluate it. Repeat it. Evaluate it. Repeat it. This works whether it's a singular event like a cold call or a specific event inside of a larger program such as a daily run for an entire marathon training program.

The important part regarding these repetitions is that you're doing them correctly, evaluating what's working, making the necessary adjustments, and not stopping.

One of the greatest examples of this type of repetition is my Job Search Challenge®. I have a large community of job seekers who need help finding their new jobs. One of the techniques I teach them is this challenge where I want them to send three emails each day to people at their prospective employers. At first, I get reluctance and a lot of, "Oh, no! I don't want to send an email to someone I don't know to inquire about a job!"

I encourage the people in the programs to keep at it and within a few days they usually respond back to me with messages such as, "Whoa. This is so much easier than I thought it would be and it works. People are getting back to me and helping!" This occurs primarily because they get in motion and it gets easier with practice. Plus, they discover no one will actually bite them through an email.

When it comes to "putting in the reps," I like to add two elements that accelerate your ability to build confidence. First, when appropriate, it's helpful to over-quota the repetitions. That is, if you're charged with making ten cold calls, try to make twenty or fifty. I ask my Job Search Challenge® participants to send three emails each day. Perhaps they could over-quota the challenge by sending five messages each day.

The second element is to increase the level of difficulty or take one extra step when appropriate. You might add complexity to your practice to make the actual, real-life execution of the activity easier. Occasionally, when I go for a training run, I'll wear heavier shoes than I'd wear in a race. I use this technique when the over-quota approach might not be wise. Adding extra miles to training runs could result in an injury, but making the individual run a little more difficult will make me stronger.

Adding these extra layers of difficulty might also help with your progressive mastery of the skill.

The main point is the more frequently you do it (correctly), the better you'll get at it and the more confident you'll become.

Taking on a Big Project

Sometimes, we become apprehensive about tackling a major effort because we're uncertain of the level of complexity or lack visibility of all the steps required to complete it. There may not only be one difficult task; there might be many of them. What's worse is we don't know what we're getting ourselves into. This initially ambiguous effort can make our confidence wane.

In these instances, people become debilitated and unable to start because they cannot see how they'll accomplish every step. On one hand, I'd argue the lack of knowing is what makes the journey fun because the project will teach us a great deal. This is the part of life and work and hobbies worth embracing—the journey of learning. For the purposes of our lesson here, however, let's consider any major undertaking with lots of steps.

We don't want the fact it appears difficult to stop you. Keep in mind, whatever your project is, there are likely people around the world who accomplish something similar every day. Whether that's starting a business, writing a book, or anything you want to accomplish, you can do it with the right mindset and actions.

The most important part to building your confidence and overcoming your reluctance is to break it down into smaller pieces. Let's take this book for example. It's my fourth book, but when I wrote my first book, I had absolutely no clue what I was doing. All I knew before I started was there were millions of books published each year. I didn't know how to start a YouTube channel or a podcast. I didn't know how to build an online training program or how I'd get people to use their credit cards to pay for the training. I was a total novice in all these examples. If I can figure it out, I'm sure you can too.

For any major project I undertake, especially something new, I try to think in terms of three to five steps ahead. Those are manageable numbers and I won't get overwhelmed. I'm not doing three steps at once. I'm simply trying to visualize and keep in mind what's to come.

For my first book, I listed the steps I knew I needed to tackle. There were more than five, but the important thing was to get them down as part of the plan. I needed a topic. I needed to draft an outline. I needed to schedule time each day to write. I needed to actually write each day. I needed to get a publisher. I'd figure out later how to find one. I'm sure there'd be artwork for the outside and inside of the book. Someone will need to edit the book. It needs to somehow find its way to Amazon and Barnes and Noble and other retailers around the world. I'm sure there are other aspects to marketing the book to the public and on and on.

Whatever your project is, breaking it down into smaller pieces will help. To make progress, the only step you need to take is the next step. To constantly remind myself not to get overwhelmed with any of my projects, I have a note on the front page of my journal to use the next-step rule. That next-step rule for me is to simply "do the next act."

When you continue to stay in motion, you will keep your momentum going. I often say, "You don't get it until you get into it," and "It's easier to redirect a moving object than a stationary one." Both of these expressions are especially true when it comes to gaining traction and confidence as you tackle your biggest efforts.

Always remember, your success, in anything, will have more to do with where you place your attention than your ability. If you have a bias for action and focus on the next step, you'll keep that momentum, make progress, and build confidence.

Speaking of making progress, there is one other key step to help you build your confidence when it comes to lengthy projects. It's also a tool to help with your reflection and evaluation. That step is to use your outline, plan, or journal to track and log your progress.

Every project, especially ones that take a long time, needs a plan that shows the steps. The plan might change over time as you learn more about the steps you need to take. The most important aspect is to keep your strategy and goal intact and adjust the plan as you need to along the way. It's better to fall in love with the planning process than the plan. If your plan is too rigid, you'll likely not reach your goal.

As an example, with writing this book, I have an outline to write the book, a proposal to offer to the publishers, a sales plan to bring it to the retail market, and a few other essential plans. I also have a writing log. At the end of each workday, I make sure I know what portion of the book I'll write tomorrow morning. I wake up, zip through my morning routine, sit down at my desk, and start writing that section. When I'm finished, I log the session number, the number of words I wrote, and a few other notes to help me track how I'm progressing.

As I type this, I'm in my fifty-sixth writing session and the unedited manuscript has over 70,000 words so far. I still need to write quite a bit, however, when I look at that log and reflect, it shows me how far I've come. I don't dwell on how far I need to go. I keep reminding myself how much I've already accomplished. Each time I sit down to write, I make more progress and get closer to my goal of completing the manuscript. Without a log, diary, or journal, I'd lose sight of all the work I've put in and everything I've learned.

This type of reflection or tracking log is vital whenever you're taking on any major initiative. It's a vital tool to help keep your psyche in order and your confidence high.

"Looking Badly"

The last major issue many people have with confidence is an appearance issue. One of the more common questions I get related to this issue is, "How can I get over my fear of public speaking?" or "What if I post a YouTube video and no one watches it?"

I have news for you. Fear of public speaking isn't a thing. You might call it that. I'd bet you can probably speak to a bunch of people wonderfully. What you have is a fear of looking badly or what other people think of you or some form of ego-based worry that erodes your confidence when it comes to sharing your knowledge with the world. You're afraid of judgment, not public speaking.

Like I've mentioned a half-dozen times earlier, whenever you have a challenge, your success will be found in where you focus your attention rather than your ability.

In these appearance-based obstacles, you're placing your attention on their judgment of you. The fastest way to build confidence in these instances and get over any fear is to focus your attention on the service or support you're providing them rather than their judgment of you. The moment you take your mind off yourself and put it onto them, the act becomes a lot easier and more natural.

I remember the first time I livestreamed on my YouTube Channel. I had very few subscribers, so only a handful of people would even be aware I was available to help them. The few that showed up to the session probably didn't know who I was.

I turned the camera on and started talking. I'm sure I fumbled my words. I tried to concentrate on what I needed to tell them, keep eye contact through the camera, and not push any buttons that would abruptly end the session prematurely.

Everyone needs to start sometime. I reminded myself once I got going, I would know a lot more about how these livestreams work. I reminded myself people need my help. I reminded myself I was practicing and serving and could review the video and learn from it.

There's a common expression content creators use. If you're not embarrassed by your first attempt, you waited too long to start. It's true. Remember this the next time you want to try something you're passionate about and want to deliver it to the world.

When you place your attention on your service rather than their judgment, you'll become more confident and your fears will evaporate.

The right success metrics means nothing ever goes wrong.

I'm sure my three techniques to help build your confidence sound all hunky-dory in theory, but you might be wondering, *What about when something goes wrong?* Of course, something will go wrong! This has to occur for you to get over the challenges, learn to handle the not-previously-encountered complexities, and ultimately grow.

Progress is not linear contrary to what most people hope. To keep yourself, your perspective, and positive attitude intact as you encounter setbacks, you need the right success metrics to help shape the way you interpret those experiences.

Most of our unhappiness, in general, comes from our expectations. That is, the lack of our expectations being met. As it relates to building confidence, we have expectations about our abilities to perform and get the results we want. When we don't attain those results, or see the progress we expected, we become skeptical in our abilities.

The way to avoid this is setting up the correct success metrics and continually evaluating your progress against them. The very best success metrics, characteristically, will be ones you can completely control.

When I started my YouTube Channel in 2016, for example, one of the success metrics I could have set was the number of subscribers. If my channel hits 1,000 subscribers in the first month, I'll call that success. If it hits 10,000 subscribers in the first year, I'll call that success.

The issue with success metrics (or expectations) like these is I have absolutely zero control over them. Of course, I have indirect influence over them. I can put out educational, high-quality videos. There are also a bunch of video settings, tags, search-engine-optimization techniques, and other algorithm-based tricks I could employ. (I knew nothing about these when I started. Still don't know much.)

If I don't achieve a particular number of subscribers, does that mean my videos aren't helpful? Should I quit? These outcome-based, non-controllable success metrics have a way of eroding one's confidence when it comes to progress.

Instead, I focused on metrics that'd guide me, ensure I got consistent feedback so I could evaluate and adjust, mix it up, and keep it fun. I used these as my success metrics when I started my channel and for the first year of its existence:

- Release one full-length recorded video each week on Tuesday morning to provide fifty-two videos within the first year.
- Build a channel that includes the complete array of job-searching topics, not solely ones that get the most views.
- Conduct three live workshops.

Notice how these three metrics are 100 percent within my control. Additionally, while in a subtle way, the second metric, regarding the range of topics, was vital in helping to guide me and stay within my strategy.

Many YouTubers would consider more subscribers the golden success metric. Subscribers generally come from the most popular videos. One of my success metrics was to build a complete channel as it related to job searching, not solely focus on the video topics that got clicks and subscribers. More subscribers for a less-helpful channel was not my measure of success. Building a one-stop, go-to channel for job seekers was my definition of success.

As I released the videos each week, viewers would comment and ask me questions. This helped me understand what their biggest pain points and needs were. I let that guide me regarding the range of topics and videos I'd release to support them.

The main point to all this is regardless of the traction I made in the first year of this important, large initiative, I'd be successful as long as I put in the effort and stayed consistent. The same applies for your undertakings. Dial in your success metrics properly and you'll be a winner every day. Now, it's time for you to start building your confidence!

Photo courtesy of Alex Rogals, Growing Community Media

110

BUILDING CONFIDENCE EXERCISE

Thought-Provokers

1. A critical task I perform frequently where more repetitions would help me "get over the hump" is...
2. The first five steps of a big project I'd like to undertake are...
3. An important project I've been hesitant to undertake because I'm concerned with judgment from others is...
4. Projects I've been working on where I can alter my uncontrollable, outcome-based metrics (specifically identified expectations) to more controllable, process-based metrics are...

Challenge

Week One: Over-quota a critical task. You already identified that key task you're not enthused about doing. Let's start your challenge with more repetitions to accelerate your learning and overcome your reluctance. During week one, set a significantly higher number of repetitions to perform. Even if it seems unrealistic, focus on exceeding your number of "reasonable" daily or weekly repetitions. If you need to make ten cold calls each day, for example, try thirty. Even if you "only" achieve fifteen, you still are 50% higher than your originally targeted number.

Week Two: Start that big project. Now's the time to get going on that passion project you've been putting off because, at this moment, you're unable to see all the steps to complete it. The unknown is the fun part! As this is a large initiative for you, it'll be helpful to get in motion. Let's keep it manageable. Identify and plan the first three to five steps. "Getting your arms around" the project will show you it's possible. You can determine how much effort you want to put into it based on your schedule, but the act of planning will help you begin and diffuse some of your hesitancy.

Week Three: Begin working on a "deliverable" that helps educate or entertain others. The most important aspect of this week's challenge is to **make sure it's something that can be "judged" by others**. Whether that's a piece of art or white paper or presentation in a meeting, the goal is to focus your attention and energy on the benefit it'll have for your audience. Where your awareness goes, your energy flows as they say. As I like to say, your success will be more a function of where you place your attention than your ability.

Week Four: Review your success metrics. This week, review your success metrics for the previous three weeks. As you set out for your tasks and projects, are you measuring your success against controllable or uncontrollable outcomes? As an example, was your goal of your cold calls to make sales? That's technically uncontrollable. Was your goal to execute the cold call? Effectively go through your script? Learn what objections the prospects might have? Be more ready with your rebuttals? This is solely for illustrative purposes, but properly dialed-in success metrics will go a long way in not only increasing your confidence, but also improving your happiness.

PART FOUR

The Communicator

CHAPTER 9

Developing Empathy

If you judge a fish by how it climbs a tree...

There was this recruitment client I'd been working with for a handful of years. She was the CEO of a technology consultancy and her company, among other services, provided technical outsourcing support to organizations to manage their high-speed infrastructure networks. Over the years, she engaged with my firm, milewalk®, to help her hire various executives, project managers, engineers, and technologists.

As you might imagine, as part of her outsourcing service, she needed technologists to answer telephone calls and emails whenever her company's customers had an issue with their networks. The technologists she hired, of course, were just that—technologists. They needed to know how the hardware and software of the network operate so they could fix issues when they arose.

Like many organizations, my client deployed a tiered level of support. There were Tier-One support staff who answered the telephone calls and reviewed the incoming emails. The Tier-One technologists generally served as the "first line of defense" to answer basic questions and solved the least-complex issues. There were also Tier-Two and Tier-Three levels of support staff who were increasingly more knowledgeable and could handle more complex issues.

One day, I was meeting with my client to discuss a new recruitment search for an executive position she wanted to fill. At the end of our meeting, she asked me, "Andy, could you help me hire the support staff for the NOC (Network Operations Center)?"

While it was not our specialty, I asked her, "Growing or having trouble?" I was wondering if she needed to hire additional support staff or whether she wanted to replace her current employees.

She responded, "Well, I have enough staff and we hire them from another recruitment firm who specializes in those types of resources. They look good 'on paper' and pass our technical [interview] screens. They seem to have a lot of trouble with the customer service and organizational part of the job. Our customer satisfaction scores are pretty low."

I asked, "How's their empathy?"

She asked, "Their what?" (She obviously knows what empathy is.)

I continued, "When you assess their empathy levels, how do they score? You *do* evaluate this in the interviews, don't you?"

The transformation on her face was priceless. The lightbulb went on full power.

I said, "No one calls the NOC to tell you how happy they are. They call because something is broken. You know this. The first skills I'd evaluate when I hire people for those jobs are not their technical skills. They're their empathy, customer service, and communication skills. The tech stuff is easy to learn. The [absence of the] other stuff will put you out of business."

Customer service representatives need to be empathetic to be truly great at their job. Nurses, social workers, human resources managers, marketers, and teachers do too. These are not the only professions that require a great deal of empathy. Everyone can become a better person and build a more rewarding and successful career by developing more empathy!

Am I supposed to feel what they feel? How does this work?

You can look up the definition of empathy in any dictionary and you'll find something along the lines of "the ability to understand and share the feelings of another." With respect to all the master dictionary writers in the world, I'd argue the sharing part is a technical impossibility. We're all unique and the way we feel at any moment in time about any situation is based on the experiences we've had.

**No two people can have the exact same experiences or, even
if they did, interpret them the same way.**

No two people can have the exact same experiences or, even if they did, interpret them the same way. We all process our experiences differently. Some have built thicker skin. Some have fabulous emotional support structures while others don't. Two people who are both divorced will never feel the exact same way about their divorces. The same goes for losing a loved one. There simply is no way to truly know how someone is feeling. We can relate, of course, to the joy and pain and suffering.

**I literally wish I could uninvent the expression,
"I know how you're feeling."**

I literally wish I could uninvent the expression, "I know how you're feeling." You simply cannot. You might be able to understand how I might be feeling. You might want to share the burden with me so I don't go through it alone. You'll never, however, be able to feel what I'm feeling because my feelings are my feelings. Your feelings are your feelings. They're irreplicable. Even so, that doesn't mean we shouldn't try!

Being more empathetic improves our capacity to communicate well with others. It helps us lead and inspire others and build more compassionate relationships.

In most instances, people you interact with don't want to be heard as much as they want to be understood. Even if you can't change the way they feel, you'll help the situation and they'll be happier, most of the time, if they believe you're truly listening to them.

The question for many people isn't why is being empathetic a desired quality. I get asked far more often, "Can I build more empathy if I'm not inclined to be empathetic?"

There's an entire menu of empathies?

Before we learn to develop empathy, it's helpful to understand the different types. You might be inclined to build one form versus another depending on your personality, upbringing, and whatever the situation calls for.

Daniel Goleman, author, psychologist, and science journalist, who wrote the mega-best seller *Emotional Intelligence: Why It Can Matter More Than IQ*, classifies empathy into three types. He suggests each type of empathy comes from a different part of the brain.

I'm not a neurologist, so I'll give you my interpretation of Goleman's claim. Let's call it the Andy-version of brain geography.

1. **Cognitive:** For cognitive empathy, Goleman defines this as simply knowing how other people feel and what they might be thinking. I'd call this the "thinking empathy." It centers on thought. It's mechanical. This type is about understanding the other person's mental models and what language you can use to connect with them. This is about you being self-aware and also applying that awareness to understand others. It's akin to seeking perspective by putting yourself in their shoes as you think through (not so much feel) what it would be like to encounter those situations.

2. **Social:** For social empathy, Goleman defines this as being able to feel physically along with others as if their emotions were contagious. To me, this empathy is about feeling as opposed to thinking. However, I'd opine it's about your feelings and not the other people's. This is in the "social brain" and about sensing—in yourself—what the others are feeling. This is about you being able to manage your emotions and use them to connect with other people.

3. **Empathic Concern:** Goleman indicates with this kind of empathy, we not only understand other people's predicaments and feel with them, but are spontaneously moved to help if needed. I'd refer to this type of empathy as the "head and heart" combination that makes us want to act. It's compassionate. It comes from the part of the brain referred to as the "ancient mammalian system for parenting." While the first type of empathy is about thinking and the second is about feeling, this third type is about acting.

Goleman's interpretation of empathy can help us understand how we might approach building our empathy as we communicate with others. I, for example, rarely, if ever, experience myself physically reacting to another's pain. Of course, I feel bad for friends or people I'm working with who are going through difficult times. I cannot feel what they're feeling, so I wouldn't call myself socially or emotionally empathetic (the second type) as Goleman refers to it. I'm more inclined to think and act than feel. That's why I've noticed I lean more heavily on the cognitive (first) and empathic-concern (third) types of empathy when I'm communicating with my wife, friends, and clients. My first instinct isn't naturally to feel, but to understand their situation and get into action to help them if they need it.

Yes, you are correct. The world actually does revolve around you.

If you'd like to build more empathy, let's start not at the beginning, but in the center. In your entire existence, you've never had an experience you were not at the absolute center of. This is inarguable. Everything in your life has happened in front of, behind, to the left, or right of you!

As you've progressed through life, your experiences, not DNA, have shaped the way you think. Over time, your thoughts become more automatic, so much so, you'd think they were hardwired at birth like your eye color and shoe size. They're so immediate, urgent, and "real."

My thoughts, on the other hand, need to be communicated to you. For you to have any sense of how I'm feeling, you need to turn the dial and take yourself off autopilot.

In order to attain any level of empathy the way Goleman or anyone defines it, we need to recognize that any feeling comes first from our thoughts. Oddly, you don't change your thoughts by thinking differently. You change your thoughts by *doing* differently. You actually change the way you think by what you do, not what you think.

Oddly, you don't change your thoughts by thinking differently. You change your thoughts by *doing* differently. You actually change the way you think by what you do, not what you think.

The repeated doing of anything sends messages to ourselves about our abilities and beliefs. When we reflect on what we've done and the results that transpired, we're providing ourselves with a way to rewire our brains to believe something. This is never truer than when we're building a habit as I discussed earlier. After cueing your environment, you do, reflect, and reward. A simple example is the salesperson who's reluctant to cold call prospects to turn them into customers. What starts out as hesitancy and a questioning of ability can turn into confidence after several attempts provided the person reflects, learns, and recognizes progress.

You can build empathy just like you build any good habit. There are two formulas I've used over the years to become more empathetic. The first includes daily practices that lay the foundation for me to develop traits that enable me to be a more empathetic person. The second is a three-step process I use for the specific situations that call for empathy.

Daily practice makes permanent.

As you've learned when we addressed how to focus and listen, there are foundational exercises and practices you can do continually that enable you to perform at your best when the moment calls for it. If you haven't designed your lifestyle to focus, for example, you won't be able to actually concentrate when you need to the most.

Becoming empathetic is no different. There are foundational traits, behaviors, and perspectives you can build over time that make it easier to demonstrate empathy when you need to support others. The earlier in your life you build these, the less reshaping you'll need to do as you get older.

These qualities, especially for most adults who aren't inclined to naturally behave this way, will take some time to ingrain. The point is to do your best. This level of self-improvement is an ongoing process. It's about progress not perfection.

To help myself become more empathetic, each day I practice five exercises. These exercises don't take a lot of time. Your ability to improve your empathy isn't about how much time you spend with exercises like these, but the frequency in which you do them. I incorporate a few of these during my end-of-day planning and reflection. I practice others when I have the opportunity to actually engage with people. You'll see from the list, these are quite easy to integrate, timewise, into your life.

While easy to integrate and practice, some of the exercises are actually quite difficult for me. To help myself, I use reminders to take myself off autopilot. I've written these reminders in places I review frequently, such as my journal and desk pad. I can see them each morning before I write my thoughts of gratitude as well as throughout my workday. Remember, changing your thoughts is tough stuff, so do whatever you need to do to intercept your automated way of thinking.

To build my foundational skills for empathy, here are my five daily practices:

Get to know others: No matter who you are, you likely interact with a diverse group of people. Whether it's your customers or teammates or friends, taking an interest to get to know people's backgrounds, experiences, and perspectives goes a long way in helping you build empathy. The more you know about someone and what they've been through, the easier it is, at a minimum, to be understanding. I have the good fortune of coaching individuals on a daily basis. My client base includes people in nearly 200 different countries. Before I coach people, I remind myself they need my help and to make sure I'm considerate with their feelings and appreciate any difficulties they're experiencing.

Be kind and compassionate: Many times, we work with people who we don't fully understand. Our inability to understand them might come from the way they express themselves, their viewpoints, their desires, or gaps in our knowledge. They might have an accent which isn't native to our ear. Whatever the issue is, it's important to remain kind and considerate. When I'm meeting with people, oftentimes from different countries, I remind myself how fantastic it is they know my language. If anyone has an accent, I know it's likely they know at least one more language than I do! I have respect for this. Remind yourself to be kind first. It might sound like a banal platitude, but the more you remind yourself to be kind, the kinder you'll be.

Listen actively: Paying attention to what others are saying without interrupting, offering solutions, or daydreaming has become more difficult than ever. Why? We practice distraction all day every day with the beeps, alerts, and built-in interruptions available to us via the computers that also make phone calls soldered to our hands. This trains our minds to get sidetracked easily, which makes it much harder to concentrate on what someone else is saying. Remind yourself before your interactions to practice active listening. Active listening is one of the reminders I review before I head into meetings, coaching sessions, or, generally, any encounter I have with another. I'll discuss this tactic more fully as we progress into the communication lessons in this book.

Practice self-reflection: When I perform my planning at the end of the workday, I spend a few minutes reflecting on the day. I review what went well and what I want to improve. During this session, I also reflect on my thoughts and feelings to better understand how they influence my reactions to others. I do this not only for my individual coaching sessions, but also on days I perform live group coaching sessions. Even though I might not be able to interact directly with the group, I review the video replay to see how kind, compassionate, and empathetic I was as I answered their questions. I always strive for a combination of being serious, witty, and encouraging to provide valuable insight that makes their problems easier to handle.

> **The one bulletproof way to know you've mastered self-forgiveness is when you've become completely judgment-free of others.**

Embrace your emotions: I often say, "The one bulletproof way to know you've mastered self-forgiveness is when you've become completely judgment-free of others." This is true and it becomes apparent when you work consistently to forgive yourself of your shortcomings and any behavior you're not proud of. Don't get me wrong. You might do something you consider unacceptable. If that's the case, work to fix it and don't do it again. You can become more empathetic toward others by acknowledging and accepting your own emotions and feelings. As part of my daily reflection exercise, I also make sure to wrap it up by forgiving myself of anything I wish I could do over. Then, I remind myself to do better the next time.

Remember, developing empathy is a continuous process and takes time and practice. The more of these exercises you can work into your daily routine, the easier it'll be to practice empathy when the opportunity arises.

It's game time. Now what?

Laying the foundation for making yourself more empathetic is a fantastic starting point. When interacting with others, there are a few helpful steps to perform during the communication. I view any engagement an opportunity to practice empathy and consider the before, during, and after aspects.

1. Before you engage, anticipate the discussion.

Before you interact with people, pause, and try to put yourself in their shoes. Consider what it might it be like to go through what they're going through. I've mentioned my Thursday live group coaching sessions on my YouTube Channel. When I'm helping a group of people in this format, as they ask me their questions via the chat, I have a routine before the session where I verbalize a few reminders. For example, I say to myself, "I'm so thankful these people would take time out of their day to listen to me. They show up because they need my help. They don't know what I know, otherwise they wouldn't need to spend their time with me. Be gentle and remember that." I say a bunch of other stuff, but you get the idea and I'm on a word count.

Sometimes, you might be interacting with people who have very different viewpoints from yours. When I encounter this, I attempt to "argue for their side" before the interaction. This is an especially masterful step when "negotiating." It works in any situation when you're developing a solution or even if you're simply lending an ear.

Of course, occasionally, we don't know we're about to get into a discussion. Perhaps someone just pops into your office unexpectedly or your spouse springs something on you. In these cases, if you don't have a chance to think about this beforehand, try a quick mental pause to catch your breath. Think for a moment about the other person's viewpoint or what they might be going through.

You can also build your ability to do this quickly if you've (as I mentioned a few times previously) considered your day. This early-morning assessment of the possibilities of your day primes your thinking and expedites your ability to be nimble when surprise visits or discussions occur.

2. During the engagement, practice being empathetic.

Being empathetic during your discussions gets easier with practice. The best and easiest advantage you can offer yourself is to use your reminders to put yourself on alert immediately prior to your discussion. That way, when you're in the midst of your interaction, it'll be much easier to actually be empathetic. Here are a few tactics I use to help me be empathetic when I'm interacting with others.

- **Show interest:** Give them your full attention and actively listen to what they are saying.

- **Avoid interruptions:** Let them speak without interrupting them.

- **Ask questions:** Show you're interested in what they have to say by asking the appropriate questions.

- **Validate their feelings:** Acknowledge their emotions and demonstrate you understand how they feel.

- **Reflect back what you hear:** Repeat back what they said, perhaps using different words, to confirm you understand them.

- **Keep perspective:** Imagine how you would feel if you were in the same situation and try to understand their perspective.

Remember, being empathetic is about understanding and connecting with others, not solely offering solutions or advice.

3. After the engagement, reflect, and ask, "How was I?"

Remember, you're constantly trying to rewire your brain and reinforce your new state of being. This can only be done—effectively—if you reflect on what you did. Make mental notes so you can channel them into your future interactions. You can do this immediately following your discussion or at the end of the day or, even better, at both times. You're continually evaluating and reflecting on what ultimately helps you get better. If you were trying to build any skill, you would evaluate your performance and make the necessary adjustments. Building empathy requires a lot of self-reflection because our thoughts are automatic and we don't easily realize how others perceive us. The more you pause to work on this, the more empathetic you'll become!

Now, it's time for you to start becoming more empathetic!

DEVELOPING EMPATHY EXERCISE

Thought-Provokers

1A. Among the cognitive, social, and empathetic-concern types of empathy, I tend to be strongest with...

1B. Ways I can improve in the other two areas are...

2A. A recent situation where I could have been more empathetic was...

2B. Looking back, I could have handled it better if I...

3A. My most common work situations where I'll need to practice empathy are...

3B. During these situations, my formula to be more empathic will be...

4A. My most common personal situations where I'll need to practice empathy are...

4B. During those situations, my formula to be more empathetic will be...

Challenge

Step Zero: Get a journal to record what you're doing, how you're interacting, and other related steps throughout the challenge.

Week One: Practice, each morning throughout the week, **considering your day**. What could happen throughout the day? How would your highest, most empathetic self handle those situations? Then, immediately before any interaction, **practice considering that interaction** and the person or people you'll interact with. What might it be like to be them? Attempt to mentally "go through" what they're going through. This step is simply to help you intercept your automated thinking.

Week Two: Pick a **personal situation** each day to practice empathy. My preference would be to pick the same situation each day (e.g., dinner conversation with your spouse, partner, etc.). It's better to groove your practice to get comfortable thinking this way. Remember, no matter who you are, this isn't a natural reaction. We process the world the way WE process the world. Everyone processes it differently. Get comfortable realizing and practicing this.

Week Three: Pick a **work situation** each day to practice empathy. Much like in your personal encounter, it's a great idea to practice during the same type of interaction. Perhaps you have a customer or boss or staff member you can consider. Choose one person or type of person to really concentrate on. Of course, you can practice as much as you'd like, but when you're learning a new skill, it's more effective to isolate, so you can evaluate (see the next step).

Week Four: Evaluate your entire month to see how you performed. It's best to journal as you go and evaluate your level of empathy immediately while these discussions are fresh in your mind. You can reflect at the end of each day and week. The more you pause to consider what happened, the easier it'll be to stay in tune with your behavior and make adjustments. At the end of the month, do a full review of how you performed, what you did well, and what you want to improve.

CHAPTER 10

Building Trust

I trust him to get a hit. He bats .300.

Everyone has their own relationship with trust. Some like to give trust to others right away. They get to keep it until they do something to lose it. Others prefer to offer trust only after it's been earned. In all cases, trust usually entails a degree of reliability. Then it becomes a matter of degree of reliability. In some instances, that reliability needs to be 100 percent. In others, you might consider someone reliable when they come through as low as 33 percent of the time. I'd certainly want my major league baseball player whose batting average is .300 to be in the batter's box with runners in scoring position.

Of course, we all have the friends who show up on time 50 percent of the time. If you find yourself artificially dialing back the starting time for these friends, it's perfectly okay to admit you have trust issues with them.

What about trust when it comes to business relationships? These types of relationships are a bit different than personal ones because we often need to get our business colleagues, partners, and customers to trust us quickly. While we can take time to develop lifelong friendships built on trust, in business, however, we often need to accelerate that timeline because our professional and company's success often depend on it.

We want to be viewed as trustworthy. Even if we are the straightest and narrowest of rule followers, we become baffled at the notion that anyone wouldn't see us as honorable, reliable, and dependable. Even so, our well-adjusted, adult selves know trust is earned and it takes more than honesty when someone doesn't know us well.

If you want to gain the trust of your co-workers, boss, teammates, and customers as quickly as possible, you need to know what truly drives trust. It's not as simple as just being authentic and following through on your promises.

People don't trust you because you're honest...

Your life would be a lot easier if you could earn someone's trust by being honest and delivering what you committed to delivering. Of course, over time, many of your personal relationships will blossom into trusting relationships when you're consistently honest over a period of time.

In business, you want, and likely need, someone to trust you as soon as possible. Why would someone do that? I can tell you what doesn't usually make a difference. That shiny degree you have or the way you talk won't buy you as much credibility as you think. Those might help, but trust generally boils down to three areas the person considers—ability, willingness, and values.

Ability

The first question that comes to someone's mind when forging a new business relationship is, "Does this person have the ability to help me?"

Trust is about perception, not reality.

For people to trust you to help them, they need to feel you have the ability to help them. The funny thing about this is it doesn't matter whether you actually have the ability or not. As a gut check, think about any time you were disappointed after you purchased services from someone who sounded smart and whose references were impeccable. Trust is about perception, not reality. I live this every day when I coach my job-seeking clients for their job interviews. They know, all too well, the most qualified person with the greatest ability doesn't always get the job. It's about perception and interpretation. (Let's ignore the "who you know" thing here.)

Make sure when you meet people for the first time, you recognize this question will be on the top of their minds when it comes to whether they'll consider trusting you.

Willingness

Assuming they believe you have the ability to help them, the next question they ask themselves is, "Will this person—in this situation—actually help me?" After ability, the question shifts to a me-you relationship. Just because you can, doesn't mean you will—for me.

This will-they-do-it-for-me consideration is even more powerful than the ability consideration. Why? Because now it has become personal. Will this coach be there for me during my career development? Will my boss have my back? Will this person do the job I'm hiring her to do? Will this company give me my money back if its product breaks?

Values

After you've passed the can-you and will-you questions, it becomes a matter of values. The question now is, "Does this person's values align with mine?"

There will always be an element of value congruence that goes along with any relationship. People trust people who they see eye-to-eye with when it comes to the way they treat each other and approach the world. This kindred-spirit element is so powerful it'll often push you over the top if the people have any hesitation about their first two questions.

Think about it. Have you ever engaged in business relationships with people just because you liked them? You liked them for reasons related to their values. They saw the world the same way you did, had similar belief templates, or reminded you of a younger you.

I've never really subscribed to the fact that opposites attract—in any relationship. Husbands and wives can have different hobbies or different personalities, but if their foundational values are different, divorce is imminent. This is true for people and companies and just about any other relationship you can imagine.

Why Does Someone Trust You?

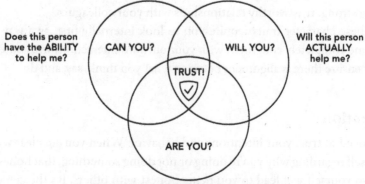

Does this person have the ABILITY to help me? — CAN YOU? — WILL YOU? — Will this person ACTUALLY help me?

TRUST!

ARE YOU?

Does this person's VALUES align with mine?

Whenever you encounter someone for the first time, and through the early stages of your relationship building, keep in mind the above graphic and work to answer the three questions for them!

Think. Say. Do. You'll never be more at peace than when those three are the same.

How do you build and keep trust? There are many techniques depending on your particular vocation. Perhaps you meet face-to-face with your teammates and customers. These situations involve being consistent with what you say and do and how you follow through on your promises. I, for example, who interact online with most of my community, use email digests and complimentary group coaching sessions every week to offer valuable career lessons. My demonstrated consistency and delivering on my promises are also vehicles to earn trust over time.

The mediums you use should help you answer "the ability" question for the other parties. Whether you're able to answer and overcome this question quickly or over time, usually, this is the easiest question for them to answer. Either they feel you have the ability or don't.

The latter two questions are a bit trickier. To help answer the "Will this person help me?" and "Does this person's values align with mine?" questions, there are four key character traits to address: 1) Intention, 2) Authenticity, 3) Delivery, and 4) Togetherness.

131

When these traits are combined with the more-obvious trust-builders such as honesty, integrity, and communication, you'll find yourself developing strong, trustworthy relationships with your colleagues.

These character traits require you to look internally first, as a way to become completely congruent with your outward interactions with others. They ensure there is alignment between what you think, say, and do.

Intention

You need to trust your intentions and behavior. When you are clear with yourself regarding why you're doing or not doing something, that honesty within yourself will lead to you being honest with others. It's the centerpiece for following through on your promises.

Intention matters, not just for them, but more so for you. Why? Trust isn't solely about gaining their trust of you. It's about your own congruence. You might have heard the expression related to the double standard when it comes to judgment. We judge others by their behavior, but we judge ourselves by our intention. How many times have you said, "Well, I didn't mean to"? Of course, you weren't guilty because you didn't intend to!

You'll never be remembered for your intentions nor forgotten for your actions.

I like to say, "You'll never be remembered for your intentions nor forgotten for your actions." You might not be remembered for your intentions, but it's a great place to start when earning the trust of others.

Authenticity

It's my belief, the thing we want most is to be ourselves. This is the feeling we all chase every day.

What do we think when someone uses the word "authentic?" Is it possible it's that exhilarating feeling that comes with not having to pretend to be something we're not?

When you consider trusting someone at its very core, by its nature, that means taking a risk and being vulnerable. The mere fact we need to trust people or they need to trust us means there is a risk they or we might not come through. Vulnerability is being our authentic selves with another person. This is essentially the source of trust from another. You being you and sharing you with them.

> **Vulnerability is being our authentic selves with another person.**

Internally, this means being authentic with yourself. Externally, this means being your authentic self with others.

Delivery

There is no greater ingredient for building trust than when you do what you say you'll do. Others are able to observe this congruence in us. It's what helps them believe we're trustworthy.

What happens within ourselves when there is a struggle between what we think, say, and do? Initially, we might be able to say something we don't truly believe. We're able to do something we don't actually want to do.

Now, recollect the times in your life when you were completely in alignment with thinking, saying, and doing. This led to being consistent externally with others in what you thought, said, and did. In these instances, you likely put their minds at ease. They were thinking, *You will do it for me.* Once this starts, they continue to think that as long as what you think, say, and do for them is consistent.

When you consistently deliver on your promises, you've provided yourself and them with the foundation for building trust. You've also given yourself the opportunity to over-deliver with one extra step. That one extra step can be anything you want. Just take it one step further.

Togetherness

Through your actions you show the other person you're willing to help them. When you add an element of sharing, unity, and togetherness, you solidify that willingness.

This is you overdelivering to show your willingness. That is, you're effectively saying, "Not only am I willing to help you, but I'll be there with you every step of the way by doing this with you!"

How does this team-oriented nature feel internally? I like to say, "We become judgment-free of others the moment we become judgment-free of ourselves."

This helps you become a good teammate for yourself. It's healthy to be your own best cheerleader, fan, and supporter. This also makes it easier for you to team up with others.

What do teammates do? They work together to achieve a common goal. They also do it in an open-minded, welcoming way. To support this team orientation, I lean on five principles that expedite relationship building. They are listening to each other, communicating to eliminate ambiguity, celebrating diversity, building each other's confidence, and giving credit.

What's the rush?

While these four character traits help you address the willingness and values questions people have when it comes to trust, there is no substitute for time and behaving this way on an ongoing basis.

When you think long-term and aren't in a hurry, your intentions will almost automatically become purer within yourself and toward others. This happens because you're not focused on the what's-in-it-for-me right now.

Long-term thinkers and trust-builders take it one step at a time, enjoy the journey and the interactions, and remain present. Short-term thinkers look for the quick fix, are generally internally and externally misaligned, and often need to repair their relationships later.

You'll, practically by default, be more trustworthy and have better results, in every form, when you consider the long-term healthy outcome for you and the other parties in your relationships. When in doubt, ask yourself, "What's the best long-term outcome of this relationship?"

BUILDING TRUST EXERCISE

Thought-Provokers

1A. Areas of my life where I feel I haven't been honest with myself include...

1B. I can take these steps to become more honest in these areas...

2A. Areas of my life where what I think, say, and do are not in complete harmony are...

2B. I can take these steps to become more congruent...

3A. Relationships in my work life and personal life I feel need a health boost include...

3B. Three steps I can take to improve each of these are...

4A. Areas in my life where I've been focusing on the short-term include...

4B. The steps I can take to become more mindful of the best long-term outcomes include...

Challenge

Week One: Practice being honest with yourself. For the areas of your life you identified you weren't being honest with yourself (your career, personal relationships, etc.), assess why that is and identify the first three steps you can take to get yourself in sync. For example, if you don't love your current job, can you speak to your boss or look for a new job within the company or externally? Should you find a new career? Is your current love relationship not working for you? What steps can you take to get it in order or move on?

Week Two: Evaluate your congruency. For this entire week, keep track (a logbook, field notes, e-diary) of whether you're following through on your actual and intended promises. Is what you're thinking the same as what you're saying and doing? Can you keep those *intended* promises you *meant* to make? If you meant to call your friend or customer, did you actually call even if you didn't tell them you were going to call?

Week Three: Give three relationships a health boost. Choose three relationships of any kind (partner, customer, teammate, etc.) and work on the steps you previously identified to enhance them. These don't need to be "broken" relationships. Simply think of three important people in your professional or personal life whose relationships you'd like to strengthen. Now, go do it!

Week Four: Step back to get ahead. Review three areas of your life or relationships where you've been thinking short term. These are situations where all your moves seem to be focused on yielding immediate results. How can you improve the quality of your actions and relationships, in the short term, by taking more thoughtful long-term steps? Are you continually reaching out to your network only when you need something? Have you considered reaching out to your colleagues to see how they're doing and whether they need anything? It's just an example, but hopefully it illustrates ways to help you start planting seeds instead of assuming everything needs to be Jack's beanstalk!

CHAPTER 11

Networking

It's not who you know. It's not what you know.
It's who knows what you know.

I have this friend named Tom. He and I went to high school together. We've remained friends over the years even though we connect infrequently. We exchange an email here or there and get together socially every now and then. Since this is the twenty-first century, we are, naturally, Facebook friends and directly connected on LinkedIn. I even have his telephone number programmed in my contacts list on my iPhone.

I've remained friends with many of the guys I went to school with (it was an all-boys school while I attended). Even though I speak to only a handful on a frequent basis, if anyone from my graduating class called me out of the blue, I'd respond quickly regardless of what prompted his message. That's how I feel about the guys who walked the same hallways of Fenwick High School as I did.

A few years back, my wife and I sold our condominium so we could move into the house we currently live in. After we moved in, my wife posted the obligatory Facebook pictures to let our friends know where to find us.

We got several, "When's the dinner party?" responses to her post. Wedged somewhere between those was a reply from Tom. He asked, "Why didn't you let me know you were moving? I'm a real estate agent now and could have helped you!"

My response was, "I didn't know that. I thought you were still managing your [other] business."

Your network is a career insurance policy that pays dividends too.

No matter who you are or what you do professionally, a healthy network will provide you with one of the greatest advantages in advancing your career. Of course, you need to keep it up to date.

People buy from who they like. Companies hire who they like. They hire friends they know and friends of friends and so forth. If I'd known Tom was a real estate agent, I would have called him to sell my home.

When it comes to keeping up your friendships, just like maintaining your professional network, the issue has always been that it requires time and energy. Nowadays, it's tougher than ever to keep up with anyone who's not in your immediate family or inner circle of friends.

We're busier than we've ever been, which leaves less time to maintain our relationships. Thanks to technology that has made our lives "easier," we're also accessible on a twenty-four-hour basis to handle the demands of our organizations. Our personal lives have become frenetic. Somewhere between the time I was a child and today, much of a parent's life has become consumed with their kids' activities. The little league baseball season, which used to be a local-park, eight-weeks-in-the-summer activity, has become a three-hundred-sixty-five-days-every-year-across-state-lines-never-ending grind for ten-year-olds. My three siblings, parents to nine child "athletes," spend more time traveling for their children's lacrosse games, football games, volleyball tournaments, and track meets than they do anything else. I need colored push pins and a cork-board map of the United States to keep track of where everyone is on any given day. How would my siblings ever have time to foster their professional networks?

Whether your lifestyle is like theirs or you're simply busy with your own career, you need to understand the value of your network, how to build it, and use a system to ensure you manage it well.

Isn't "the network" the thing my computer system runs on?

Before we get into the how-to, it's important we're clear on what professional networking is. To me, it's about building relationships, supporting them, and expanding yours and others' networks.

Networking is making a real-life connection, not plopping a contact in your phonebook. A contact is nothing more than a name. A connection is a full-blown relationship.

Networking is making a real-life connection, not plopping a contact in your phonebook. A contact is nothing more than a name. A connection is a full-blown relationship. Of course, you'll have the occasional quick acts of help from acquaintances and referrals from colleagues. When you want to truly be helpful and gain the value of a healthy network, you need to put forth the effort to ensure that happens.

That means networking becomes more powerful when you treat it as an all-the-time, consistent effort. Consistency is what keeps it growing and your bonds strong. It's not about being perfect or hitting the exact right person at the right time. It's about taking the right steps and putting in the energy on an ongoing basis. That steadiness is more important than the once-in-a-lifetime homerun relationship.

It's also best if you build and maintain your network proactively. Specifically, make your efforts targeted based on your goals. The best tool you can build for yourself to help you stay on track with your goals is a networking map. Your map might look like an organigram to help you visualize, and be deliberate, about who you want to meet and how you can "get to" that person. Think *I'm here. They're there. How do I get introduced to them or how can I reach out to them directly?*

You're not only nurturing your existing relationships, but also expanding your network and hopefully the network of others.

How do I build a network? What if I'm a recluse?

Let's first address how to build your network. The best and easiest way, of course, is to get an introduction from someone you already know. Whether that's an email introduction or a friend who introduces you to another at a party, these reference-based avenues usually go over well.

You can also put yourself in positions where it's easy to meet people. For example, attending a networking event is helpful because everyone there has the same goal and they're willing participants. You're not likely to get "turned down" when you open up a conversation.

139

Of course, you can meet people at committee meetings, country clubs, alumni dinners, and any of a number of interactions. These types of formats tend to be local-based and a matter of similar interest more than anything else.

Thanks to the digital age we live in, networking doesn't need to be limited to the people in our community, industry, or location. We can use online mediums, to which most have grown accustomed, to meet new people. Vehicles such as email, direct messaging, and chat, are simple to use. It's not the tools, or your ability to reach someone, that are the problems. The challenge is knowing what to say to a "stranger" that will elicit a response.

After substantial trial and error and data analysis through my corporate marketing and networking efforts as well as my personal relationship-building attempts, I've determined there are seven key ingredients to an effective networking message. By "effective," I mean one that actually gets a response.

Your first and only goal when you reach out to people is to get them to respond. That gives you a starting point and you can see where it goes from there. You can do something with a "No, thanks." You can't do anything with silence.

The seven pieces of information that make your networking message powerful include:

1. **Who you are:** You need to let them know who you are. While this may sound extremely obvious, I'm amazed at how poorly many people manage the opener of the message. This part needs to be clear and straightforward such as, "My name is Andy and I'm a career coach."

2. **Why you chose this person:** The second part of your message explains the rationale behind why you selected this person. This is vital if you're sending the message to someone without a referral because it highlights why you chose them as opposed to someone else. This level of uniqueness has a way of warming up the rather cold nature of your reach-out. It shows people you took the time to notice them. You might say, "I noticed you work for [insert company here] ..." or "I saw from your profile you are in charge of [insert that here] ..." If you received the person's name from

someone, you would simply mention that. For instance, "Chuck gave me your name and mentioned you are in charge of..."

3. **What you want or the reason you're contacting this person:** It's best if you get right to the reason you're reaching out. State, "The reason I'm reaching out is..." or "I was hoping you could help me with..." A best practice with networking is to give first and ask second. That means, "what you want" could technically be what you're giving to the person.

4. **You did your research or investigated properly:** The fourth part of your message shows you did some investigation that led you to this person. For example, "While I was looking for [...] I came across you and noticed..." If it sounds more natural based on who the person is, you can combine this fourth part with the second part. The important aspect here is to demonstrate this is a one-of-a-kind message. It can only be sent to this specific individual. You're showing the person you aren't sending this "form letter" to hundreds of people hoping someone gets back to you. You are implying, *I'm sending you this one-of-a-kind message in the hope you (specifically) get back to me.* The combination of numbers two and four is what substantially increases the likelihood you'll receive a response.

> **You're showing the person you aren't sending this "form letter" to hundreds of people hoping someone gets back to you. You are implying, *I'm sending you this one-of-a-kind message in the hope you (specifically) get back to me.***

5. **What you offer them:** You want to include the value you can immediately offer this person. There needs to be something in your message that conveys the reason why it would be beneficial for this individual to respond. This will depend on the nature of your networking message, but one immediate valuable asset can be your network. I also teach this technique to my job-searching clients. In these cases, what they can offer in their networking messages are their experiences and services as employees. The range of value you can provide to somebody may be infinite, but you need to help them see the value immediately.

6. **You are grateful:** Make sure to thank them for their time and consideration. This is quite easy to forget. More importantly, make it simple, keep it tight, and don't be obsequious. Everyone is busy and there's no need to say, "Thank you so much. I know how busy you must be blah, blah, blah." A simple, "Thank you so much for considering this…" works wonders.

7. **What the next step is:** There needs to be a call to action to serve as a prompter regarding what you want this person to do next. This is the individual's cue to get back to you. The more specific the call-to-action the better because it's easier to respond to something narrow than something wide. For example, "Do you know anyone at the milewalk Academy® I can contact?" is more effective than "I'm looking to network with people in the recruitment arena and wanted to see if you know anyone?" I realize you might want to get the names of people in recruitment, but it's important to make it easy on the person to respond. Think about them first and yourself second. The more difficult it is to respond or the more (mental) work you're asking the individual to do, the greater the likelihood of delay or total disregard. Keep in mind, your goal is to get a response. Make that as easy for them as possible.

> *You don't need to hit me over the head thirty-one times.*
> *Thirty is plenty.*

I'm sure you're wondering what a "cold" networking message might look like, so I have a story and a sample for you.

In 2016, before I offered my first online training program to the world, I was focusing on two vital success steps—building a network and a community.

At this point in my career, I'd been working for twenty-eight years as a technology consultant and executive recruiter. To say I had a gigantic professional network would be an understatement. I managed people, supported clients, recruited job candidates, and had business colleagues across the globe. I'd kept everyone's phone number and email address, so my "phonebook" was filled with tens of thousands of people.

The size of my network wasn't my problem. The people in it, however, weren't ones who could help me establish my online training business nor did they know me as a career coach. I also had a community of exactly zero people who knew I'd soon be providing paid services to individuals in addition to the corporations I'd been supporting for nearly three decades.

I did what felt natural to me. I started looking for individuals who could educate me on my new business venture. I sought coaches and trainers and watched their videos, read their books, and attended their in-person seminars. I established relationships with coaches as well as the people who attended their seminars.

To start building my community and awareness of my venture, I started creating videos on YouTube and offering complimentary, down-loadable templates. This would help people on the other side of the internet benefit as it related to their job searches and career development. This would also give them a glimpse of my subject matter expertise and hopefully start us down the path of a trusting relationship in which they could greatly benefit.

One day, I was watching a video training session of one of my coaches. He indicated many of the online e-zines welcomed articles from contributors. If you were successful in submitting yours, it could open a path to helping more people and becoming known to a larger audience. Some e-zines offered these opportunities via their websites. He indicated *The Huffington Post*, now *HuffPost*, was one of those sites.

Before I submitted any articles, I added Arianna Huffington, who is the founder, and a few editors of the e-zine to my network map.

At this point, I had been blogging and vlogging for a while and accumulated quite an inventory of articles and videos. I asked a member of my team, Rhonda, to help me get one of my articles selected by *The Huffington Post*. Her charter was to enter one of our articles into their online submission form every morning for the next thirty days or until we got a hit, whichever came first. She did exactly this and we heard exactly nothing.

Over the course of the month, I did more research and discovered I didn't know anyone who knew Arianna Huffington or the editors. Naturally, I did what any sane person would do and emailed her directly. In fact, I emailed her at exactly 4:34 PM CDT on Thursday, July 14, 2016. She must have been busy because it took her all the way until 10:45 AM CDT on Friday, July 15, 2016 to get back to me. This is our exchange:

Dear Ms. Huffington,

My name is Andy LaCivita and I'm a career coach. I'm a huge fan and admirer of what you've built and how it contributes to the benefit of our world. I'm writing because I'd love to join your effort and see whether you think I'd be a valuable contributor to The Huffington Post.

I've dedicated my life to helping people find their passions and purposes so they can lead rewarding careers and fulfilled lives. I've done this through my recruitment firm milewalk®, three published books, and (top 5 Human Resources/Careers) blog Tips for Work and Life®. Although I've built a nice platform and following, I'd like to help more people.

This past year, I was encouraged by Brendon Burchard's (Experts Academy) training to pursue contributing to The Huffington Post. I've submitted 30 articles via your website and am still awaiting response.

I hoped reaching out to you might help my consideration.

Thank you so much for reviewing this. I'd welcome any insight or feedback you can provide.

Sincerely,
Andy

Her response:

Dear Andy, many thanks for your note. I checked you out and we would love to feature your voice on HuffPost. I am cc'ing our blog editor Madeline to send you a password so you can start blogging on the site.

All the best,
Arianna

While I have spent considerable time working on the networking-message formula since my original message to Arianna Huffington several years ago, you'll notice the seven elements embodied in my message.

While my network-message copywriting skills have improved since that time and my letter to her could have been more effective, the important takeaway for you is to hit the dang "send" button! Get your messages out to the people you want to connect with. It's better they are sent than perfect. Be consistent with your initial reach-outs and not pesty with your follow-ups.

After I received Arianna Huffington's response and my blogging credentials from Madeline, I took the first article we (Rhonda and I, that is) submitted and loaded it into the *Huffington Post* website and hit "Publish!"

The next morning, Saturday, I was running errands and pulled into the grocery store parking lot. I wanted to call my wife to see if there were any additions to the shopping list. As I looked at my phone, I noticed we received 9,786 downloads of one of our free templates. At first, I'm wondering, *What the heck?* Then, I realized what happened.

In less than one day, nearly 10,000 more people would benefit from something I created simply because I was unafraid to hit the "send" button to someone who could help me. I hope you remember this story next time you're hesitating to reach out to someone you want to meet.

Don't be a one-hit wonder or solely a digital nomad.

Consistency, at anything in life, is what makes you successful in the long run. Be consistent in reaching out and networking with new people each month. Be consistent in nurturing your existing relationships because they'll atrophy if you don't cultivate them on an ongoing basis.

Building a great network takes time and should be viewed as a long-term effort. The more short-term your focus, the poorer and less genuine your results will be.

It's not solely about the frequency, but also the mediums. We've grown accustomed to texting and emailing, but networking is much more effective when you're able to communicate directly. The online formats are wonderful for openers and logistical purposes, but are not productive for truly building and nurturing relationships. I realize, of course, if you're networking with people on the other side of the planet, it will be more difficult to shake their hands. In these instances, I'd recommend video chat or some format where you can see each other.

The main exception to meeting in person is when you're serving as the conduit to facilitate an introduction between people. Any way you can connect two people is a good way.

It's one big trust-building effort.

Being genuine and building trust are critical to creating a healthy network. If you're focused on the long-term vitality of your network as a whole and the strength of the individual connections as the parts, you're more inclined to take the proper steps to build a trustworthy reputation and trusting relationships.

One of the best and easiest ways to build trust in these instances is to follow through on your promises. I even have a little formula I created. I call it "I will by via." That's my shorthand for…

I will do [insert action] for you by [insert date] and I'll follow up with you via [insert medium].

For example, I'll reach out to Joe for you by Thursday and I'll follow up with you via email to let you know what he said.

You can structure this any way you'd like, but the important elements are to be specific, have a follow-up date, and a call-to-action (that is, next step). If you leave it open-ended without a specific date, it likely won't get done. People get busy, the act becomes less important, especially because it's no longer top of mind and has nothing driving the urgency for its completion. Treat your word as your bond and you'll make sure to follow through.

Be a linchpin.

Networking isn't solely about building your personal connections and fostering those relationships. It's equally important to expand other people's networks. It's about growth for all parties involved. I like to say, "Be a link, not an endpoint." Do whatever you can to make sure the networking chain doesn't die with you.

Be a link, not an endpoint.

One of the best ways to help someone and offer them value is to introduce them to someone who can also help them. To give myself a little scoot when considering how I might be able to expand people's networks, I ask myself:

- Who do they need help from now? This can be someone they requested specifically or others I know in general who can help them.
- Who do I think would be good for them to meet? I consider their areas of expertise, interests, geographies, or any other appropriate parameters they might have in common with people I know.
- Who are my "just because" people? Sometimes, I know people who are energetic, connected, and always willing to help others. I always think about matching people I think will just "hit it off."

It's important to be proactive in helping others grow their networks. People don't know who you know. Be generous when it comes to your introductions.

What was that thing you said about pushpins
and a map to keep track of everyone?

I'm sure you realize by now you'll never be able to keep up with your network, let alone grow it, if you don't have a "system" to keep it in order. You can use any techniques that work for you, but successful systems will generally have four "tools:"

- **Network map:** Capture the people you want to meet. This can be in a form that resembles an organigram, list, or any vehicle that keeps visible the people you want to meet.
- **Calendar:** Provide yourself reminders to proactively reach out to individuals in your network and contact new potential connections. Perhaps you can do this on the first of every month or every other Friday. The key is to alert yourself so you actually do it.
- **Templates:** Prepare standard email or direct-message templates for when you reach out to someone. Create starter versions so you can begin quickly. This will help you reduce the time you actually need to spend each month or week. Remember, each message you send, even if you start from a template, should look like it's a one-of-a-kind message.

- **"Gifts"**: Identify various offerings you might use when reaching out to people. These can be articles, books, presentations, videos, or anything of common interest.

The most important factor beyond being organized is your execution. You need to actually put in the time to connect with your network and reach out to new individuals that will enhance your life.

Here's a pro-tip when it comes to making your networking more consistent. Each December, identify 80 to 100 people you want to contact in the upcoming year. You can, of course, do this whenever you're reading this. You can also add to your list throughout the year as you meet new people.

This might sound like a huge effort, but if you contacted ten people each month, that would be 120 people over the course of the year. That's essentially five people every other Friday. Based on who gets back to you, you can go from there.

Figure out what works for you. Be consistent. Be generous. You'll get back what you give off!

NETWORKING EXERCISE

Thought-Provokers

1A. My professional goals include...

1B. People (whether specific names such as John Smith or functional names such as coach, author, agent) who can help me attain my goals are...

2. People I already know who I'd like to spend more time with are...

3. People I can introduce to the individuals I identified in number two are...

4. People I can start following (specific names or functions) on social media so I can learn from them and interact with their professional communities are...

Challenge

Week One: Start building your networking map. During week one, take steps to begin developing your networking map including: 1) Identifying five people in your current network and one way you can help each of them with anything, 2) Adding ten people (names or functions) you need to help you achieve your high-level goals (i.e., the ones you included in the Thought-Provokers section), and 3) Adding new people you want to meet "just because."

Week Two: Reconnect with gifts. During this week, reconnect with your professional friends. Here are four great ways to do this: 1) Make five phone calls to people just to catch up (text and email does not count!), 2) Write five LinkedIn recommendations without asking for reciprocity, 3) Share an article, book recommendation, or something you enjoyed with five people (that's five unique messages), and 4) Send five handwritten cards to friends or colleagues to thank them for whatever you can!

Week Three: Make introductions. During this week, introduce five people to five other people. No overlapping. That means you need to contact at least ten people!

Week Four: Build your "system." From weeks one through three, you've developed some great momentum. You have emails and gifts which you can turn into your starter templates. Now, develop your entire system including a more formalized networking map (from week one), a calendar of reach-outs, plus an inventory of email templates and gifts. Add to your system as you see fit and, more importantly, focus on executing it!

CHAPTER 12

Communicating

Which grunt was that?

Communication makes our world go around. In whatever form, whether verbal, non-verbal, or written, we cannot survive—happily—without being able to communicate with others.

Every species has some form of communication. Zebras use their noses, ears, tails, and even facial expressions to communicate their moods. They use a two-syllable call to signal to the herd predators are coming.

My four dogs, all the same breed (Dachshund), each use different signals, barks, and acrobatic maneuvers to tell me they're happy. It's a stitch, not to mention my canine vocabulary is next-level good. Plus, I have my wife, as always, to inform me whenever I'm wrong.

Regardless of the medium or tactics you use to communicate, one thing is certain when it comes to communication—it's about message transfer, not the technique you use. You either got your message across with zero distortion or, technically, you miscommunicated.

A mutual understanding…

Let's talk about how effectively you communicate. Do you know what your communication intelligence quotient is? There's a quotient for everything nowadays. Ever since pioneers such as Alfred Binet coined IQ (Intelligence Quotient), Wayne Payne's EQ (Emotional Intelligence), and a host of other "Q's" that popped up from who knows where (e.g., BQ =

Body Intelligence, MQ = Moral Intelligence), anyone can throw a "Q" out and start typing.

One of my favorites is CQ, Communication Quotient. I didn't coin the phrase, but have encountered it over the past several years as I've evaluated and studied concepts related to interpersonal communication. (Incidentally, in 2012, I published an entire interpersonal communication book and wrapped it in a job-interview setting. Check out *Interview Intervention: Communication That Gets You Hired* if you're job searching!)

I've come to believe the way we communicate leads to the way we think, not the other way around. More importantly, this impacts our judgment and the choices we make.

I've come to believe the way we communicate leads to the way we think, not the other way around. More importantly, this impacts our judgment and the choices we make.

In my studies, I've yet to find a definition for CQ I think encapsulates its true meaning. I, therefore, developed my very own:

Communication Intelligence: An individual's level of proficiency in accurately exchanging thoughts using verbal and nonverbal cues to achieve a mutual understanding.

If you can't remember my entire definition, simply stash the last two words. A mutual understanding seems to be difficult enough in life and almost impossible in time-compressed business meetings, hallway exchanges, and job interviews!

I cannot stress enough how important good communication is to good judgment. This holds true because when you have complete and accurate information and a mutual understanding, you are, at a minimum, making an informed decision.

I cannot stress enough how important good communication is to good judgment. This holds true because when you have complete and accurate information and a mutual understanding, you are, at a minimum, making an informed decision. With a clear exchange, you've also enabled your partner in the communication to make an informed decision.

There is one other point I want to call out on a "mutual" understanding. This is one to which you likely don't give much thought. What about when you communicate with yourself?

Here's a common, funny little saying, "Good judgment comes from experience. Unfortunately, experience comes from a lot of bad judgment." This expression is entertaining, but not accurate. There's no law which requires you to exercise bad judgment to gain experience. We all know, probably because of too much evidence in our personal and professional lives, individuals with experience don't necessarily exercise good judgment. This tends to occur for the same reason history repeats itself—because people don't listen the first time. In the case of exercising poor judgment, it's because people don't listen to themselves.

People who exercise the best judgment and make the smartest decisions aren't necessarily the ones with the most experience or good intuition. They are typically ones who are introspective and actually listen to themselves. They also rarely have unexpressed or misunderstood expectations—the very same expectations that shape what we see and hear, but more disturbingly what we value.

Realize, of course, it's extremely difficult to listen to yourself. Your head is filled with biases you don't work to rid, residual emotions from hours or days earlier, all smashed between a crowd of preoccupations from your work and personal life.

How do we make our best effort to rid our crowded noggins and focus on a positive exchange of thoughts with ourselves and others? It's not as simple as listen first and then say what you want to say. I wish it were that easy.

Let's consider all the factors that enable you to listen before you actually listen and the confirmation to know you actually received the message the way the person intended it. Remember, it's not the words used. It's the message transferred. That technically means the person who is communicating with you might not use the correct expressions, but you actually understood what that individual intended to communicate.

To build an extremely high CQ as it relates to receiving and sending communications, we need to consider everything that enables or prohibits our ability to listen and speak effectively. Whether you're listening or speaking, there are problems to be aware of, practices that will help you become better at each form of communication, and performance tactics that ensure you accurately exchange your messages. Let's take a look at each of these areas as you listen and speak.

I've got two ears. Isn't that enough?

Listening Problems

Why do we listen in the first place? Listening is vital to our everyday being and ability to operate in this world. We listen to share in another's life, help people when they seek our advice, provide that "ear" when someone needs to vent, capture information when we're given instructions to carry out, and many other reasons that make life worth living.

What if you had to listen to remember? Remember when you needed to remember? That was way "back in the day" when we didn't have cellphones which stored someone's telephone number. How did we do it? It was easier back then.

Why is it so difficult to listen now? There are many reasons, some of which we've already covered. When considering this from several angles, I've noticed six challenges most people have when it comes to listening.

- **Lacking focus:** As I covered in the lesson on focusing, much of our daily lives is filled with practicing distraction. Practice distraction enough, you get really good at it. The problem is this interferes with your ability to concentrate when someone is speaking to you.
- **Distracting environment:** Oftentimes, we attempt to listen in environments where it's loud or you see people walking by the conference room glass walls or the television is on or your cell phone is beeping.
- **Expending energy on the wrong stuff:** Instead of listening with an open mind, we're expending energy mentally filling in assumptions, crafting our rebuttals, worrying about our responses, fretting the fallouts, or whatever other futuristic speculation we can manufacture during the moment. Additionally, we tend to fill in the blanks with assumptions instead of capturing information that would help anchor our memory.

- **Judging, not empathizing:** If you can imagine, or simply make the attempt to imagine, what the other person might be going through, you will, by default, become a better listener. Instead, many people stock up on judgmental thoughts that prohibit their ability to empathize.
- **Missing intent:** Great communication and, in turn, great listening skills, are incumbent upon one's ability to receive the message accurately. If you haven't, in this case, received it accurately, you've miscommunicated. Most people don't confirm they've received the information. Saying, "I got it!" is not actually confirming the intention of the message.
- **Filling in with biases:** You can listen for what you want to hear or you can listen with the experience that has shaped you or you can listen with a blank mind. The last one is the most effective when it comes to absorbing the message. It's also the hardest to accomplish.

Understanding the obstacles and challenges is a great place to start. Once we're aware of the challenges standing in our way of becoming a great listener, we can work to overcome them!

The command "Just listen" never helped anyone actually listen!

Listening Practices

Let me guess. You've been told thousands of times to "Listen to me!" I'll bet mom, dad, your teachers, and probably a bunch of your friends are guilty of this ludicrous command. Just like you've never been taught to focus, you've probably never been taught how to actually listen. Hearing sounds is not synonymous with listening. Listening is a skill and a perishable one at that.

As with any skill, there are a host of steps you need to practice to perform at your best when it's "game time!" You can't simply turn it on and listen if you haven't built an "entire system" to enable you to do this.

There is an overall "listening" lifestyle that enables you to be at your best so when the time comes to listen, you can easily execute tactics that enable you to listen well. I practice five techniques daily, all of which I consider prerequisites to the act of listening.

These five practices are part of other routines I perform daily as they relate to focusing, planning, and being empathetic. As you can see by now, all of the skills, behaviors, and abilities are integrated into a singular lifestyle that helps you remain focused on what's important to you. Most importantly, these techniques, practiced frequently, enable you to draw the best from yourself and to serve others.

Silence and then "Noise" Practice. When was the last time you heard no noise while you were awake? Each morning, at the beginning of my meditation practice, I spend a couple of minutes working on my hearing. I sit in a quiet spot in my home. I close my eyes and simply listen to the quiet. I'm not focusing on my mind or trying to concentrate. My goal is to get connected to my ears. Then I'll listen for isolated sounds that are faint or distant. Occasionally, there will be birds outside my windows. My home is approximately 300 meters from a fairly desolate street. Very early in the morning, there will be rare few cars passing by. I listen closely until I hear one. This level of concentration to locate sounds and isolate them helps strengthen your hearing. It also makes it easier to block out noise and distraction. This hearing exercise improves your ability to detect sounds among background noise and also trains you neurologically to detect even the softest sounds.

Focus Practice. Of course, focusing and listening are different skills, but you need to be able to focus so you can listen effectively. If you practice focusing each day as I outlined in the focusing lesson earlier, you'll be able to listen better thanks to your capacity to concentrate on the person speaking to you.

Consider the Day in Advance. A big reason why people have a hard time listening is because they go from one activity or conversation to the next. They move at a breakneck pace. They accumulate stress. If you spend a few moments each morning anticipating your day (as I outlined in the Planning and Running Your Day lesson), you'll free your mind of excess noise enabling you to listen more effectively during your conversations.

Consider the Act Immediately Before. It's not only a great exercise to consider your day before you start it, but also consider each act as you're about to start it. You can do this during your transitions. As this relates to listening, you'll become more empathetic if you take a deep breath, think about the people, what they might need, how you might help, what you want to accomplish, and how you'll react before you listen to them. You can do this as part of your "recharge and reset" technique.

Minimize Your Filters. We all have cultural, language, and belief biases. We also tend to have intentions, expectations, and a number of other unhealthy precursors to our interactions and conversations. If you've considered your day in advance and also took a step to pause and consider the act immediately prior to your engagement, you'll be in a much better position to minimize these filters. You won't be able to remove them without lots of practice, but intercepting them frequently works wonders. I take it a step further, especially when I'm coaching someone. Before I start the session, I ask myself, "What if I didn't know what I know?" and "What if everything is actually the opposite of what I think?" This helps me remain open-minded and empathetic as I do my best to help the person.

At this point, you are conditioning yourself to be a great listener and you haven't even started listening to anyone! Whether it's focusing on anything or listening to anyone, you need to set up a regimen that enables you to command your abilities the moment you need them. This is akin to someone who wants to build a healthy lifestyle, become more vibrant, and ward off illnesses. When your body is at its strongest, you're able to do all of this more naturally and easily. It's the same when you want to listen to someone.

Listen closely enough to hear what the other person is feeling.

Listening Performance

Ever have a friend, loved one, or business colleague just start talking and you're wondering *what does this person need from me?* I don't mean this in a negative way. I mean, when someone is speaking to you, that person wants something. Otherwise, there'd be no reason to speak to you.

They might need to vent or want your advice. Your boss might need to inform you or have you carry out instructions. In each of these situations, you'll actually listen differently. The only act that'll be the same is you'll be hearing sounds. You might hear with your ears, but you listen with your brain because you need to process the information you're being given.

You might hear with your ears, but you listen with your brain because you need to process the information you're being given.

Once you know why the person wants you to listen, it becomes substantially easier for you to actually listen. If you don't know the person's intention, you need to hold onto all the information being shared. Furthermore, you don't have any context upon which you should hold it. That's tough stuff.

Step one to listening effectively is knowing why you're listening in the first place. What's the purpose of the communication? The very best communicators open up their conversations with clues, if not outright statements, of their intentions. These statements sound like...

- I'd like to bounce something off you...
- I'd like your advice...
- I need to fill you in...
- I want you to help me with...
- I just need to vent...

This offers you a chance to listen with intention and put everything you hear into proper context. This makes it much easier for you to "save" the information you need and know how to use it. You can listen and think four times faster than someone can speak. That means, you have ample time to collect what you need, assuming you're not filling that extra time trying to think of what you'll say next.

You can listen and think four times faster than someone can speak. That means, you have ample time to collect what you need, assuming you're not filling that extra time trying to think of what you'll say next.

When you understand the intent, it's easier for you to focus on the main ideas the person is sharing. This, in turn, enables you to retain the details more effectively because you're now assembling the "story" in your head. If there are many details you need to capture, you're likely interacting in an environment where you can take notes to collect this information.

What if you don't hear one of these expressions early on? Politely ask what the purpose of the conversation is. I'll often ask, "Sorry to interrupt you, but can you let me know what you'll need from me after you share this?"

As your conversation rolls on, it's helpful to let the speaker know you're actually listening. One of the best ways to do this is called active listening. Active listening is about engagement, not interruption. It's a technique you can use in business and social settings to let the speaker know you're paying attention.

Remember, communication is about accurate message transfer, which means the person speaking needs to know you received the message correctly. Active listening is a way of listening and engaging with the other person, through verbal and non-verbal cues, questions, and statements, to ensure you have that mutual understanding.

Active listening is a way of listening and engaging with the other person, through verbal and non-verbal cues, questions, and statements, to ensure you have that mutual understanding.

Here are six techniques I use to actively listen:

Practice curiosity to dig deeper. Asking relevant questions can show you're listening. This is more of a scoot than an interruption. You're moving the story along in the direction the person is going. You're not sidetracking it, but letting the person know you need additional insight so you can better understand. Questions such as "Why did you do that?" or "Why is that important?" or "Why did that matter?" or "How did that make you feel?" are ideal when using this tactic.

Get clarification. Occasionally, you'll need clarification. This is one of the more challenging active listening techniques because you might not be completely sure whether they'll clarify the issue as the story continues. This could be misconstrued as an interruption, but you'll usually be safe if you phrase your questions in a manner such as "Can you please clarify because I'm not sure if I understood what you were saying about...?" Alternatively, you can use an expression such as "Did you mean...?"

Use mini confirmations. When appropriate, especially in lengthy stories, it's effective to let the person know you're still engaged. Simple expressions such as "It sounds like you mean..." or "What I'm hearing is..." are effective. You can keep these phrases short so as to not completely interrupt the speaker, but they do serve as feedback you're still listening and receiving the messages.

Pay attention to body language. Albert Mehrabian, Professor Emeritus of Psychology at the University of California, Los Angeles, in 1972, outlined the Rule of Personal Communication in his book *Silent Messages*. Based on his research, his conclusion is we show our feelings and attitudes using a relationship between verbal, vocal, and facial or body expressions. Specifically, 7 percent of our feelings takes place through the words we use in spoken communications, 38 percent takes place through tone and voice, and the remaining 55 percent takes place through body language. He labeled it the 7-38-55 rule, which effectively states 93 percent of your inference of another's communication comes from something other than actual words! This is why it's important to notice the other person's body language and tone. It's also a great reason why you can actively listen to people by maintaining eye contact, smiling, and directly facing them to show you're engaged.

Let them finish. It's much easier for you to retain and understand what the person is conveying if you listen until the end. This, of course, shows you're respectful. The minor exceptions, of course, are to enhance the interaction with these active listening techniques.

Confirm the intent. I like to call this the "intent check!" If you want to ensure the message was transferred accurately and completely, it's helpful to reiterate what you heard in summary form using different words than the speaker used. This provides you both with an extra layer to confirm the message was transferred and received properly because you're focusing on the meaning instead of the words used to exchange the message. You can use phrases such as "To confirm..." or "It sounds like you mean..." or "If I heard you correctly, you want..."

That's a lot of listening. When do I get to talk?

When we communicate with others, we often assume they'll understand what we're sharing because we incorrectly assume they have the same knowledge we do, think the way we think, and are also beneficiaries of similar experiences we've had. We make this mistake—repeatedly—because, as we evolve through life, we forget what it's like not to know what we know. We also think the intersection between what we know and what someone else knows is much larger than it is. This is yet another reason why we tend to undervalue ourselves.

I once worked with an athletic trainer who had a habit of expressing herself this way: "Your gluteus maximus isn't engaging quickly enough, which puts more pressure on your gastrocnemius and soleus muscles to keep the lower part of your leg and ankle stable while your foot pronates. That's why your posterior tibial tendon is swollen and your navicular bone is dropping." I'd be thinking, *My what is doing what? Where's my gluteus maximus? You mean my butt?*

The first part of being a great communicator when sending your messages is to put yourself on alert there will be ambiguity and need for clarification. Starting with this mindset helps slow down your internal mechanism that tends to trip over misunderstandings at the speed of your emotions. My trainer's care for me and my well-being coupled with her excitement to impart her knowledge simply makes her blurt out stuff as it sounds in her head. We all do this.

A master communicator takes responsibility upfront to consider the other person and identify potential miscommunications by asking themself, "What would it be like to not know what I know?" and "What's the most important piece of information this person would want to know?" and "Is there a commonly understood example I could use to illustrate my point?" Simply being considerate and spending a few moments intercepting your automated thinking will often do the trick.

Speaking Problems

Aside from the built-in ways we misunderstand each other, there are a host of other issues we face when we want to communicate our messages to others. We, of course, have the same focus and environmental issues we face as listeners. We also have a host of additional challenges as the communicator.

- **Providing unnecessary information:** Rarely do we take the time to strip down our communication to what the other party needs to know. Keep in mind, it's much easier to remember less than more.
- **Forgetting what it's like not to know what we know:** As we speak, we're factoring in all the knowledge we have, not solely related to the topic or project we're discussing, but also our entire lives.
- **Confirming receipt of our intent:** We often communicate and assume the other person registered the message accurately. A simple "Got it!" from them doesn't actually confirm the receipt.
- **Considering the person's experiences or feelings:** We listen with biases, but we also speak to others assuming they feel the same way about the subject we're discussing. We need to consider how they might feel about the topics based on their position, interests, motivations, and experiences.

Speaking isn't just speaking, but more like painting with a language palette...

Speaking Practices

Now that you have an understanding of the problems you have as a communicator, let's address some practices you can employ before and during your communication to help overcome the challenges and convey the messages you want. Much like anything else, it all starts with your preparation.

When we're the listener, much of our practice and preparation involves being in the right state of mind to receive the information. We don't always know what information is coming or when we'll receive it, so we can create a lifestyle where we're alert and receptive.

Sending your message, however, can be well planned. In fact, if you go through the proper pre-game steps, you'll be able to share your message effectively and elicit the type of response, action, or inspiration you want.

I try to think, *How can I make it easy for the other people to understand? What can I do to help them "follow" the story I'm telling them?* I do that by, as you recall when we were wearing the listener's hat, letting them know—upfront—why they're listening to me and what I want from them. This allows them to "start with the end in mind" and hold onto the information they need to so they can do what they need to do with the information.

Here are seven critical steps you can take before delivering your communication:

Consider them. Take the time to think about them, who they are, what they know, and what they might be feeling. This is a great first step not only to shape what you want to share, but also become empathetic to their situation.

Identify their vocabulary. Contemplate the terminology that will resonate best as well as analogies they'll understand.

Expect misunderstandings. Based on who they are, what they know, and how they generally communicate with you, spend a few moments thinking about how they might misunderstand you. They might misunderstand because there exists a knowledge gap between what you know and what they know. They might misconstrue your intentions. You might think you're communicating something to help them. They might think you're communicating something self-serving. Take a step back to consider your communication from all angles and ask yourself questions such as "How might they misunderstand my information?" and "How might they misunderstand my motivation?"

Anticipate reactions. Think through all their possible reactions and how to elicit the ones you'd like as well as prepare your rebuttals for any objections or unwanted reactions.

Determine your primer. We prime our exchanges to move the other party's emotional state to where we want it. Opening up with "I'm excited to share..." or "I've got great news..." are effective ways to get them relaxed or enthused. There is a valence to your primer that refers to the intrinsic nature, positive or negative, of the event, issue, or situation. An expression such as "Let's meet to discuss [whatever]" doesn't carry the same sentiment as "I'm excited to meet Thursday to run over your great ideas related to..."

Decide on your frame. While your primer focuses on shaping the person's emotions, the frame of your communication is what moves the person's beliefs and interpretations. With priming, you address how you want the person to feel. With framing, you shape how the person sees the information you're sharing. Through any combination of metaphors, stories, or comparisons, you can move the focal point of someone's thinking. For example, "You could spend your time trying to figure it out. That'd take you ten hours and cost you $100. I could do it for you at a cost of $50/hour and it'll take me one hour. That way, it'll only cost you $50 and you'll save ten of your own hours." The person's initial focus was the time and cost it would take. The frame moves the focal point to the savings.

Include the necessary information. Depending on the purpose of the communication, you need to ensure the person has the requisite information to carry out the instruction, make a good decision, provide feedback, or whatever the exchange requires. What do they need to know to complete their call to action?

Thinking through these areas will put you well on your way to preparing a thoughtful, effective communication.

The beginning-middle-end formula has many uses...

Speaking Performance

Planning your communication will significantly help when actually delivering it. At this point, the only thing left for you to do is communicate what you planned! Every communication has some type of opener, body, and close. Simple for sure, but these three areas will help you with the packaging and delivery.

In this general lesson on communicating, I'll share the tenets that accompany delivering these three parts of your communication. This will help you understand the overall delivery structure so you can raise your CQ and send your communications effectively. In the next lesson on crafting compelling messages, we'll take a deep dive into how to build your messages with the right ingredients so you can accomplish the goals of your communications.

Opener

The opener is where you "help them help you!" You have a purpose to your communication and, as immediately as possible, want to let them know what that is. That way, they have the proper context for what they're about to hear and can position themselves to listen effectively. As the listener, you want to be on the lookout for those expressions I mentioned earlier that alert you as to why you're listening. As the communicator, open with those expressions to help your listener. Start with, "I want to share this with you," "I need your advice," "I want you to help me with..." and others such as these to help them listen with the end in mind.

Body

No matter what the purpose of your communication is, you want the listener to remember what you shared and act accordingly. As we communicate in business, there are secondary (if not also primary) goals related to anything we communicate. In general, we want to be likeable, believable, and memorable. This helps us build our trust, influence, and overall reputation throughout our companies and industries.

In 2007, brothers Chip and Dan Heath released a book called *Made to Stick*, with the byline highlighting why some ideas survive and others die. It's a fascinating book that reviews why some stories are memorable and others are not. The book covers examples ranging from selling a product to reliving stories for friends. It highlights techniques to grab and keep people's attention so they're alert, interested, and engaged.

In summary, they determined through extensive research that "sticky ideas" had six key qualities. They were simple, unexpected, concrete, credible, emotional, and story-like.

As I read the book, it was apparent these same qualities applied to job interviewing. As an executive recruiter at that time, I looked for creative ways for my job candidates to sell themselves during interviews using effective storytelling techniques and started using the *Made to Stick* conclusions when preparing candidates for their interviews.

In 2012, I released my interpretation of these storytelling principles, modeled after the Heath Brothers' work, in *Interview Intervention: Communication That Gets You Hired* and realigned them so they were appropriate for interviewing purposes. In addition to interviewing effectively, these principles universally apply as we communicate anything we communicate.

For the body of virtually any major communication you prepare, whether it's a casual presentation during a meeting or a tactical conversation with a coworker, you can apply these six key principles as I've adapted them. They are:

Keep it short and simple. Share whatever information you need to share in as few words as possible because superfluous information hinders their ability to remember. Think need-to-know basis and want-to-know basis.

Capture and keep their attention. They can't remember if they're not listening. There are several techniques you can use related to framing your message, breaking typical patterns of what the listeners expect is coming, and using topics that will hold their attention.

Talk in their lingo. Speak in a language they understand. Use vocabulary they are familiar with as well as examples, analogies, and stories they recognize so you can get your points across.

Make them believe you. Use details to make yourself believable. The organization of your message combined with specific facts and cited authoritative references help improve the plausibility of your message.

Get them to care. Highlight the benefit to the individual. People want to understand how they'll be affected by your message. It needs to be clear why this would matter to them. That helps get them to care about not only the message, but also you.

Get them to act. Engaging with them will help them feel connected to you provided you show genuine interest in them. As a final step to your "body." or perhaps first step to your "close," be clear regarding the call-to-action that is the next step.

Close

Your close can be whatever is appropriate based on your communication, but frequently will involve details and next steps related to their call-to-action. While you've likely already introduced what the next steps will be, now is the time to confirm the details regarding the next steps. This information might include who's responsible for which actions, when they are due, and what's to be included.

The most important aspect of the close related to any business communication is that you're clear regarding anything and everything involved in the next steps. Clarity is the key.

Now that you have an understanding of exchanging effective communications, it's time to practice so you can raise your CQ!

COMMUNICATING EXERCISE

Thought-Provokers

1A. When it comes to listening, the biggest distractors I have to focusing on what the other person is saying are...

1B. A single step I can take to reduce each distraction is...

2. Some ten-to-fifteen-minute activity(s) I perform in the morning that I can forego so I can reallocate that time to silence/focus practice and considering my day is/are...

3A. When interacting with people at work, the most common biases and misconceptions I have are...

3B. The steps I can take to open my mind to become a better listener to these people are...

4A. The people I communicate with most frequently at work are...

4B. The most common misunderstandings with those people are...

4C. The steps I can take to reduce the number of misunderstandings are...

5. A simple checklist I can use when creating my communications will include these steps (e.g., consider them, primer, frame, potential mis-understanding related to information, etc.)...

Challenge

Prerequisite Step: During the entire challenge, each morning, take some time to practice your listening and focusing skills. Consider your day and with whom you'll be speaking, what the best outcomes would be, and what would constitute success. It's also helpful to do this immediately before you're speaking with someone if you have the luxury of it being scheduled. You'll be amazed at the difference in your overall communication.

Week One: Casual communications. While this communicating lesson focused on business interactions, your most important relationships and communications are likely with your family, spouse, partner, children, or close friends. For the first five days of the challenge, pick one conversation and focus on the communication principles. Considering the other person, remove assumptions, open your mind, listen actively, and confirm you understood their intent.

Week Two: Colleague communications. During week two (and always), continue the practice of week one with your casual communication. Now, include practicing the communication principles during the conversations you have with your teammates, customers, and other business colleagues.

Week Three: Boss and management communications. Let's continue to ingrain your communication practices in week three by adding focus to the communications you have with your boss and management team. This will be especially important as you conduct meetings and prepare and deliver your presentations. Concentrate on considering them, planning your priming and framing, and executing the discussions.

Week Four: Written communications. As you start to practice this month with verbal communications, you'll get more proficient at advanced planning and properly anticipating their reactions and the outcomes. Now, put those practices into your writing, whether this is a simple email exchange or more formal write-up.

PART FIVE

The Influencer

CHAPTER 13

Crafting Compelling Messages

When I became a coach, I took an oath to educate,
inspire, and entertain.

If I had to take it again, I'd add the word iterate.

Understanding how communication works in general is not something that's intuitively obvious as you likely gathered from the previous chapter. Even though we naturally listen and speak from the time we're toddlers, our experiences, environment, and biases affect the way we see and hear anything. As we become adults, the experiences that shape us become more cemented unless we constantly intercept them using evaluation and reflection.

If we pay attention to our interpersonal communications with family, friends, and colleagues, we'll discover clues as to the effect we have on others. Do we have solid, supportive relationships? Do we tend to repel? These types of communications affect the health of our relationships in the everyday-life kind of way.

As we progress in our careers, irrespective of our profession, we tend to need very thoughtful communications to not only build trusting relationships with coworkers and customers, but also inspire, persuade, market and sell our ideas or products, and other forms to influence.

I'm not speaking solely of some grand presentation you need to put together to convince your Board of Directors of the major initiatives your company should undertake next year. All forms of communication, written and verbal, when prepared effectively, have a number of elements and steps in common.

Each week, for example, I develop several different types of written and verbal communications for my business. These communications are usually emails, documents, presentations, workbooks, and other forms I use to educate and advise. Specifically, I write emails to my community, newsletter digests, and blog posts. I craft teaching lessons in the form of recorded videos, presentations for my live shows, and audio podcasts. I also develop workbooks and guides for my online training programs. All of these communications are to build my community, help people with their careers, and support my business.

I'm sure as part of your job, you need to write and speak in some of the same formats as I do. Of course, you might have different goals or purposes, but preparing a great message is important nonetheless. You might need to write an email to your boss assessing a major project or pitching a great idea to your entire team or writing a status report for your internal client. You might have the opportunity to present at a company meeting or speak with a customer or train the staff. In all cases, you need to craft messages that advise, persuade, and inspire. Whatever the goal, you'll likely need someone to act on the information you're providing and that's what influencing is all about!

How do we go about building communications like these? What goes into those communications so you can achieve your goals? Over the years, I've developed a formula, which I perform by going through a sequence of nine iterations, whenever I prepare any major piece of written or verbal communication. These steps help ensure I advise and educate and positively influence the people receiving it. If my communication is a long-form format (i.e., book, teaching lesson, lengthy email, blog post), I perform these steps serially. That means several iterations, with a focused purpose each time, to ensure I have all the elements I need to achieve my goal.

You can use this nine-step approach to craft your compelling messages, irrespective of their formats, to share important information and get the receiver to act.

1. Outline the main points.

Ask yourself, "What needs to be communicated?" Make a list of the pieces of information you want to share. This can be a simple list or checklist. Then, sequence it properly. This might be as simple as "three points I need to share" or as complex as a seven-part lesson or twenty-step white paper. When we get into the writing of this communication, whether it's written in its final, delivered form or shared verbally, we'll likely update our main points, add to them, or remove some.

For every communication I create, whether it's a long-form email to my community, a live-group-coaching lesson for my Leadership Coaching Program, or a workbook for one of my training products, I use what I call a "standard clock" to help me finish on time with the best final product. This "standard clock" as I call it, is a schedule of communication development. The clock starts when I draft the main points. I'll cover what the "horology" of my communication development looks like in the next section.

I use what I call a "standard clock" to help me finish on time with the best final product. This "standard clock" as I call it, is a schedule of communication development.

2. Write out the main points.

If you're developing a communication that needs to be fleshed out completely such as a paper, book, or long-form email, write it out. That means, just write. That does not mean write some words and then edit them and then edit them again and again. During this part of the iterative development, just get it down on "paper." This is one of the biggest mistakes I see people make. They want their first drafts to be perfect. Our goal is not solely to create well-thought-out communications, it's also to create them as quickly or with as little effort as possible.

If your communication will solely be delivered verbally, write out your notes in this step. You can use bullet points or whatever form of notes works best for you. The important factor is to make sure you have them all.

3. Clarify your message.

Now that you have your communication written out, review what you wrote. Ask yourself, "Does this make sense? Does what I'm sharing have all the pieces people, who don't know what I know, need to accomplish their goals?"

In this step, I also like to review whether the sequence of my points makes the most sense. This is a vital step because it gives you an explicit chance to review your communication as the receiver as opposed to yourself. While I understand it's very difficult to review your own work as if you didn't know what you know, your final communication will be much better if you give this a try.

4. Incorporate examples, analogies, and stories.

When you add examples and analogies it helps them not only "get" the messages, but also ingrain them and put them into practice in their lives. Examples and analogies are also built-in "intent checks" because they provide additional viewpoints of what you mean. Instead of them needing to replay back to you what you said, you are proactively providing them multiple ways of interpreting the same messages. These extra layers ensure they receive your messages correctly.

> **When you add examples and analogies it helps them not only "get" the messages, but also ingrain them and put them into practice in their lives. Examples and analogies are also built-in "intent checks" because they provide additional viewpoints of what you mean.**

Wrapping your communication into a story-like format or sharing a specific story are powerful techniques to help your receivers understand, remember, and enjoy the communications. Including stories also makes it more engaging and easier to remember. You can use characters to serve as doppelgängers, so to speak, and other storytelling elements to make the message more relatable. This is what helps the receivers connect emotionally with the communications. Stories also have a structure to them that enables the receivers to retain and recall your messages more easily.

5. Make it succinct.

Perhaps you've heard the expression, "If I had more time, I would have made this shorter." I can't actually verify who said this because when I Google the quote, I find various attributions. No matter who said it, it's true. Writing a more concise letter, email, or book whose goal is to convey a large amount of information, takes longer to package. Your communication is worth making as effective as possible using the least amount of information. The goal isn't solely to make it brief. The goal is to make it as powerful as possible while taking up the least amount of time of the people with whom you're communicating.

When you make this iteration through your communication, ask yourself, "Did I communicate everything I needed to in as few steps or words as possible?" Strip out everything that isn't absolutely necessary to know.

6. Evaluate it for emotion and the action you want them to take.

As I mentioned, when you clarify your messages, you want to keep them in line with the receivers' and your goals. If you're teaching and they're learning, they need to be informed. If you're providing instruction they need to carry out, they need not only the information, but also inspiration to act with vigor. Whatever the goal, ensure you're shaping your communication to help achieve it.

Most communications, especially in a corporate setting, have a by-product of building long-term trust. Even so, the majority of these communications have short-term goals of getting people to think, act, or become motivated. The consistency in which we follow through on our communications and actions will build trust over time.

When we want someone to act or feel, however, we need our messages to contain emotion. This is most easily accomplished in the form of a challenge. It doesn't need to be an explicit "I challenge you to…" It can be a leading expression to carry out a project or drawing their attention to a desired feeling they want to attain.

Depending on the type of communication I'm sharing and my goal, I use six techniques (or a combination thereof) to elicit positive emotions:

Ask a question. Oftentimes, a simple question to get them to think or focus on an issue is all it takes to stimulate the emotion you desire.

Identify a problem. Identify a specific problem or challenge you're helping them overcome. For example, opening up with "We have this issue where our customer service level is dropping..." can lead right into the emotion.

Cite an aspiration. Include aspirations they might want. Generally, our lives and businesses are filled with nothing more than problems we need to solve or aspirations we want to achieve. What goals might they have? Asking "What if we can gain twice the number of customers with half the expense?" will often prime the emotion.

Raise myths or oddities. Often the easiest way to sound intriguing and invoke emotion is to debunk a myth or counter the norm. State, "You might think this is true, but in fact..."

Mention the feeling. If there's a certain way you want them to feel, you can use the exact word. Many times, I'll start email digests to my community with an opener such as "Isn't it frustrating...?" or "Wouldn't it be exhilarating...?"

Clarify the benefits. One of the biggest mistakes I see people make, when communicating, especially when they want someone to carry out instruction, is to assume people know the benefits of their subsequent actions. It's so important to be explicit regarding this. People, of course, respond to "what's in it for me." I have noticed, however, that citing the benefits to the greater good has a powerful way of getting people to act. Saying, "When we complete this program, this is what it will mean for everyone..." is vital in motivating them.

7. Talk it out if it's a "speech."

Getting it out of your head and down on paper is important. Talking it out will bring it to life. It's amazing how much more clarity you'll get when hear your own words. You'll start to notice whether you have the parts in the right order. You'll also hear how expressions sound. This provides you with an opportunity to practice your tone, cadence, and wording. As we covered in the previous lesson on communicating, keep Albert Mehrabian's 7-38-55 rule of personal communication in mind and recognize how important tone and body language are to getting your points across.

When I practice my presentation for my weekly live teaching shows, I spend more time isolating the most important messages I need the audience to retain as part of the lesson. How you say particular words and expressions will help emphasize their meaning, significance, and consequence. It's difficult to "hear" this when you're writing out your notes. That's why this iteration is so vital.

8. Edit it if it's a long or "print" format.

If your communication will be delivered in "print" format, edit it in full again. This is just as it sounds. If you're developing a white paper, blog post, lengthy email, presentation, or anything that will be distributed with the actual words, perform a detailed review to ensure it's well formatted with proper sentence structure and without typos. (Yes, I get the irony. Even with all these reviews by yours truly and the three reviews by the publisher, there will still be some typos that slip through. Do your best.)

9. Take a last pass.

After I call it complete, I review it one last time to make sure it's good to go!

For production and creativity, here's Communication Horology 101. It's all about the clock.

The nine-step, iterative process I shared is the approach I use for every long-form communication I create. Some projects, such as my weekly digest, are short and others, such as this book, are long. Regardless of the length of the communication or amount of time it takes me to complete it, I use my standard-clock technique to manage my effort, plan the iterations, and ensure quality of the final output. These "clocks" are effectively pre-determined schedules for communication development. They help me plan what's due each day if it's a shorter clock or each week or month if it's a longer clock.

Over the years, as I've monitored the development of my emails, lessons, workbooks, and other communication vehicles, I've captured the amount of time it takes as well as reviewed my creativity to help me produce high-quality communications.

You might be thinking, *That sounds great, but what if I don't have the experience or know how long something will take me to develop?* Even if you're not sure or are doing a unique, one-time project, you can still implement a technique like this. You need to start at some point. Now is as good a time as any!

Each communication has its own standard schedule. As I mentioned earlier, the schedule starts on the day I outline the main points for the communication. For example, my monthly Leadership Coaching Program members and I meet (you guessed it) approximately every four weeks. To ensure I have the very best lesson prepared, I use a four-week standard clock to pace my development of the lesson. During the first week, my only goal is to ensure I have the main points outlined for the presentation. I want the lesson to "live and breathe on simmer" in the back of my mind over the course of the four weeks. Determining my talking-points outline gives me something to ruminate for the next few weeks.

During the second week, I'll write out the main points and clarify my message and start incorporating examples and identifying stories I want to tell. During week three, I'll review it to ensure it contains the desired emotion.

When the fourth week arrives and I'm getting ready to deliver the live group coaching lesson at the end of the week (we meet on Fridays), I'll make sure to complete and edit the workbook between Monday and Wednesday. I reserve Thursday to talk it out and update any stories or examples I'd like to use.

I follow this same schedule every month. It's my standard clock for these lessons and communications.

Of course, not all my communications require this much time and effort. My weekly live shows (every Thursday) and newsletter digests (every Tuesday) have three-day clocks. For my Thursday live show, the clock starts on Monday when I outline the main points of the lesson. On Tuesday, I write out a few notes for each point. On Wednesday, I talk it out.

There is a reason I have a pace to each of my communications. It started when I noticed I seemed to come up with the best points and stories right before the shows or coaching sessions were starting.

Crafting communications is about developing them quickly, creatively, and with high quality. For me, the best way to do this is to start early for productivity's sake and finish later (that is, on time) for creativity's sake.

Crafting communications is about developing them quickly, creatively, and with high quality. For me, the best way to do this is to start early for productivity's sake and finish later (that is, on time) for creativity's sake. Why might this approach work for you too? When something is "done," we stop thinking about it. If I wrote the lesson and workbook three weeks before I delivered them, I wouldn't have a chance to "marinate" on them. I'd think they were done. Conversely, if I procrastinated and tried to build, write, and rehearse the lesson the day before, it wouldn't be nearly as thorough, creative, and effective.

Planning your next day the night before works effectively to unload your mind so you can sleep well. That planning you do the night before, as I mentioned earlier, keeps your mental short-term memory clean. For longer-term projects that run over days, weeks, or months, however, I don't want to stop thinking about them. I also don't want them in the forefront of my mind every day taking up my short-term memory and energy. I want them cooking on a low simmer in the back of my mind. That's why I leave these communication projects undone. I'm hitting the deliverables according to my scheduled standard clock, which continually reminds me I'm progressing accordingly. From a creativity standpoint, the ideas and stories and pointers are marinating like a fine dish. This is where the creative part comes in.

There was a study done in 1927 by a Lithuanian-Soviet psychologist named Bluma Zeigarnik (*On Finished and Unfinished Task*). She concluded based on her research an activity that has been interrupted might be more readily recalled. Now labeled the Zeigarnik effect, she hypothesized people remember unfinished tasks better than completed tasks. The main reason is that once a task is done, the brain doesn't think there's any need to hold onto that information. (Think about all those tests you took in high school and college. Remember much of those?)

While each one of us leads different lives and careers and our activities and schedules vary greatly, consider my approach and Zeigarnik's study to see how it might apply to you. Give it a try. Keep what works. Continue to refine your "standard clocks" for your major communications until you have them dialed in like, uh, clockwork!

I always seem to need to convince someone of something.

One of the most common activities we perform in our professional lives is persuading someone to act. This might be nothing more than pitching your teammates or boss a new idea or why your daily process should change. Other times, you need to go into a full-blown presentation to recommend an approach to your steering committee.

To me, your ability to persuade is one of the greatest skillsets you can develop. We do this constantly whether we like it or not. You don't need to be on the sales or marketing teams to continue to tap into this ability. It seems to naturally surface no matter who we are.

We need to be able to "make our cases" when we're pushing for anything we believe is important. Whether you want to sell that big project or you're seeking a promotion, we need to factor in the elements that "sell it!"

From my many years of experience as a consultant and corporate executive combined with selling products as services as a business owner, I've learned there are essentially seven key tenets required to be convincing.

These tenets will also help you become—as importantly—thorough in thinking through your project or effort. This level of thoroughness not only helps ensure you're making a solid case, but also puts the listeners or decision makers at ease knowing you've done your homework.

1. Provide context.

It makes no difference what the subject or argument is. You need to give your listener context regarding what you're about to share. People think and remember in compartments. They want to see the house framing before they fill it with furniture. This is critical because once people understand the context, they won't continue to wonder where the story is going.

It's "the wondering" that tires them out and also causes them to forget the other details because you're asking them to exert unnecessary energy.

As we discussed earlier, as a listener, we want to know the purpose of the discussion so we know how to listen. As a persuader, it's equally important to provide the background and a "discussion map," in the form of context, so your listeners can properly evaluate what you're sharing.

You get two great benefits by providing context. First, they won't have to work harder to figure out where your story is going. This frees their minds to focus on the important keys you want them to focus on. Second, you've properly framed what you're about to tell them so they know exactly where they are in the process.

2. Explain why it matters.

You have a much slimmer chance of convincing someone of anything if they need to ask why it's important after you've made your pitch. Why? Obvious benefits are easy to embrace. Hidden benefits are more difficult to grasp and need to be overtly explained if you're selling your boss, team, or the world on a grand effort.

Sharing the benefits at the beginning allows people to make correlations as you lay out the details. This continually reinforces the benefits to them. Each time they make these correlations, you make mini "sales" of your idea along the way.

3. Wrap it in a story.

We already discussed the benefits of including a story in your communications and how it relates to remembering. When you're making a pitch to persuade someone, stories help listeners connect emotionally. They especially love stories they can relate to about people or businesses who've struggled just like they have.

You can choose your stories and the way you tell them based on your audience and goals. When speaking with a colleague, questions and statements such as "Have you ever [insert the situation]? I've encountered that too! Here's where I struggled with it. Here's what I learned. Here's how I got results…" work really well.

When pitching your boss on a big project, your story might start with, "I'm noticing we're always doing this and it prevents us from..."

Storytelling, when it comes to persuasion, knows no boundaries. My wife, who's an elementary school teacher, was interviewing for a job a few years ago. I shared with her when she is responding to interview questions, there are very effective ways to connect with the interviewer. Your natural reaction to answering a question might be, "Here are the steps I took to teach this child..." The interviewer might like your approach. When you start your response or add to your response with, "There was this boy named Charlie...," the interviewer will register your actions differently. The imagery of the child brings to life the steps you took. The interviewer will start filling in your results as you're telling your story.

4. Share what's in it for me (WIIFM) and what's in it for them (WIIFT).

At this point, they have context and understand why it's important to them. As you explained why this matters, you highlighted for them the benefits to them. They are the "me" in the WIIFM.

Now, you can take the additional step of explaining, if you haven't already, how the greater good will also benefit. Get them to think about what's in it for the company, your customers, the market, and as many others as possible.

I believe people genuinely want others to be happy and successful. I also feel people truly want to help others because nothing is more powerful than serving others. In the corporate world, this is vital to your company's success and when persuading people to take on big projects.

5. Explain the here's-how.

A major ingredient in persuading someone is showing them you know the approach and steps to bring your idea to life. This can be as simple as, "Here are the five steps..." or as complicated as, "Here are the twenty steps..." The most important factor is to outline exactly what needs to take place.

6. Prove it with a case study.

The "here's-how" part looks a lot more life-like when you provide a case study. Providing examples of what you or your company has done is extremely powerful. More importantly, it helps the listeners look past the theory and envision real results.

Your case studies can be comprised of real results from previous participants or customers. If you don't have a track record of performance, use market investigations, anecdotal information, or any available research.

You might wonder how you can find case studies if you haven't done this project before. Here's how I pulled this off when I was working for a technology consulting company. I was in charge of creating new products which we were going to sell to new customers. That means, we had never technically done what we were selling. I had two major problems. First, what would we sell? Second, how would we convince a company to hire us if we hadn't technically done it before?

To handle the first issue, I assessed macro and micro market trends for the two sectors, financial firms and insurance companies, we wanted to support. I evaluated the technology trends in these sectors for the previous ten years. Based on these trends, I projected the future business problems these organizations would have and need to address.

Once I found the trends and real issues, I called software companies whose products solved those problems. I asked them for their case studies so I could use them when pitching our services. Of course, we'd be happy to establish a partnership to work together. The most important point is I needed proof my predictions were viable and someone had already solved them and proven this.

Think creatively regarding where you might get your proof if you don't have it already.

7. Cover the risks.

If you're persuading an individual or group to undertake a large-scale initiative, it's important to cover the risks. In fact, it's a must. Risks are potential issues that arise from uncontrollable factors. Perhaps your project will be affected if the housing market rises or falls. You might be implementing a software product and need new features to be available by a future date. Of course, you're relying on the software developer to complete them on time. These examples illustrate how you might not control all factors required for success.

Before you make your persuasive pitch, identify all the risks you can imagine so you can plan to mitigate them or implement contingencies in the event you're unable to avoid them.

Assess, for each risk, the probability it will occur, how you'll mitigate it to hopefully avoid it, who and what will be impacted if it comes to fruition, how much it'll cost if you encounter it, and the contingency plans you'll implement if you're unable to avoid it.

When you make your argument, explain you've already considered the major risks and have planned for them. This will go a long way in gaining the confidence of the people you're trying to persuade. The most important point when capping it off is to share you realize there is no such thing as smooth sailing and you're ready for it.

Now, let's start working on these practices and building your standard clocks!

CRAFT COMPELLING MESSAGES EXERCISE

Thought-Provokers

1A. The obstacles that prevent me from concentrating during my creative sessions are...

1B. Steps I can take to remove them are...

2. The steps I can take to optimize my physical environment so it's more conducive to creating quickly are...

3. I've noticed the best time of day for me to create is...

4A. The most common problems I address (product issue, team dynamics, customer issue, etc.) in my communications are...

4B. The most-frequent solutions to those problems are typically...

5A. The people I most frequently communicate with at work are...

5B. The issues these people face most often are...

Challenge

In the thought-provokers portion of this exercise, you addressed to whom you're frequently communicating and which topics you tend to tackle most often. Now, let's perform a challenge to start building and practicing your **"standard clocks"** and **persuasion skills**.

You can do these challenges serially or concurrently. The short-form challenge is set as a four-day clock, but you can make it a two-day clock or five-day clock or whatever is appropriate. The long-form challenge is set as a four-week clock, but, again, you can compress or elongate based on what works best for you.

Prerequisite Step One: Choose two communications you develop frequently. Select one you'd typically create within one week and another you'd create within one month. This will offer you opportunities to develop two standard clocks, one for a short communication and another for a more involved communication.

Prerequisite Step Two: For the longer communication, the primary focus is to build and practice your standard clock. However, if you have the opportunity to select a topic which requires persuasion, it's a wonderful opportunity to feed two birds with the same piece of bread. If this option is available to you, before you start the long-form challenge, think through the elements I outlined in the lesson: 1) Context, 2) Why it matters, 3) Stories, examples, or analogies, 4) WIIFM and WIIFT (that is, the benefits beyond them), 5) Steps, 6) Case studies, and 7) Risks.

Day One (short), Week One (long): Outline your main points. Identify what needs to be communicated. This is as simple as making an outline of what you need to communicate. This might be the single greatest success factor because it provides you with a great structure. Don't start writing out your points as tempting as it might be. Work on letting your ideas marinate overnight or over the week. You can confirm your outline before heading into that step.

Day Two (short), Week Two (long): Write out your points, clarify your message, and add the relevant stories and examples. The second part is to build out 90 percent of the message. We're now adding meat onto the bones. For the short-form communication, you can do this in a single day. For the long-form, you can spread this across three days throughout the week or complete it all in one day during that week. Remember, this is about learning and practicing what development process works best for you.

Day Three (short), Week Three (long): Make it more succinct and ensure it contains proper emotion. Now that you have the bulk of your communication in place, this step is about making it as short as possible and ensuring it elicits the proper reaction. You can use the prompters I outlined in the lesson to capture their emotions (i.e., ask questions, cite problems and aspirations, reference myth and oddities, call out feelings, mention benefits).

Day Four (short), Week Four (long): Talk it out, edit it, and take a last pass. Once you have everything in place, talk it out if it's a speech and edit your final written form of the communication. Then, it's time to sling it out into the world so it can live and breathe!

CHAPTER 14

Inspiring with Your Personal Story

Your greatest opportunities will be found in the sounds of other people's complaints.

It was Friday afternoon, November 19th, 2004. While I don't remember the exact time, I'll never forget the date or the mere minutes that would become a defining moment in my life. The CEO called me into his office.

I had just spent the last 312 days—my entire tenure with this consulting company—serving as a Vice President of Business Development. I created, designed, and sold consulting "products" to the tune of slightly over $4 million. The company was a mere $12 million dollars in total revenue before I joined, so I'm thinking I'm doing my part.

The CEO tells me he "needs" to make changes and, as part of those changes, I have "two" options. The first option was to take a $100,000 salary pay cut and become a sales representative. He generously points out, through good production, I could earn back my reduced salary in the form of sales commissions. The second option was to take a $25,000 pay cut and manage consulting projects.

I literally thought he was kidding, but since he didn't have much of a sense of humor, I knew this was no joke. I wondered, *What the heck is going on?* I discovered a few months later that he was getting ready to sell the company, and didn't want my compensation reflected in next year's cash-flow projections.

189

After a brief exchange, I said, "Give me the weekend to think about it. I'll check in with you Monday morning with one of my four answers." Then I walked out.

As I left, he asked, "Four?"

I didn't bother to turn around to explain. I could have picked any number because the number of choices then, now, and forever will be infinite.

Let's do the math. I had the two unattractive options he gave me. I could quit, which didn't take much creativity to come up with on the fly. I felt there must be another option, but couldn't grasp it at the moment.

As I headed back to my rather unflattering cubicle, I stopped at my best friend's desk. My next-door neighbor and childhood buddy, Tony, who I've known since I was eleven years old, was our staffing coordinator. He managed the list of our clients at which our company's consultants were deployed. He also tracked which clients were waiting for us to put our staff resources on their projects.

I asked him, "How much money are we 'losing' each month because we don't have 'butts in the seats?'" ("Butts in the seats" is endearing slang in consulting-speak for filling a client request for a resource.) That is, I wanted to know what we could have been earning if we simply had the consulting resources our clients wanted.

He said, "It's big."

I asked, "How big? Can you give me the number down to the dime?"

He said, "$249,000 and change."

I asked, "A quarter of a million dollars? How about the previous few months? Similar?"

Turns out, over the previous four months, our company could have earned an additional $1 million in consulting revenue if we had the resources our clients would have happily paid for! I'm guessing that stung the CEO a bit. That would have looked nice on the profit and loss statement, especially considering the company was about to be sold.

I did some thinking over the weekend. I thought about what I wanted. I thought about how I could leave this company on my terms. I focused positively on this new opportunity. That's what his ultimatum was—a golden opportunity. That's the date a professional executive recruiter was born.

On Monday, I walked into his office.

He asked, "Which option did you choose?"

I said, "I chose the one where I open up my own recruitment firm and you become my first client."

The look on his face was absolutely priceless. I wish the iPhone had been invented back then because nothing would have stopped me from snapping that picture and framing a twenty-by-twenty-four blow up of it.

I continued, "We're losing out on a quarter of a million dollars each month because we don't have the resources. That's every month! You need help. I know our company and positions better than the corporate recruiter and you'll never find a recruiting agency who understands this business like I do. You get the help you need and I'll even discount my standard rate 20 percent for you."

He said, "You already have a standard rate?"

We laughed.

I said, "Yes, it's 25 percent (of the employee's first year compensation) and you can have it for 20 percent. Either way, what does it matter? You're not paying me anything unless you hire the people."

We signed the contract before the Thanksgiving holiday.

I had my first client and I didn't even have a company name yet.

If, a few days earlier, people had told me I'd be a business owner the following week, I'd have laughed in their faces.

Why we undervalue ourselves…

You might be wondering, *Who cares about my story?* Most people think this because they consider their stories in terms of what it means to them, instead of the value it provides to someone else. This is the exact same reason people undervalue themselves. They think of what they know or what they've experienced in terms of what it means to them instead of the value their knowledge and experience could bring to someone else's life. I've already mentioned a few times, your experience is not what happened to you. It's the meaning you attach to what's happened to you.

**You might be wondering, *Who cares about my story?*
Most people think this because they consider their stories
in terms of what it means to them, instead of the value it
provides to someone else.**

Why do we do this? Because we forget what it's like not to know what we know. We also think the intersection between what we know and what someone else knows is a lot bigger than it is. The actual intersection is usually microscopic, but we tend not to feel this way because we're so used to knowing what we know.

We also don't recognize the emotional and inspirational value our story provides. Think about the empathy and understanding you can offer someone else—even someone you don't know—who immediately identifies with what you've been through and how you overcame it. They don't feel alone anymore.

I'll take it one step further. You have many personal stories and it is important to share them. The story about my boss and the transition to start my recruitment firm is merely one chapter in my life full of stories. I shared that particular one with you because it not only helps me illustrate the points of this lesson, but also, hopefully, connects us. Perhaps it'll help you understand there are so many more options available to you in this world. Maybe you'll remember it at some point in your life when you feel backed into a corner without many options. Then, all of sudden, you'll recall my story and it'll give you an extra push to identify better alternatives. It can be the inspiration to open the business you've been wanting to for many years but haven't drawn the courage to do so.

Your personal stories are important to share because they'll help you inspire others and build trust with them. Sharing them will also have great benefits for you personally because they'll require you to practice your communication skills, especially as they relate to persuasion and motivation.

Attach meaning to the "unimportant" events in your life.

I was born in 1966 at St. Elizabeth's hospital in Chicago, Illinois. At the time this book is released, I'm fifty-eight years old or older. Let me tell you my personal story. I can just hear you shutting the book now.

Your story doesn't need to start at birth. It doesn't need to be an hour long. Different stories have different purposes. The most important aspect of personal storytelling is knowing it's a vehicle for you to positively influence, teach, and connect with others.

This can be the beginning of your keynote speech or a two-minute pick-me-up story for your friend. It can be part of your "sales pitch" or an analogy you use to share a product-advertising idea with your client.

Once you recognize the value and how you can use your personal stories, you can start collecting the scenes from your life.

Consider your "life résumé." Perhaps there are stories about your mom, dad, church, or volunteer group. Hopefully, you've lived a healthy life, but if you've had a serious illness, I assure you there will be value in your struggle and recovery. Review your "professional résumé." This includes your entire work history. Were there challenges you overcame? Were there promotions you didn't get, but kept charging forward? Your hindsight is the source to identify your victories among the mundane. These will usually be found in your low points where you managed to dig yourself out. Think in terms of the ripple effect and how your story goes beyond you.

Your hindsight is the source to identify your victories among the mundane. These will usually be found in your low points where you managed to dig yourself out. Think in terms of the ripple effect and how your story goes beyond you.

As you perform this exercise, remember the meaning you assign to the events in your life is what ultimately controls the quality of your life. The quality of your life also has a habit of altering your interpretation of the events in your life.

The meaning you assign to the events in your life is what ultimately controls the quality of your life. The quality of your life also has a habit of altering your interpretation of the events in your life.

Not exactly "he said, she said," but more like "here's a version for you" and "here's another version for you."

After my defining moment with my CEO boss, I started my recruitment firm milewalk® and I had no experience in recruiting, no track record for the business, no client testimonials, or just about anything else I'd need to successfully sell my services. I had no form of income. None of this mattered because I had a story. Actually, I had several stories from my professional life and several versions of the same story related to the defining moment that helped me transition into recruitment.

I was an information technology consulting professional who held various positions throughout my eighteen years in this profession. I developed software, managed projects, sold consulting services, marketed, built products, established and operated large practices, developed methodologies, and had a keen sense of running a business.

As I transitioned to being an executive recruiter, I realized the job candidates I'd recruit for my new clients would love the fact I held the same corporate positions they do. How wonderful would it be, as a job seeker, to have a recruiter helping you who actually understands what you do as a professional? I told job seekers the story of my evolution into recruitment and that helped them trust me and feel more comfortable working with me.

Of course, I also needed to secure clients, the businesses on behalf of which I'd recruit. I started with what I knew, which included technology consulting and software companies. I shared with them the stories of how I was a consulting practitioner, grew businesses, and understood the types of employees they needed. How nice is it to have an external recruiter who understands the skillsets and traits you desire in an employee and can actually evaluate them even before you see the job candidates? As my firm grew, I developed, in a consultant-like fashion, a proprietary recruitment methodology based on predictive analytics. This organized and proven framework simply augmented my personal story. I wrote about this recruitment methodology in *The Hiring Prophecies: Psychology behind Recruiting Successful Employees*. My story now includes handing my potential client an award-winning hiring book.

My entire business started with the experience I had and a couple of versions of a singular defining moment. Let's get to how you can find yours so you can start building your stories!

Think about the scenes before you write the story...

When I built my recruitment stories for my clients and job candidates, I needed to collect the scenes from my professional life. Some of these were mundane. In fact, most, especially at this point in my life, were afterthoughts. They weren't even important to me as I continued to grow as a professional. Why? For the very same reasons I shared when it comes to undervaluing yourself. I hadn't yet attached any beneficial meaning, for my purposes or anyone else's, to my experiences.

Building your personal stories starts with collecting the scenes from your life. Think back to your most pivotal, defining moments. These will usually include a struggle in your personal or professional life. You might have gone through a breakup, divorce, illness, or death of a loved one. Perhaps you got fired, lost a client, or your business failed.

The most important factor is your stories start with a low point or at the beginning of a very long journey. Think back to moments which changed the course of your life. They required you to fight and you persevered. These are the stories with the most valuable lessons. How did you fight? Ask yourself this as you start drawing out your story.

When my boss called me into his office and told me he needed to make some changes, he was in a position of power. I fought to get that power so I could make a decision that suited me. In the end, I thought creatively and came up with a solution that benefited both of us. There is a lesson in there about having more options than you first realize. I packaged that into a shareable story for you because all great stories have a lesson.

I've never heard a great story start with something such as, "I got a scholarship to Harvard and everything took off from there!" It'll sound more like, "Ugh. I couldn't get into any college, but I kept at it and at it. I figured it out. Here's what I did…" Share what you learned because the value is in the lesson for them.

You won't believe what happened next…

You've got your scenes, but we need to write the "complete" story. I've adopted my storytelling structure from novelist and playwriter Gustav Freytag. In 1863, he formalized his *Technique of the Drama* based on five storytelling stages that many books and movies follow today.

He illustrated his framework using a pyramid that showed the five stages including the exposition, rising action, climax, falling action, and catastrophe or denouement.

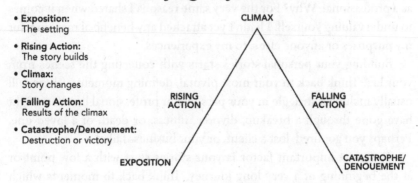

Freytag's Pyramid

- **Exposition:**
  The setting

- **Rising Action:**
  The story builds

- **Climax:**
  Story changes

- **Falling Action:**
  Results of the climax

- **Catastrophe/Denouement:**
  Destruction or victory

CLIMAX

RISING ACTION

FALLING ACTION

EXPOSITION

CATASTROPHE/ DENOUEMENT

- **Exposition:** The opening includes the setting, which identifies the characters and environment in which the story takes place.

- **Rising action:** This part includes the buildup, which typically means "things got worse." You make a bad choice or the villain hurts the main character or any conflict that sends the story downward.

- **Climax:** The middle part, or peak, is where we learn the fate of the main character and serves as the turning point in the story.

- **Falling action:** After the climax shows the turning point in the story, the falling action reveals when the story gets better or worse.

- **Catastrophe, denouement:** The last part uncovers how the story ends, which can be a tragedy, victory, or, occasionally, an untidied outcome.

The LaCivita twenty-first-century version of storytelling…

Freytag's storytelling structure is applicable today and a wonderful way to tell dramatic stories. I've modified his methods slightly so it becomes easier for you to share your personal stories with business colleagues and friends.

Here's how the storytelling structure looks in seven steps. I've mapped these steps back to Freytag's framework so you can see the correlation and also put sample expressions next to each so you can easily imagine how your personal stories might begin within each stage. I also mapped pieces of my original story, along with paraphrases, to show you how they fit into each step.

Setting (Exposition): "I was strolling along..."

It was Friday afternoon, November 19th, 2004. I was working at a company as the Vice President of Business Development.

Incident: "And then this issue occurred..."

The CEO called me into his office and gave me two options.

Buildup (Rising Action): "So I gather myself, do this and that..."

As I headed back to my rather unflattering cubicle, I stopped at my best friend's desk. [...] I did some thinking over the weekend. I thought about what I wanted. I thought about how I could leave this company on my terms.

Peak (Climax): "All of a sudden, BAM..."

He asked, "Which option did you choose?"

Resolution (Falling Action): "So I decided to solve it this way..."

I said, "I chose the one where I open my own recruitment firm and you become my first client."

Outcome (Catastrophe/denouement): "Here's what happened..."

I opened the milewalk® recruitment firm and, subsequently, the mile-walk Academy®.

Lesson: "The moral of the story is..."

Look for the opportunity! There are more options available to you than you think. Life happens *for* you, not *to* you!

A story from Spanxville...

There is this woman. Her name is Sara. At one point in her life, as she tells her story, she wanted to be a lawyer, but she failed the Law School Admission Test (LSAT) twice. Then, she wanted to go to Disney and be the character Goofy, but, apparently, she wasn't tall enough, so she settled on being one of the chipmunks. She evolved into selling fax machines door-to-door for seven years because she needed the money and health insurance.

As her life was rolling along, she was heading out to a party one evening. She realized she didn't have the right undergarment to provide a smooth look under her white pants. She used a pair of scissors to cut the feet off her control top pantyhose. She put the pantyhose on and then pulled up the jeans to see how everything looked. Just like that, voilà, she thought, *This should be an invention.* She worked on that invention for two years.

She didn't have much money at the time so she wasn't able to hire a lawyer. She decided to buy some books on patents, then created the patent, and started to work in department stores pulling twelve-hour shifts. While she was giving it a go in Neiman Marcus, she pitched her clothing to one of the buyers. She hoped the buyer would purchase the clothes and stock them in the stores.

The buyer was reluctant, so she asked the buyer to join her in the dressing room to see what this garment looked like on an actual person. She showed the buyer the "before" and "after" looks. The buyer said, "I'll take them. We'll put them in seven stores."

Today, Sara Blakely's company, Spanx, is one of the leading providers of women's bras, underwear, leggings, and activewear. She's a self-made billionaire.

Consider this story I shared. It's a superfast, powerful recollection of her struggle, creative thought, hard work, and grit.

Here's how her story breakdowns when considering the seven-step process I shared:

Setting: She wanted to be a lawyer.

Incident: She failed the LSATs twice.

Buildup: She worked as a chipmunk at Disney and sold fax machines for seven years. She wanted to get the right look for her outfit as she dressed for a party. She felt she had a novel idea and worked on her invention for two years. She bought books on patents, studied, and started selling her clothing in stores for twelve hours each day. She had an opportunity to pitch her clothing to a buyer in Neiman Marcus.

Climax: The buyer from Neiman Marcus was reluctant, but Sara persuaded her with a demonstration. Instantly, seven stores started carrying her product line.

Resolution: She built a clothing empire and line of women's undergarments and activewear.

Outcome: Spanx is operating successfully.

Lesson: There are so many lessons in her story related to everyday people coming up with brilliant ideas to hard work paying off to being creative in the way you convince people.

There is such a this-can-be-you feel to her story. Now, when you see her, you might think she's rare. That's because you've discovered her recently or in the capacity you know her (perhaps because you've purchased her products or seen her deliver a speech). What's rare about her is her belief in herself that she could make it happen. You can too.

Like any great food dish, inspiring stories have ingredients too.

The most important part about the personal stories you share is knowing what your goal is. Obviously, when we're developing relationships with other people, we share ourselves with them as a way to get to know each other. The personal stories I'm discussing here, however, always have a purpose. That's what makes them magical. You need to decide what that purpose is so you can choose the right story for that situation.

Whenever I tell a personal story, I consider these factors so the story becomes valuable to the other person.

What is your goal for sharing the story? What do you want to happen as a result of sharing your story? When I share stories about my company milewalk®, for example, sometimes the goal is to make a sale. Other times, the goal is to build a relationship. What is the purpose of your discussion? Are you trying to cheer someone up? Motivate them?

How can you bond with or relate to the person? What is your common ground with the person? When I speak to another business owner, I can relate to them on what it's like to struggle as a company owner. When I speak with a person who is looking for a new job, I can relate to them on my experiences in searching for my jobs. This bonding element is exactly why the Harvard-scholarship-style stories would make you unrelatable (unless, of course, you're speaking to another Harvard alum).

199

What motivates the other person? With whomever you share your story, it's important to understand what they care about. Why would they want to listen to your story? Will the lesson in your story be valuable to them?

Is it an actual story? Can you package it into an "entertaining" story that keeps their attention. One of the reasons Freytag's technique works so well is because there are different scenes and a buildup. It's easier to keeps someone's attention when the story is moving along and there is some level of suspense.

Will they be able to see their potential transformation? The most inspiring stories show the possibility of growth and transformation. While we want to be clear about the lesson, the element that gives the story inspiration is when people can envision what's possible for them. That hope is what uplifts their spirits. The proof you were able to overcome it gives them belief. The combination of these two is what inspires them to go out and do it.

> While we want to be clear about the lesson, the element that gives the story inspiration is when people can envision what's possible for them. That hope is what uplifts their spirits. The proof you were able to overcome it gives them belief.

Now that you have the formula to leverage your personal stories to help others, let's get to building yours!

PERSONAL STORY BUILDING EXERCISE

The Personal Story Building exercise combines thought-provokers and activities within the steps so you can develop and practice your story(s) to empower and connect with others. I recommend completing it over a five-day period to allow you to "marinate" on ideas and reflect on key moments in your life. Remember, experience is not what happened to you as much as it is the meaning you attach to what happened to you. Your experiences contain valuable lessons for you *and* others. Spice this up by wrapping those lessons into stories!

Day One: Collect your scenes. Start with collecting the scenes from your life. At first, you might think what you've experienced or accomplished in your life isn't all that important. It's not the events themselves that need to be interesting. I mentioned how my boss called me into his office. We talked. That's borderline coma-inducing. The events can be mundane. It's the meaning you attach to the events—in hindsight—that will make the mundane truly remarkable when you ultimately tell your stories. In this step, simply collect them. There is no need to evaluate or "judge" your scenes. These can be highs, lows, anything in between, starting a family, launching a business, getting passed over for a promotion, an illness, or whatever you want!

—Ten (yes, ten!) memorable scenes from my life are...

Day Two: Identify your defining moment(s). You have a running start with some of the scenes from your life. Now, think about *the* moments that changed the course of your life. Think about the times you were required to fight for something. You simply were not going to let it beat you. You not only survived, but thrived. It could be a fork in the road. Maybe there was an "adversary," but there sure was adversity.

—Moments that definitely changed the course of my life were...

—The shareable lessons in these moments are...

Day Three: Connect your story(s). You've got the scenes and major, pivotal moments. Before you construct your story(s) (in the next step), consider the purposes of how you want to use your stories to connect with others. Specifically, what are your goals for sharing your stories? Do you want to inspire others? Help them avoid a crucial mistake you made? Make a sale? Move your business forward? Ultimately, how will you use your stories?

—The goals of my stories are...

Day Four: Construct your story(s). Let's bring it all together using the seven major storytelling stages. For each of your stories, develop your first drafts using the outline I previously provided including: 1) Setting, 2) Incident, 3) Buildup, 4) Climax, 5) Resolution, 6) Outcome, and 7) Lesson. Refer back to the main lesson for more detail on each stage as well as the sample expressions if you need to get a running start!

—The stories I want to tell and the way I'll tell them are...

Day Five: Practice your story(s). The only thing left is to practice your stories and start telling them to others. In this step, simply talk out each story. How does it sound? Are there sentences or parts of your story you want to emphasize? Should you elevate your voice or pause or both? What are the proper facial expressions you should use? You get the idea here. Have fun with these and deliver them in your own style because they are *yours*. Remember, more importantly, you're serving others and that's what matters most!

CHAPTER 15

Mastering Your Trade

Show me your calendar. I'll tell you your future.

Sara, a sales director, and I were meeting for our first high-performance coaching session. Although titled a "director," she was truly a mid-level salesperson who sold information technology consulting services to small-to-medium size businesses in the central region of the United States. She was responsible for selling her company's services to organizations in her designated territory, which included five different states.

She had a wonderful job and, like many ambitious professionals, wanted to become better at her trade, gain more responsibilities, advance in her company, get assigned larger clients, and, in turn, earn more compensation. She figured if she could reach all these goals, becoming the number-one sales representative in her company was well within her grasp.

Sara enlisted my help to build her skills, learn more advanced sales techniques, hold her accountable for putting in the effort, monitor her results, and make the necessary improvements along the way.

During our session, after we got to know each other a bit and discussed her goals and aspirations, I asked her to show me her calendar. It's a request I make with any new high-performance client.

She responded, "Oh. Do you want to schedule some of our future sessions?"

I said, "No. I want to see how you currently plan your time to work on all the skills you'll need to build to meet your goals."

Her answer was among the most common I receive in the wake of this question. She said, "Well, I figured as I implement the techniques you'll teach me, I'd get better and learn to manage the larger accounts over time."

I said, "Sara, anyone can read the playbook and learn the tactics. Rapid advancement and becoming the best never happens between 9:00 AM and 5:00 PM. That's when the game is played. It's how you practice between 5:00 PM and 9:00 AM that makes you win."

All successful people have three things in common.

In my lifetime—I'm not kidding—during my stretch as an executive recruiter, I've personally interviewed (that's actually spoken directly with) 15,000 professionals who were open to or actively pursuing new employment. I've interacted with countless more as a consultant and career coach. That's a lot of evaluation and data.

During my assessments of these individuals, I noticed the most successful had three traits in common—passion, vision, and commitment. To me, these qualities are part of who they are, not how they became the way they are. All of these traits enable them to take on the challenges required to master and become the best at whatever they do.

Passion: You're not born with it. It's something you develop. It's a love for something you were exposed to from the time you were born until now. You fell in love with it. You became interested in it and then passionate about it. You genuinely love it.

Vision: Your ability to see where you want to take your passion. How will you grow it? How will you nurture it? Where will it take you?

Commitment: Your dedication to fulfilling your vision. This commitment is what ensures you get past the bumps and "failures" along the way.

These three characteristics shape their attitudes in everything they do, but especially in their most meaningful, vocational pursuits. Your attitude and mindset as you approach your quests need to be completely intact to reach great heights. It all starts here. To be clear, I'm not speaking about being positive and cheery. Positivity is great. Appreciating the implications of your efforts, however, makes your success a necessity. That necessity will continue to drive you because it matters to you and what you do matters to the rest of the world.

Optimism is something you manufacture from your attitude and inspiration is something someone else manufactures from your optimism.

I believe this about attitude. Optimism is something you manufacture from your attitude and inspiration is something someone else manufactures from your optimism. Starting with this mentality, and never forgetting it, is what keeps you forging ahead through the toughest times. If you want to master your trade and become the best, there will be very tough times ahead. Keeping in mind your attitude helps not only you, but affects those who surround you, can serve as great motivator when you encounter those challenges.

Beyond these three traits, I believe there are ten major steps, success factors if you will, the best-of-best employ to become masters of their crafts. Let's cover each of these in detail.

Build Your Capabilities

As I mentioned to Sara, anyone can buy the playbook to learn the game. Sales executives can purchase the books or attend training programs. Project Managers can study the techniques associated with being a Project Management Professional (PMP), take a test, and get a stamped-credential next to their names. Every profession has a how-to manual. If you read it and execute the steps on a daily basis, you essentially become the same as everyone else.

If you're still reading this book, you are, fortunately, not like everyone else. You have ambitions. You want to become the very best you can be. Becoming the best at your craft requires building skills not found in the playbook. These skills are the ones that transcend the specificities of your trade.

These specificities are related to exactly what you build, sell, market, and account for related to your company's products and services. For Sara, that means learning how her company's consulting services work.

It's learning how to sell those specific consulting services. It's like the mechanic who knows exactly how his automobile maker's engine works.

Capabilities transcend specificity. They're the foundational abilities, that when applied, will make you better irrespective of your specific product, service, or function. For sales executives like Sara, example capabilities include psychology, organization, relationship building, human behavior, and customer service. For the automobile mechanic, it's problem-solving and diagnosing, time management, and dexterity. Sara wants to build skills that will make her the best salesperson, not just the best consulting services salesperson.

Take Jerry Rice, for example, who many argue is one of the greatest, if not the greatest, National Football League (NFL) wide receivers. He holds many of the NFL's wide receiver records. He is certainly not the biggest, strongest, or fastest to ever play the position. I'm sure he knew his teams' playbooks very well. As documented and covered in many places including the book *Talent Is Overrated*, by Geoff Colvin, however, Rice had a legendary workout regime. In the offseason, he'd train six days every week. He'd run ten forty-meter wind sprints up the steepest part of his hilly five-mile trail. He was consistent and practiced it again and again. He honed his strength, speed, agility, elusiveness, quickness, and other abilities that made him great.

The book you're now holding includes several wonderful capabilities that most white-collar professionals need. Research your profession to learn the most valuable foundational traits and, like I said to Sara, make sure to carve out time each week to practice them.

Find the Right Teachers

I've never met masters of their crafts who became that way on their own. Oftentimes, it takes an entire stable of coaches, mentors, and teachers, especially if the range of capabilities and skillsets you need to learn is vast. In Sara's situation, you'll note a few of the capabilities I highlighted for her. Each capability has a guru. Someone is the best psychology coach for her. Someone else might be the best organizational coach. She can find the best expert in each of the areas who teaches the way she prefers to learn.

That takes some time to research and find the right coaches because it's very unlikely you have a group of experts readily available to you.

I like to build what I call a "Franken-mentor." That's, as you might imagine, several experts who help me with various parts of my business and personal development. I've had coaches who taught me how to market my products and others who helped me understand how to incorporate YouTube into my community and marketing platforms. I have others who helped me learn my meditation practice. You get the idea. It takes a village, but how do you know which coaches are the right ones for you?

First, you need to identify the skills and capabilities you want to learn. That's part of the previous steps. Once you identify those, it's time to start researching, following, and learning from potential teachers. I review eight areas whenever I'm considering and selecting coaches.

Knowledge and tactics: As you read, listen to, and watch them, is what they're saying accurate? Have you tried implementing any of the tactics and do they work? Do they draw your attention to the most important techniques? Is it eye-opening?

Results, case studies, and testimonials: Their success is technically based on your results, not the number of followers they have. When you review their "social media proof" or testimonials on their websites, do their case studies seem credible? If they're very extreme, can you verify them?

Teaching delivery and style: Not all experts can teach. They might be knowledgeable in their subject matter, but can they reverse engineer what they know and package it into a format you can understand and implement? Does their style of teaching motivate you to put in the effort and enjoy the journey?

Love of their subjects: To be great, long-lasting teachers, they need to love what they're teaching. Of course, people can be adept at something and teach others, but to have lasting power as teachers, trainers, or coaches, they need to love what they're doing or they'll quit. If they quit, obviously, they're no longer your teachers. If their hearts are in it, that'll genuinely come through the words, cameras, and microphones.

Availability: In today's modern world of online everything, teachers that'll have the most impact on you will likely be the ones who are most available to you. That is, they'll continually provide you with lessons through their books, blogs, YouTube channels, podcasts, communities, real-time live shows, and other platforms. These easily available and easily accessible mediums offer your coaches ways to adapt their lessons to appeal to your preferred way of learning.

Generosity: I'm quite partial to this evaluation point. I genuinely believe offering complimentary lessons is one of the best relationship-building and trust-building activities. Often referred to by many coaches as "freemiums," these vehicles, which can be eBooks, documents, webcasts, live events, and countless other formats, shouldn't be marketing ploys by coaches to get your email address so they can spam you with sales messages. As part of your research effort, download various freemiums from potential coaches. Review the level of breadth and depth of their freemiums. This will be a preview of what it will be like to work with the coaches on a deeper level.

Modality: I know a lot of smart teachers who only write books or speak on stages at conferences. These types of teachers, while I might enjoy their books, won't be in my stable of go-to coaches. I want more "access" to them. I want to watch, listen to, and learn from them on a weekly basis. Personally, I want coaches who offer videos because it's my medium to learn from them and gives me the best way to gauge their authenticity and love of their subject matter. It makes no difference what your preferred medium is, but make sure your coaches provide the modality that fits your learning methods and lifestyle.

Inspiration: The ultimate acid test for coaches I want to follow and work with is whether they inspire me and build my confidence. Anybody with a cell phone can turn it on and call themself a coach. It's scary. I know. Any coach can also recite the steps. Many coaches, in fact, regurgitate steps they learned by copying other coaches. This doesn't make them great coaches as much as it makes them frauds. You'll notice a great coach not only teaches you the steps from practical experience, but also inspires you to take on the challenges, put in the work, and keep going. They'll focus on enjoying the journey because the joy must be in the doing. Otherwise, you'll give up.

Practice the Right Way

Now that you've identified the capabilities you need to build and teachers to help you develop them, you need to practice building them the right way. Whatever you practice generally becomes permanent (not perfect), so it's vital you practice effectively.

Whenever I practice anything, there are two components to it. First, I make sure I'm doing it correctly. That is, get the proper instruction and steps. Second, I practice and plan for next-level proficiency. I'm not speaking about being impatient with my progress. I break down my growth and development into stages so when I practice, I'm working toward getting proficient at one stage while keeping an eye on what I can do to improve it to reach the next stage of progress. I refer to this as progressive mastery.

Here's progressive mastery in action as I learned to use the video camera to communicate with my community. As an executive recruiter, I performed my business on the phone and in person. When I committed to becoming an online coach and trainer, I started by writing a blog, which turned into a podcast too. Then, I added videos on YouTube as well as a weekly, live coaching show. To become more effective at teaching using the video camera, I needed to practice using the video camera. That's quite different than having a conversation directly with someone!

The first stage of using the camera to communicate with my community was to get comfortable keeping my eye contact on the camera. This, in essence, means I'll have eye contact with whomever is watching and listening to me. I could use notes to ensure I covered my teaching points.

The second stage was to make our interaction as natural as possible. I'd practice so I could do my shows with as few, if any, notes as possible. This would help me make the online experience feel more life-like and conversational.

The third stage was to perform the lessons without any notes and make it even more engaging and interactive for the community.

The fourth stage, as I continued to progress, was to make the shows more entertaining and inspirational. My early videos and shows, while educational, probably lacked some zest because I expended energy focusing on delivering the teaching points. As I continued to practice and conduct more shows, I improved my level of engagement so the audience's experience got better.

This evolution took time and practice, but I condensed the amount of time it took me to become proficient because I practiced deliberately and worked in stages as opposed to incorporating all improvements at once.

The last element that expedited this process was my persistent evaluation of my performance. I watched each of my shows multiple times to review them for improvements. I still review all my shows. I evaluate whether I delivered the material as I intended, whether I was empathetic, thorough in my answers to questions, and all other components that ensure I can be the absolute best career coach.

To cap off practicing, I want to be clear. It's not about being satisfied with your performance. I want you to work at it and be happy with your progress, but also keep that thirst for getting better in a progressive manner.

Show up the Same Way

Practicing the right way each day will help you achieve progressive mastery in your craft. Showing up the same way each day will make you a legend in your career. This is a big reason why great careers are made from repeated excellence.

Practicing the right way helps you develop skills to become better at what you do. Showing up the same way helps everyone around you be their best. Everyone around you depends on you being consistent.

> **Practicing the right way helps you develop skills to become better at what you do. Showing up the same way helps everyone around you be their best. Everyone around you depends on you being consistent.**

Your consistency is not only for you, but the entire organization. If you commit to being the best, they'll commit to being the best. If you're demanding of yourself, they'll demand more of themselves. If you're detail-oriented, they'll be detail-oriented. If you cut corners, they'll cut corners.

This is true regardless of whether you're a company of one who helps others or you're the CEO of a *Fortune* 500 company. During my weekly, online, free, live coaching sessions, I remind jobseekers and professionals to be consistent with their searches and careers. I show up every week to be an example of that consistency. How can I ask them to be consistent if I'm not consistent?

There is an expression in professional sports although I'd extend this saying to pretty much anything—the best ability is availability. I'd also add the expression "count on." I can count on them to show up on time. I can count on them to be there when I need them. This is a big reason why availability is one of the eight criteria I recommend when choosing your coaches!

Get the Right Tools

Getting the right tools can really help your progress and development. They'll save you a lot of time and money if you choose the right ones. Point of caution here. First, determine your goals. Then, decide which tools you need to support those goals.

The tools I'm speaking of can be training programs, people, doctors, journals, mobile applications, or anything that enhances your ability to perform better.

A tool for me, for example, was a training program I enrolled in to learn how to develop and sell online training products. I have a handyman who fixes things in my house. When he rolls his pickup truck onto my driveway, it's filled with the necessary tools he needs to fix whatever he's attending to in my house.

Start simple and use the least expensive tools possible. See what works and whether you want to invest more as you get better with your craft. Going back to my camera example, when I first started shooting videos and doing livestreams, I used the computer's built-in camera. Then, I invested in a $99 web-camera. Now, I use a camera and lens that cost

$2,000. I didn't buy the expensive camera and lens until I was six years into my profession!

If you want to build a new habit, you can make your own paper-based habit tracker in a journal or you might find a free mobile application to let you track it. Use whatever helps you.

Build the Right Network

There are three kinds of people in the world. Those who support your goals, those who detract from your goals, and those people you don't know.

> **There are three kinds of people in the world. Those who support your goals. Those who detract from your goals. Those people you don't know.**

Managing your network is a living, breathing exercise that never stops. I constantly curate my network and keep the people who support me and my goals. I remove anyone who detracts me.

As far as the other people, it's beneficial to find the ones who'll be major contributors to your goals. Ask yourself, "What do I want to accomplish? Who can help me accomplish that?" The answers can be specific names of people. The answer could be "the organizer of that event." Whatever the case, find them. Introduce yourself.

I covered many of my favorite mechanics for growing your professional network and helping others build theirs in the earlier lesson on networking.

Listen to the Right People

Who are the people you should listen to to get better at your craft? Nobody, and I mean n-o-b-o-d-y, will make you better at your craft faster than your customers. Every person has customers. Find yours and listen to them. Your customers might be your company's actual customers. They might be an internal corporate group you and your team support.

There will never be greater opportunities for you to succeed—not to mention anything as satisfying—as helping others. I've long said, "Your greatest opportunities will be found in the sounds of other people's complaints. If you solve their problems, you'll become their hero."

Your greatest opportunities will be found in the sounds of other people's complaints. If you solve their problems, you'll become their hero.

The world will always provide clues of what to focus on. All you need to do is listen. The problem with most people is they're listening to the wrong people. It's not your competition. It's not your fellow colleagues. A very small percentage of the world is your customers. Find out who they are and listen to them. They'll tell you what they need.

Repeatedly Create MVPs

To become the best at your craft, you need to contribute actual value to the world. The only way to do that is to create products, services, tools, and anything else that can actually be used by others. Those others can be your customers, community, teammates, executive management team, or anyone who benefits from your work.

The easiest and most effective way to add value to the world is by creating MVPs—Minimum Viable Products. MVPs allow you to get something up and running as quickly as possible so the rest of the world can start benefiting and offer you feedback on how to improve it.

Don't get me wrong. I'm not speaking about the engineer who needs to ensure all the parts of the airplane are in working order. Some products need to go through months of development and years of testing because our lives depend on their proper function. I'm speaking of the other 99 percent of our world's creations.

This book you're reading, for example, required decades of experience for me to gain the knowledge. Developing the outline for the book took fifteen minutes. Writing the actual book took a few months of daily, morning writing sessions. After I reviewed it for whatever typos I could find, I sent it to my acquisitions editor who initiated the rest of the publishing process so the retailers could ship it to you. You, hopefully, are benefitting from it.

Instead of doing it in this manner, I could have created a product that offered you everything in my heart. In that case, you'd still be waiting for a book that would be three-times the size with thirty additional lessons. Essentially, you wouldn't be reading this sentence right now.

It was more important to me to create a wonderful book and balance the speed, quality, and, most importantly, get you value as quickly possible. If you like this style of book with lessons packed in, I'll write you another book or you can join my Leadership Coaching Program!

You might not be writing a book, but there are MVPs awaiting all around you. They can be a better process your team uses or a white paper you share with your community. Perhaps those pieces of paper with critical numbers in them can find their way into an Excel spreadsheet that can be viewed by your manager.

Your product doesn't need to be perfect.
It needs to be breathing.

People who become the best at what they do continually perform their progressive mastery on real-life "products." Your product doesn't need to be perfect. It needs to be breathing. That way, you can see what worked and what didn't. As I like to say, you can scale version 1.0, but you can't scale version zero. Iteration is your key to success.

Iteration is something perfectionists struggle with because everything a perfectionist wants to create needs to be, well, perfect. The issue with this mindset is that perfectionists consider every step they take to be a "final" one. That is, they think it's final so it needs to be perfect. When I coach perfectionists, I try to focus them on the fact that what they're creating at any moment in time is something they will change in the future. You're working within a strategy that has a long-term goal and the key to achieving that long-term goal is by iterating your MVPs along the way.

Use the Right Success Metrics

Most human suffering comes from expectations. We expect. Our expectations are not met. Now, we suffer, or at least get annoyed.

The next major culprit, even if we have zero expectations, is looking at the wrong success metrics. I coach several people who want to build their online businesses. They wonder, *Why don't I have more Instagram followers? I must not be worthy or desirable. Why didn't more people buy my product? I'm a failure. I'm a fish. Why can't I climb this tree as fast as that squirrel did?*

A key factor in reaching great heights is knowing what success looks like for you and making sure it's something totally within your control. The issue for most people is they often select success factors which are out of their control.

You might have a success metric of earning $100,000 annually. Whether you're an employee or business owner, that's an outcome your boss or customers control. It's possible you don't get that promotion and pay raise. What happens then?

When I decided to augment my firm to include business-to-consumer coaching, I'd never sold a product or services directly to an individual. I'd never created an online training product. I had never performed email marketing or a host other first-time endeavors.

When I offered my first online training program in 2016, I could have had success metrics such as the number of people who enrolled in the program and how much revenue my "big" sale generated. Those are metrics many business owners would track and work toward.

I did have some of these metrics in mind, however, I focused more on metrics related to these questions:

- Did I run an effective marketing effort, provide value to the potential customers, and make it clear how my product would improve their lives?

- Did I hit my target date to release version 1.0 of my product?

- Were the customers able to enroll easily?

- Did the customers get the welcome kit and everything they needed to use the product?

- Did I capture all the relevant statistics to help me evaluate what worked effectively and what I might improve for version 1.1?

As you can see from this list of success metrics, none are dependent on anyone but me and my team. Other metrics such as how many people enroll and how much revenue we generated are lagging indicators of how effectively we implemented the other areas.

To become the best at your trade, you're going to encounter many challenges along the way. Many outcomes won't go the way you hope. In fact, if you're "doing it correctly," most will not. In these instances, it's especially important your success metrics are dialed in properly because your ability to stay focused on your goals is dependent on it. Achieving your very long-term goals will be more a function of where you place your attention than your ability. Focusing your attention on the right success metrics will keep you enjoying the journey at every step.

> **Achieving your very long-term goals will be more a function of where you place your attention than your ability. Focusing your attention on the right success metrics will keep you enjoying the journey at every step.**

Reflect to Gain and Keep Perspective

No matter how much you accomplish, you'll never feel successful unless you reflect properly. Reflection, in this instance, isn't simply looking back. It's considering what happened and adding context to what happened so you can learn and grow from it.

I often say, "Experience is not what happened to you. It's the meaning you attach to what happened to you." Effectively, reflection is synonymous with attaching meaning.

As practicing the right way is required to progressively get better at your trade, reflecting the right way is required to keep your perspective so you maintain momentum through the tough times.

> **As practicing the right way is required to progressively get better at your trade, reflecting the right way is required to keep your perspective so you maintain momentum through the tough times.**

Reflection is also a tool to use whenever you get stuck. If you're unable to determine your resolution or path forward, it's best to step back to gain a broader perspective of what's actually occurring. Think the forest-through-the-trees analogy here. This is how you can keep moving forward even when you hit the inevitable bumps. The best of the best knows this, which is why they reflect daily!

MASTERING YOUR TRADE EXERCISE

The Mastering Your Trade exercise combines thought-provokers and activities within steps to help you build a plan to focus on and develop your trade-specific skills. While this entire book provides an overall approach to developing skills throughout your career, this exercise is aimed at highlighting and practicing skillsets primary to your area of expertise. Choose from a ten-day or ten-week period or whatever pace works for you.

Day/Week One: Develop the right attitude. The right attitude will help keep your momentum intact. High performers think in terms of abundance. Low performers think in terms of limits. Reflect on this and identify what's been working for you attitude-wise and what needs adjusting.

—The of attitude I want to develop and maintain is...

Day/Week Two: Identify the right capabilities. While specific on-the-job skills are important, your capabilities will lead you to become the best.

—The capabilities most related to my area of expertise I need to develop are...

Day/Week Three: Identify the right teachers. Once you know the capabilities you need to develop to become a high performer, you need to find the right teachers and coaches to help you. Start with your capabilities and search for coaches who are knowledgeable on those subjects. Build your Franken-mentor!

—The initial list of teachers I want to follow includes...

Day/Week Four: Practice the Right Way. You have identified the right capabilities and teachers to help you develop them. Now, you need to make sure you're practicing the right things the right way and striving for progressive mastery.

—The techniques I'll use to practice the capabilities I need to develop are...

Day/Week Five: Get the right tools. No matter what your profession, you need the right tools to be successful. Every job in the world requires you to have some set of tools. These can be computers, phones, tablets, and processes.

—The tools I need to make sure I perform my best are...

Day/Week Six: Build the right network. You're very much a byproduct of the people you surround yourself with. They need to be supportive, uplifting, and challenge you in the right way through encouragement. Anything less than this will hurt your ability to be the best you. (To supplement this step, you have a more-complete exercise in the Networking lesson.)

—The people I need to spend more time with include...

Day/Week Seven: Listen to the right people. Listening to the right people is different than surrounding yourself with the right people. You surround yourself with the right people so you have support in your efforts, and you listen to others who will make you the best—the fastest—at what you do professionally. Those people would be your customers or whomever you serve.

—My customers often complain about or tell me they need...

Day/Week Eight: Produce the MVPs. Don't wait another minute to bring life to something valuable. Most people spend the majority of their lives planning and very little time producing. The only way to know if your outputs, ideas, or efforts are valuable is to get them in the hands of people who can benefit from them! Plan. Build. Release. Improve.

—Those "products" I've been hemming and hawing to develop are...

—The first step I need to take to get each of them in motion is...

Day/Week Nine: Watch the right success metrics. A big part of human pain and corporate suffering occurs because we're not monitoring the right success metrics. As people learn new activities at work, they often struggle initially because they're not yet proficient. What's worse, they beat themselves up mentally because they're measuring themselves against (unrealistic) final outcomes. It's more telling, not to mention encouraging, to focus on the intermediary steps—the "in between goals" so to speak.

—Outcome success metrics I've been using, which are not a true reflection of my growth include...

—More appropriate success metrics include...

Day/Week Ten: Reflect the right way! No matter who you are, how successful you are, how much money you earn, how many accolades you've racked up, you'll never feel successful unless you properly look back on what you've accomplished. Focus on the impact and results of accomplishing what you've achieved. Your acts always have a ripple effect. Reflecting on the ripples is what ultimately shows you what you've truly achieved.

—The real outcomes of my accomplishments include...

PART SIX

The Developer

CHAPTER 16

Coaching and Mentoring

I'll treat you all fairly, but I won't treat you the same way.

During my consulting career, I ran several multi-million-dollar projects that required team sizes in the hundreds of people. As a corporate executive, I managed large operating units comprised of various large teams. No matter what the situation was, I learned there is one common characteristic about management that transcends organizational structure, team sizes, and numbers of units contributing to the goal. That is, you do not manage a team. You manage individuals.

The challenge with achieving that greater sum is there usually isn't anything common about the people who are contributing to the "common" goal.

If you manage the individuals correctly, the total achievement of the team will be greater than the sum of its individual parts. The challenge with achieving that greater sum is there usually isn't anything common about the people who are contributing to the "common" goal. You might think this is an extreme claim. We're all unique in our traits, experiences, and the way we process the world. Companies, of course, want to do whatever is possible to recruit and build teams made up of individuals with similar traits. Even when they're successful in hiring people with similar skillsets and traits, people generally respond to different styles of communication to ultimately register the sentiments companies want.

In the easiest-to-manage scenarios, you have individuals working on a singular team to achieve a common team goal. For example, you have the technologists developing a singular application. In other situations, this issue of uniqueness is exacerbated when you're managing multiple teams to achieve a common goal. Ask any Chief Operating Officer who's responsible for running the sales, marketing, and operational departments.

I once managed a project which had approximately 100 people. There were architects, analysts, organizational designers, trainers, administrators, and a host of other resources. My immediate eight direct reports were people from different parts of the world with different educational and professional backgrounds. Some were from "broken homes" and others had solid familial upbringings. They ranged in age from twenty-five to thirty-seven years old. They collectively were one amazing team I wish I could work with for the rest of my life, but they were far more different than they were the same. This is the issue we face as we coach and mentor others. It's the challenge we encounter when we're trying to motivate a unit to reach great heights.

This lesson on coaching and mentoring is to help you whether you're running a team at work or helping one person develop a skill. Regardless of your situation, this is about helping people with their development to attain their or their team's goals.

I'll give them a head start and catch up. I'm a quick study.

When I started my online career coaching business, I searched the internet. I checked out other coaches on YouTube and social media sites. There were, of course, dozens of skills I needed to learn, build, and refine. When most people want to grow, they fall victim to one of the worst mistakes you can make when you're beginning. They compare their beginnings to other peoples' middles.

If I do what they're doing, I should be able to get 10,000 subscribers without a problem! Why didn't that work? Why is it taking so long? What's worse, coaches and bosses do this to the people they're supposed to be helping! This causes the individuals they're coaching to become deflated, feel like failures, and give up.

Instead, focus on the first key to success when coaching people. Identify where they are in their current stages of development. Sometimes this is obvious. Sometimes this is not. I use a few easy-to-understand labels. The most important part of your initial assessment of the people you're coaching, mentoring, managing, or directing is you're clear on where they're starting.

Beginner: As a beginner, they're starting out, just beginning to learn, and typically unfamiliar with the activities, processes, or techniques. They need constant monitoring and frequent corrections to stay on track. The most important coaching technique to deploy is to get them to put in the repetitions so they get adequate amounts of correct practice.

Intermediate: As they progress and become more accustomed to what they're doing, they're able to do the activities and complete them effectively. Their limitations are they have yet to become proficient in developing an overall approach or strategy. That is, they can follow the activities in a "system," but cannot develop the system. The most important coaching technique to deploy for their growth is educating them on the big picture and how the pieces fit together.

Expert: After enough practice and education, they're able to develop the approach or methodology and practices within the methodology. They can also teach the components to others. The most important coaching technique to deploy is teaching them to use analysis for improvement as well as indicators to spot trends as they look forward and anticipate.

Master: At this stage, they can see in all directions, anticipate trends well in advance, and motivate everyone around them. Their mindset is in order and their outlook is clear and steady irrespective of external conditions. The most important coaching technique to deploy is introducing them to new challenges and providing opportunities for them to learn new areas.

These four levels of mastery are intended to serve as starting points for you to make your own. You might alter my definitions or add additional layers. The most important factor is to have well-defined levels so you can identify the correct developmental starting points and clearly communicate to your staff or protégés how to reach the next level. Remember, from the lesson on Mastering Your Trade, we strive for progressive mastery as we build our skills and work toward our goals.

There are five love languages? I have enough trouble speaking one!

Coaching people is about providing direction. Whether you're directing your team of people at work or helping an individual develop, you guide them on a path to achieving their next-level goals. The best coaches not only provide that direction, but do it in a manner that motivates and inspires the individuals.

The language you use to provide that direction, including the vocabulary, tone, and level of clarity, is one of the single greatest success factors in expediting their ability to grow and accomplish their goals.

Whether you're coaching an eclectic group of people or one person, you want them to respond to your messages. They can only do so by understanding them, being clear on the action they need to take, and becoming inspired to take that action. After all, it's possible for people to understand what you want or what they should do, but aren't necessarily motivated to do it. While this is more of an issue when managing a team of less-than-motivated individuals, it's still equally important with someone who willingly enlisted you as a coach or mentor.

Regardless of their personal motivations, you and they will get the best results if you communicate in their "developmental language." I use this term to refer to the language to which people best respond when they are being coached or instructed. It's akin to the love languages outlined in the book *The 5 Love Languages: The Secret to Love That Lasts* by Gary Chapman. In his book, Chapman illustrates how people express and receive love in five different ways, called love languages: quality time, words of affirmation, gifts, acts of service, and physical touch. When you're communicating in a language your loved one responds best to, you can strengthen and elevate your relationship. If, however, you shower your loved one with gifts, but your loved one prefers more of your attention in the form of (quality) time together, you'll have a rougher go of it.

The same applies to managing, coaching, and motivating people at work or in business. To be an effective coach and help people maximize their results, you can take some time upfront to observe their behaviors and determine the developmental languages to which they best respond.

Using Chapman's five love languages as the basis, excluding physical touch for so many obvious reasons, I'd parallel development languages this way:

Actions: Actions speak louder than words as they say. For some individuals you coach, you'll notice they need to observe your actions in order for your instruction to register. That is, how does my coach execute that presentation? How does my coach handle that meeting with the Board members? The people who respond best to this developmental language learn by seeing you do it. You'll need to let them shadow you frequently. (The love language analogy is acts of service.)

Rewards: Some people respond to "show me the money" more than others. You'll find yourself coaching some individuals who require incentives such as compensation, pay raises, higher-level titles, and other items of this ilk. In these cases, you'll need to dangle the carrot so to speak. (The love language analogy is gifts.)

Attention: Some individuals simply require and want more dedicated time and attention. They might need you to explain a technique a few different times and a few different ways. Sometimes, it's a matter of them wanting to "talk it through" to make sure everything is in order. (The love language analogy is quality time.)

Affirmation: All people need reassurance they're on the right track. This is as plain and simple as positive reinforcement by explicitly stating so. While all of us need some type of general feedback, some individuals will need more verbal feedback than others. (The love language analogy is words of affirmation.)

Each person you coach might "use" one or more of these languages. That is, someone might prefer a blend of "actions" and "affirmations." The important aspect for you is to observe which one or combination is most effective.

Empathy is part of a coach's not-so-secret sauce.

While we covered developing empathy at length in The Communicator section, I think it's important to touch on it here as it relates to your success as a coach. Empathy enables you to do anything better when it comes to interacting with others, but it's especially important when helping, teaching, and motivating them. The very definition of this lesson on coaching and mentoring others means you're likely more experienced at whatever it is you're helping them with. As we become more seasoned in our trades, we tend to forget what it's like not to know what we know.

Even if we're able to remember that, our task is further complicated by the fact we've never operated in the current environment our staff or protégés are operating in now. They're performing their tasks and building their skills under a different set of conditions than we were. This will enhance or detract their abilities to learn and process depending on what you're teaching them.

For example, today, you can Google anything. Information is immediately available. This will expedite certain activities. The opposite is also true. For instance, many young professionals have never been without a cell phone since they could speak (eh, text). Their professional communication skills are generally lacking because of the medium they use so frequently. This is something which will require a Herculean effort to alter for young professionals. As a coach, you must remember this and factor it into whatever lessons you're providing them.

As you learn to manage a team or mentor your protégés, make sure to revisit the types of empathy you can employ for your situations. All three types, whether social, cognitive, or empathic concern, will come in handy.

Earn trust first, give direction second.

Mom might have been able to get away with "Because I said so." This isn't going to fly for you.

In the company I "grew up in," you followed orders without question otherwise you were shown the door. This type of environment rarely exists anymore, not to mention it isn't really effective in building quality relationships with your staff or anyone you're helping develop.

The combination of earning their trust, showing them you care, and being empathetic are what will help you win the day. Much like with our deeper dive on building empathy, revisit the building trust lesson to ensure you're answering the "ability," "willingness," and "values" questions for those you're coaching. I also hope it's becoming clear how these skillsets build upon each other as you advance your way through your profession.

Questions > Statements.

The Socratic method is a dialogue technique to elicit thinking, answers, and ideas by asking questions. It's a wonderful technique to use no matter your relationship with your staff, but especially if you have yet to earn their trust or encounter tension from these individuals.

The reason this is so important is because you can focus your questions on outcomes you'd like to attain. When eliciting ideas to achieve outcomes or goals this way, you neutralize any personal feelings while simultaneously getting the person or group to focus on the independent goal. Remember, wherever you focus, that's where your energy flows.

Depending on the individual's or team's goals, you want to help their development as well as your company's outputs by asking questions that offer them ownership in the outcomes. That is, their responses are contributing factors to the ultimate outcomes. Some example questions include:

- What's the purpose of this exercise?
- What kind of customers do we want to attract?
- How would we like our customers to feel?
- What forms of service would help us achieve that?

Asking these types of questions to your group gets them to focus on the goal rather than whose idea or suggestion is the winner. It takes their minds off how they feel about you and each other.

When you ask questions such as, "What ideas do *you* have to attract more customers?" the focal point is on the individual rather than the goal. It becomes more of an indictment of their performance in facilitating the outcome rather than helping them develop their next-level thinking. Of course, we want the individuals we manage and coach to know we care about them and are attentive to their needs. In many situations, however, it's important to balance both needs.

Most importantly, in interactions like these, it helps them feel like owners in the creation of the solution. This is just an example of how to get them focused on the approach, outcome, and common goal rather than focused on your relationship with them.

An added benefit of this technique is it's a way to help manage any personal conflict among the staff or multiple parties. Sometimes, when teams work together, there exists tension among the members. That tension is usually more of a personal nature than business-related. Getting the team members to focus on the goal, rather than whose idea the solution was, is an effective way to neutralize those often-unwanted emotions.

Get the map before you go on the hike.

You can build trust and form solid relationships with the people you're managing and coaching, but if you don't have a plan or they don't execute it, they won't grow.

When beginning a coaching journey with people, it's helpful to understand their goals, their starting points, the steps they need to take to reach the next levels, timeframes to work on those steps, and a way to track their progress.

If you're missing any of this information and haven't planned accordingly, the individuals won't grow or will grow slowly. Beyond the growth aspect, a big part of being a successful coach is helping the people stay motivated. This is often difficult, especially for ambitious professionals, who are constantly looking at where they are not or how far they need to go to reach their goals.

One of the easiest ways to help them overcome this issue is to show them how far they've actually progressed. You cannot do that unless you have a map that shows their progress.

Sports coaches have data, video, and other mediums to look at a "before" and "after" version of someone's progress. White-collar professionals can use a Word document, Excel spreadsheet, or any other system or tool. The tool matters less than identifying and tracking the right information to show the actual progress!

I use five major groups when helping people develop their skills and advance in their careers. I've laid it out in a table format for illustrative purposes. You can use this template as a starting point and use whatever tool or application you'd like to communicate and track progress.

Any questions?

Ideally, you planned their development, are executing it, and everything is moving along hunky-dory. Anyone who's ever done anything

Inventory of Skills to Develop	You Are Here, Current Level of Proficiency	Desired Level of Proficiency and Target Date	Actions to Develop Skills, Attain Level of Proficiency	Scheduled Checkpoints, Feedback Dates
Identify all the skills the person needs to develop. This can be compiled from a formalized Career Development Plan or dialogue between you and the individual.	For each skillset, determine the person's level (Beginner, Intermediate, Expert, Master). Choose whatever nomenclature works best so everyone knows the definition of each level.	Identify the level and dates the person wishes to attain progression in each skill. These dates do not all need to be the same as you will not work toward all next levels universally.	Identify the specific steps the person needs to take and frequency to perform those steps. That is, some actions will require daily repetitions while others might be weekly.	Identify the type of feedback and next date to formally discuss progress. Feedback should be continuous, but there should also be a specific date to "sit down" more formally.

knows my previous sentence is utterly false. We simply don't live in a perfect world.

Along the way, your protégés will need your help. They'll ask you questions. Your responses to their questions are what will set you apart as a great coach and mentor.

Most people, because of their extensive experience, will be inclined to respond quickly. After all, you have the answers and want to demonstrate that. That's why you're the coach. I'd like to challenge you, however, to consider four questions before you respond to them.

- Am I being empathetic?
- Could they be asking this question because my initial advice and direction wasn't clear?
- Was that concept initially difficult for me to grasp?
- Have I factored in their current parameters, variables, and experience versus mine when I was learning this?

You might be thinking *this would be exhausting to consider these questions and factors each time I receive a question.* My goal isn't to exhaust you. It's to intercept your automated thinking, help you become more empathetic with practice, and recognize it's very difficult to remember what it was like not to know what you know.

Great coaches look at themselves first before considering the people they're coaching. I don't mean this in a selfish way. I mean this in a take-accountability way.

Great coaches look at themselves first before considering the people they're coaching. I don't mean this in a selfish way. I mean this in a take-accountability way. When you respond, it's good practice to...

- Cover what they need to know.
- Explain why it's important.
- Keep them focused on the item, but consider the context of the bigger picture.
- Make sure they know the one next step to take.

If you're able to establish a process for development, communicate it effectively, manage it along the way, and do that in a nurturing manner, you'll become a master coach in no time!

COACHING AND MENTORING EXERCISE

Thought-Provokers

1. Situations in which my expectations of the staff's performance levels weren't aligned with their current proficiency levels (e.g., expecting beginners to operate as intermediates) include...

2. Situations when I could have more effectively managed the staff if I was more familiar with their "feedback" languages include...

3. Three major differences in my staff's "operating environment" compared to mine when I performed their similar duties are...

4. Three questions I can use as prompters with the staff to stimulate ideas and build ownership for building important solutions are...

Challenge for Managers

Week One: Assess the members of your team. Take some time to "grade" and benchmark the levels of each of your team members based on their responsibilities and skill levels as they relate to those responsibilities. That is, label them as a beginner, intermediate, expert, and master and be explicit as to why they've attained that label.

Week Two: Review the team members' developmental "love" languages. First, reflect on this and take the time to observe. Then, have a discussion with them regarding this. You'll be amazed at their responses to your awareness and interest in helping them become better.

Week Three: Work with the team members to **put their developmental plans together**. Do this together. In fact, you can even have them make the first draft. The most important elements here are 1) Putting a plan together, 2) Making an honest assessment, 3) Prioritizing, and 4) Working on the plan, which includes the feedback checkpoints.

Week Four: Begin working on the staff development plans. Now that you have their plans in order, make sure they and you have "officially" launched them!

Challenge for Individual Contributors

Week One: Inventory your goals and skills you'll need to develop to attain them. This is the ultimate assessment of, "Where am I now?" and enables you to see the specific abilities you'll need to achieve the levels you want.

Week Two: Consider how you'd like your managers or mentors to communicate with you. A big part of your development is knowing what you need from others. Your developmental language is vital in helping you respond to instruction and direction. Take this opportunity to share with your managers your self-assessment and ask for their thoughts regarding what they think will be effective.

Week Three: Build your development workplan. You don't need a manager to do this for you. You can be proactive. Once you develop it, share it with your manager. (It might be a good idea to mention to your manager you're performing this exercise.)

Week Four: Prioritize the skill(s) you think will give you the greatest return on your investment. You likely won't have time to work on all the skills at once. Prioritizing and focusing will help. Now, start your development!

CHAPTER 17

Delegating

I wish everyone could have a Kara.

I have this rock star who works with me. Her name is Kara. If you've ever visited my recruitment firm, milewalk®, or career coaching firm, mile-walk Academy®, any time since March 9, 2009 when she joined, you probably know who she is. Everyone should have a Kara. I thank my lucky stars every day I have this particular Kara. No, you cannot have her.

Kara and I met in 1999. We worked at the same consulting organization for a number of years. After I left that company in 2003, she and I stayed in touch. Somewhere along the way, she took time off work to start her family. While she was still raising her two young children, she responded to one of my email newsletters. She wanted to say "Hello!" and let me know how happy she was for all my success with my recruitment company.

I replied and asked her if she'd be interested in helping me. She wasn't quite ready to go back to work on a full-time basis, which fit well with the level of support I needed at that time.

I said to her, "That's great. All I need is someone to help me with researching, identifying companies to prospect, and searching for potential job candidates for our clients. It's nothing too strenuous. It's internet surfing, organizing, and stuff you can do in your sleep."

She said, "Okay. Sounds great."

We agreed she'd start by working ten to fifteen hours each week and we'd see how it goes.

Kara is sensational at building systems, organizing data and information, and anything process-oriented. She has a background in technology consulting and is a wizard at problem solving, so the researching and evaluating type of work was in her wheelhouse.

On Wednesday, March 11, 2009, not a full three days into her "organizing" position, I naturally said to her, "I need you to get on the phone."

She said, "You need to me to what?"

There was silence.

She knew I meant I needed her to call job candidates, evaluate them, and perform a host of other cold-call-like activities of which she was not familiar nor would ever want to do. The noise from her pigmentation changing from white to red made the silence on the phone hiss.

I said, "It's easy breezy. (Nothing could have been further from the truth.) I'll teach you. Think about how nice it'll be to call people who are currently happy with what they're doing [professionally] and offer them an even better life."

Although this was a long while ago, I'm fairly certain, if memory serves, there was more silence.

I continued, "Don't worry. We'll build you a system."

She asked, "How are you going to do that?"

I said, "I've recruited so many people, I know everything anyone could ever possibly ask or say and exactly how to respond to them. I know all their objections. I'll teach you what to say no matter what they say. For the people who are happy to speak with us, I'll give you a list of all the questions to ask, how they'll answer them, and what you need to say based on their answers. I'll make your conversations like one big if-then program for you."

I'm pretty sure the if-then comment was what got her to agree.

She and I met. I explained how to open up the conversations and how to introduce herself and our firm to them. Once she said her introduction, they would have one of three responses. I told her, "If they say, 'Yes,' I want you to say this. If they say 'No,' say this. If they say, 'I'm not sure,' say this."

I continued to outline how she could conduct an entire one-hour session with all the questions to ask and all the potential answers the candidates could provide to every question.

A couple days later, Kara showed me how she kept track of what I taught her. She had created an if-then flowchart of all possibilities! That way, she just needed to follow the flow diagram and capture what the potential candidates said.

After a dozen or so of these calls, she had the process down pat. The candidates who wanted to proceed with our process would then speak with me. She became so effective at this so quickly, within a few days, the job candidates I was interviewing would remark how wonderful she was and how surprised they were to speak to someone from a recruitment firm who was actually knowledgeable and deeply caring!

Unfortunately, most people delegate as if they're playing hot potato.

Before you can delegate an assignment or suite of responsibilities correctly, you need to understand what delegation is. It's transferring the *responsibility* of developing, delivering, or producing your company's or team's deliverables from you to someone else. It is not transferring the *accountability* and ownership of the production to the other person.

It's transferring the *responsibility* of developing, delivering, or producing your company's or team's deliverables from you to someone else. It is not transferring the *accountability* and ownership of the production to the other person.

What's the difference? When you delegate an activity, you, the delegator, are still ultimately accountable for the quality and timely delivery of the end product. You might have someone else or a team responsible for producing it, but you still own it and are the final reviewer. If you no longer have accountability, that's technically not delegation, but an actual removal of your duties. Ultimately, you can only delegate something for which you still have ownership.

The act of delegation and transferring responsibilities to another is quite simple, but we need to keep in mind the actual goals of delegation. Financially, we delegate activities because it helps our businesses run more economically as we align the production of activities with the expenses of the final outputs. That is, we don't need a $100-an-hour employee performing activities a $15-a-hour employee could handle. That would increase business costs and decrease profits.

There is another important goal as it relates to the growth of the employees. The faster you're able to develop your employees by providing them opportunities through delegation, the more experienced, valuable, and happier they'll become.

Did Abbott and Costello invent the RACI chart? Who's accountable? What's responsible? He's consulted. Why's informed.

Many companies, when running large projects or managing sizable teams, will use a RACI chart to clarify for all team members the distribution of the duties. RACI stands for responsible, accountable, consulted, and informed. The responsible person for each activity is the one who actually *does* the work. The accountable person is the one who *owns* and *approves* the work product the responsible person completed.

To round out the others involved, the consulted parties are those whose input is sought in the performance or production of the deliverables. These "consultants" usually have subject-matter expertise in the area. The informed parties, as you might imagine, are ones who need to be aware of what decisions are being made because the outputs will affect them or their teams.

RACI charts are effective because they clarify who's doing what with whom. The actual practice of delegation, however, between the manager and staff members, is quite difficult to get right. Anyone who thinks this is an easy process is likely not doing it correctly. Master delegators know you need to get the who, what, when, how, and why correct! What complicates matters further is there are a host of psychological and tactical issues that plague even wonderful managers.

Self-importance is the enemy of delegation.

Before we get to the elements that help you effectively delegate, I'd like to address some personal influences that make it difficult for most managers. Even if you understand the mechanics of effective delegation, you won't get it right if your personal issues stand in the way.

From my experience managing thousands of individuals as well as many large units, I notice six common personal issues that prevent managers from delegating effectively. Once you understand what those are, you can work to eradicate them if any stand in your way of becoming a master delegator.

Losing knowledge: It's natural to feel a loss of control when letting go of responsibilities, which, in turn, propagates a lack of knowledge. This lack of knowledge comes from not seeing the detailed work that goes into the day-in and day-out development of the deliverables. As time goes on, this gap of familiarity widens as processes, tools, and techniques improve to accomplish the deliverables. Managers who feel uncomfortable with not knowing the details have a difficult time delegating.

Becoming replaceable: As an extension of the losing-knowledge issue, some managers will start worrying they'll become expendable because they no longer possess the detailed experience. In fact, this issue has more to do with managers focusing their attention on the loss of delegation rather than the gain. The primary reason to delegate activities is to free up the manager's time to do more important, higher-level activities. This transition is what should make the manager more valuable, not more expendable.

> The primary reason to delegate activities is to free up the manager's time to do more important, higher-level activities. This transition is what should make the manager more valuable, not more expendable.

Lacking confidence and trust: Some managers do not trust their staff members to complete tasks to the level of quality they expect. This can stem from a lack of confidence in their abilities or lack of trust in their judgment. This particular issue is a bit more difficult to overcome because trust is developed over time through repeated demonstration of production. In these instances, the manager can expedite this by designing practices and processes the staff can use as crutches or guiderails to ensure quality output. It's also helpful when the activity can be performed repetitiously so you can provide frequent feedback and the staff can get feedback of their own through iterations.

Maintaining excessively high standards: Some managers have high standards for their work and believe they are the only ones who can achieve those standards. There's obviously nothing wrong with having high standards and expecting quality production from yourself and your team. This only becomes a problem when it causes managers to inefficiently distribute their team's workloads and activities. Whether managers maintain responsibilities they should delegate or overtax one of their staff members, it's still an inefficient way to operate. While these managers might not technically be perfectionists, they are demonstrating perfectionist qualities. Perfectionism, in general, has much to do with how a person views any production. They interpret whatever is "completed" as a "final" product, which needs to be perfect. This is true whether it's an intermediary deliverable or an end-product. To overcome these issues, it's helpful to view everything they and their teams produce as a product that can be iterated. It's exactly like I outlined in the Mastering Your Trade lesson when it comes to creating MVPs—Minimum Viable Products. The more geared toward MVPs a manager can become, the easier it is to rid the perfectionist obstacles.

Worrying about appearance: Occasionally, managers become leery of appearing lazy. They feel if they pass off work to others, their management team or boss might misconstrue them as being lazy or incompetent. Much like with the issue of becoming replaceable, you can overcome this issue by focusing attention on the more-important, higher-level activities. If managers pass off some responsibilities, they should theoretically be able to fill that freed-up time with more valuable activities. This is the entire point of delegating in the first place.

Lacking fulfillment: The I-like-to-do-it-myself issue will come into play for virtually all of us. There are simply some tasks that bring us joy and fulfillment. If we delegate those, our personal enjoyment drops as a result of the void. As an example, when I worked on my first programming assignment as a consultant, I developed software. Each time I completed a program, I was proud my customer had a workable product to perform their business. As I became more proficient, my duties were elevated to that of a "designer." As a designer, I handled the more-difficult tasks of drafting the business logic required for the program to work correctly. I'd provide the programmers with this deliverable so they could build the final, programmed product. I personally didn't get to *feel* the sensation of completing a usable product. Someone else did. To get over this emotional hurdle, I realized the design was my "final" product, but more importantly and enjoyably, teaching the programmers was also one of my "final" products.

There are many other issues that influence how we feel as managers and, in turn, affect how well we delegate. Even if we're able to overcome these personal obstacles and are more-than-willing to happily delegate, we need a formula to help us delegate effectively.

There are many factors we need to get correct when we delegate. They are who the person is, what responsibilities, when to start, how we communicate those responsibilities, and why we'll realize a business benefit from this entire process.

Before I offer you my formula, I'd like to discuss a popular one I want you to avoid!

Pareto's principle does not apply to delegation!

Our personal issues aren't solely to blame for poor delegation. Being bad at math doesn't help either.

There was this Italian polymath, Vilfredo Pareto, who made many important contributions to economics, particularly as they related to income distribution. (He was not bad at math.) His quite-well-known Pareto principle states that for many outcomes, roughly 80 percent of the consequences come from 20 percent of the causes. You might know this as the 80/20 rule or law of the vital few.

What's so fantastic about his principle is that it seems to apply, albeit in various ranges, to basically everything in life. 20 percent of your effort will yield 80 percent of your results. 90 percent of output, in some areas, is caused by 10 percent of the input. At extreme levels, the world's richest 1 percent has generated nearly two-thirds of all new wealth in the past few years.

Someone, who apparently Google cannot find, attempted to apply Pareto's genius when it comes to delegation. This unknown person created a popularly used guideline called the 70 percent Rule of Delegation.

I felt compelled to mention it for fear you might one day be Googling how to become a more effective delegator and discover it. The rule states that if others can complete the task at least 70 percent as well as you can, you should delegate it to them.

There are a number of problems with this rule. First, how are we to apply a universal 70 percent rule across managers? I'm sure your version of 70 percent might be different than mine. We managers, as judges of the 70 percent, have different scales, filled with biases, related to the quality of our and our staff's work.

There was a study done in 1997. According to Jeffrey Pfeffer, Robert Cialdini, Benjamin Hanna, and Kathleen Knopoff as conducted in "Faith in Supervision and the Self-Enhancement Bias: Two Psychological Reasons Why Managers Don't Empower Workers," they concluded there are reasons managers are reluctant to empower their staff. Their study shows our interpretations of quality are skewed based on the situation not the outputs.

They cite "a faith in supervision effect," which reflects the tendency of managers to view work performed under control of a supervisor as better than identical work done without as much supervision.

They also point to "a self-enhancement effect," which reflects the tendency of managers to evaluate a work product more highly the more self-involved they are in its production. Because empowerment practices dilute managers' individualized supervision of work, they can also reduce managers' biased perceptions of work quality.

They drew these conclusions because the participants assigned higher quality to the identical work product as supervisory involvement increased. They did so at elevated levels when they had more self-involvement in supervising the work. A team-based, empowerment orientation curtailed both of these biases.

Our measuring sticks, subjectivity, and biases are not the only issues. Activities are not created equally when it comes to our ability to evaluate the efficacy of the final outputs.

I know people who could perform nine of the ten acts required to build and conduct one of my online workshops. The single act they're unable to perform would completely void my ability to bring the workshop to life. Ten percent of the input, in this case, will contribute to 90 percent of the delivery and results. Even though someone could handle 90 percent of the workload, the workshop would likely perform at 10 percent of the production.

What if I want to delegate the management of a client account to a salesperson on my staff. My client trusts me 100 percent and, generally, trust is not transferrable. Should I have the salesperson "shadow" me for six months so the client trusts the more junior person to handle their account 70 percent as effectively as I could?

Let's look at it from the opposite angle. What if someone can perform a task at 0 percent of the level you can? Does that mean you should not delegate it? I'll submit into evidence, on Wednesday March 11, 2009, Kara had exactly zero hours of experience performing live recruitment calls. The next day, I officially turned her loose (with the fancy flowchart she built herself) and off she went helping me find and recruit job candidates for our clients.

How is this possible? It comes down to two major factors. First, you need to be able to teach the staff the process, provide them with a structure and parameters to follow, and make sure they get enough repetitions so you and they can get immediate feedback to improve the results.

Second, and every bit equally important, you need to ensure the people you're delegating to have the requisite foundational abilities to perform the tasks you're delegating.

> *Consider delegation an opportunity and, for that matter,*
> *let's consider all the other "itys."*

Delegation is entirely too complex to use a simple formula such as the 70 percent Rule of Delegation. What can we do as managers to know when it's the right time and which tasks we should delegate?

The first thing I do is think. Thinking is good! People don't seem to do it as much these days as they have in the past. Here are the questions I ask myself when I consider opportunities to delegate. The combination of these answers helps me decide if I should evaluate it at a deeper level.

Responsibility

Let's start with what's currently in your scope of duties. Delegation starts with transferring your responsibilities, so let's inventory what might be available to be delegated.

Each morning, I spend twenty minutes performing a brainstorming exercise I call my excellence planning. I'll share more on this technique in the next lesson when I cover generating creative ideas. As part of that brainstorming exercise, I ask myself questions to stimulate ideas. One of the questions I ask myself daily is, "What can I do to optimize my internal systems?" This question effectively covers delegation at a high level.

To take it a step further, each month, I spend one or two days diligently tracking every single task I do. I generally track my tasks, how I schedule them, and what deliverables need to be produced as I outlined in the lesson on Planning and Running Your Day. In this exercise, however, I audit my tasks with the intent of examining cost efficiency.

I'm now truly looking for opportunities to delegate or outsource my activities by asking myself for each task or related set of tasks:

- Am I the only person who can do this?
- Could someone else with a portion of my skills do this activity to completion even if it's not to the same level of quality?
- Could I break up portions of a set of activities to delegate them?
- What skills would the person need to complete each activity?
- Can anyone, even without the requisite skills, do this activity?
- Can I build an instruction sheet with steps of how to do this? Is it straightforward or are there many variations and decision points that will inevitably occur?
- Is there an artificial intelligence tool that can perform this activity?

This provides me with an idea of whether it's possible to effectively delegate an activity. For example, if I'm building a webpage in our system, that would be a great candidate to delegate because someone with knowledge of how our system works could perform that activity.

We all know it's not that simple because when you dig further, in this case, you need to factor in the time required from me to explain what I want, how it should look, and important design requirements. I'd need to determine whether someone on my team has availability or whether we should outsource it. Before you can make a smart, economical decision, there are other considerations. I'm sure someone can build a webpage to 100 percent of my ability, but that doesn't necessarily mean I should delegate it.

I also need to factor in the upside if I've actually created more time for myself by delegating this task. It's possible I could be spending the same amount of time, but on a different, related activity. Instead of designing and building the webpage, I've transferred that time to explaining to someone else all the requirements to build exactly what I want the page to look like.

Opportunity

If you have a task, such as my webpage example, you feel is a worthy candidate for delegation, you need to add to your consideration the best use of your freed-up time. How can you and your company benefit from the time now available in your schedule? I believe this is the most important aspect of delegating that managers often overlook. Typically, managers focus on the cost of someone else doing those activities to a lower level of quality. This is natural. As humans, pain associated with loss hurts more than the joy we receive when we gain.

We need to consider the downside; however, the upside needs to be factored into the equation to know the true return on investment of the delegation.

> **If managers can perform tasks at 100 percent quality and the staff members can do them at 80 percent quality, there are obvious losses with relation to quality. The question that must be answered now is what are the managers doing with the freed-up time from the delegation?**

If managers can perform tasks at 100 percent quality and the staff members can do them at 80 percent quality, there are obvious losses with relation to quality. The question that must be answered now is what are the managers doing with the freed-up time from the delegation? Are they securing more clients and generating more revenue? Are they streamlining processes and saving costs?

I consider these questions when evaluating the upside of the delegation:

- What will I do with this freed-up time after delegating this task?
- What gains or improvements can I make in the areas I'm now focusing on as a result of my freed-up time?
- Will these gains outweigh the loss of production or quality when the staff member performs it?

Liability

Just like there's an upside to benefiting from your newly created free time, there is a downside that must be evaluated when delegating. What is the cost, in terms of loss not expense, associated with someone else doing an activity not to the level of quality you could?

There are extreme liabilities such as the inexperienced scrub nurse who doesn't clean the operating room to perfection. Someone could die in this instance.

There are the not-so-serious consequences such as turning over the distribution of the social media messages and videos I circulate across the channels on my online platform. If I let someone else write the social media text and that person isn't as effective at copywriting as I am, does that mean less people will read, click, and engage in my work? Is that a good tradeoff? Is it something I could monitor to see if there's any falloff?

There might not be a downside or any loss of production or opportunity, but it is something to consider before delegating. When it comes to the downside or liability, I ask myself these questions:

- What is the potential impact in terms of loss (e.g., revenue, clients, miscommunications, credibility)?
- Is the loss something I can monitor?
- Will I be able to make adjustments to minimize or eliminate the loss?

Ability

If you're going to delegate a task, you need to determine whom you'll delegate it to and whether the person has the requisite skills and abilities. This is more complicated than it might first appear.

In Kara's case, when it came to the live recruitment phone calls, she didn't have any experience with how to conduct them or elicit the information from the candidates let alone sell our company or positions we might offer the candidates.

I considered she's articulate, could follow a formula, would learn quickly, and capture the information diligently. Her initial calls might lack a little oomph because she's concentrating on asking the right questions while following her script. She'd be able to get better at this and become comfortable quickly because she would be conducting quite a few of these calls. The more repetitions she had, the faster she'd learn. The more she'd find her rhythm and "become herself" in these interactions.

The biggest key to success for us was we were able to build an "instruction manual" she could follow.

In other instances, your staff might need a certain level of technical expertise or greater level of executive presence or whatever the situation requires. As the manager, you'll need to gauge this based on your activities and whether the upsides and downsides balance out effectively.

From your earlier evaluation of your responsibilities, you know which skills the person would need or whether you could teach them. Now, there are a few additional questions to consider related to the specific people to whom you might delegate your activities:

- Do these people have the specific skillsets needed to perform the activities?
- If they don't have all the skills, can they quickly build the ones they lack?
- Can they follow the steps with proper instruction?

Availability

No matter what activities you'd like to delegate, there needs to be someone available to perform the activity. If there aren't any people on your staff, you can consider outsourcing the activities if that's an option.

This becomes rather straightforward after you consider whether the people have the requisite skills or can learn them. I ask these questions:

- Do they have the availability to take on this particular activity?
- If the best person to handle this delegation doesn't have the availability, are there others on the team or outside the organization who could handle these?

Delegating effectively is part art and part formula. It requires continual assessment, feedback, and adjustments to get right. The most important factor is that you are considering all the factors!

DELEGATING EXERCISE

Thought-Provokers

1. Reflecting back on times I delegated responsibilities to the staff, three practices I need to stop and three practices I need to continue are...

2. Based on the evaluation of the existing staff, when replacing or building the team with new members, the character traits, cultural values, and skills of the new employees that will make delegation easier and more effective are...

3. The skills and projects I can work on with additional time freed up from delegation would be...

4. With my existing activities and new efforts (from the delegated, freed-up time), the areas I can find the most fulfillment are...

Challenge

Week One: Audit your activities. To get started, take a couple of days (or the entire week if you can manage that) and diligently capture everything you do *and* how long it takes. Ask yourself the key questions related to your activities including:

1. Am I the only person who can do this?

2. Could someone else do this activity to completion even if it's not to the same level of quality?

3. Could I break up portions of a set of activities to delegate them?

4. What skills would the person need to complete this activity?

5. Can anyone, even without the requisite skills, do this activity?

6. Can I build an instruction sheet with steps of how to do this?

7. Is there an artificial intelligence tool that can perform this activity?

Week Two: Audit your staff's activities. Much like you assessed your activities, do a similar exercise for your team. Have each staff member do this for themselves. It might be tempting to have them do this while you're doing your audit, but please *do not*. Go through your personal exercise first. Your experience will help you better assess what you're doing, teach you ways to look for opportunities, and adjust the audit process for them. Have each staff member ask themselves these questions:

1. How long did this activity take to complete?
2. Is there a better process or tool I could use to decrease the time to complete this activity?
3. Could someone with less experience perform this activity?
4. What skills would someone need to perform this task to the minimum level of acceptance?
5. Could I break up portions of this activity and allocate them to someone with less experience?
6. Can I build an instruction sheet with steps of how to do this?
7. Is there an artificial intelligence tool that can perform this activity?

Week Three: Review the audits and develop a delegation plan. Based on your and your staff's findings, prepare a plan to delegate the appropriate activities. The goal is to develop a plan that contains short-term and long-term opportunities. There will likely be some immediate shuffling of responsibilities you can do as well as ideas that require more evaluation (such as hiring new people, outsourcing, automated tools). Do not limit your opportunities to reallocating responsibilities to *people*. There are many new artificial intelligence tools available now that can handle jobs previously performed by a person!

Week Four: Delegate and monitor. Consider this week's effort in two phases. Immediately delegate those activities that can be shifted. Monitor them closely throughout this week and upcoming weeks. Adjust as appropriate. For the areas that require more evaluation, put your "investigation teams" and plans together to actually evaluate these opportunities. Again, think creatively about how you might accomplish the completion of your work!

PART SEVEN

The Visionary

CHAPTER 18

Generating Creative Ideas

Meet Mr. 97, also known as Keith.

I have two signature online training and coaching programs. One focuses on job searching and the other on leadership development. Keith is a member of both.

One day, Keith and I were doing a one-to-one coaching session to help him with his job search. He mentioned, while he was interviewing with a company, he needed to take personality and aptitude tests as part of their recruitment process.

I asked, "Did the company give you any feedback on how you did?"

He said, "Not really, but the recruiter did tell me I scored in the ninety-seventh percentile on the aptitude test."

Of course, his nickname was born.

A few weeks later, I was teaching on the topic of creativity during my monthly leadership group coaching session. Mr. 97 asked me, "Is it possible to develop a visionary?"

He continued, "I've had little success developing people to reach this level. It feels, to me, like they are either born with it or not. I need to get a visionary in my organization to replace me when I leave. I feel like I can develop people to a certain level, but when they start to rise, they just slip back down the mountain. Should I be looking for something specific when I interview them? How can I find that twinkle when I'm speaking with them? Can people learn to be visionaries or am I just spinning my wheels?"

253

Before we get to my response to Keith, let's consider what a visionary is. The dictionary definition is someone who thinks about or plans the future with imagination or wisdom. I agree with that.

The way I've defined it for you, in terms of your professional growth, is using your expertise to create and implement market-moving ideas. I want you to create the future with unique, creative ideas! This is actually much easier than you might think because the critical success factors in becoming a visionary and creating brilliant ideas are not what most people think they are.

Many people mistakenly think you cannot be a visionary without enough expertise. Of course, you need knowledge and experience, but you can develop that over time easily enough. Others get hung up on the word "creative." They confuse creative ideas with being "artistic." That is, they think it's more about "the packaging" than the contribution the idea will have. Creativity is not found in the sexiness of the marketing brochure or the graphics of the social media post. Creativity lies in coming up with the idea in the first place. Think in terms of creative thoughts versus creative art.

Creativity is not found in the sexiness of the marketing brochure or the graphics of the social media post. Creativity lies in coming up with the idea in the first place. Think in terms of creative thoughts versus creative art.

I've discovered, through my personal experience as a business owner and entrepreneur, as well as teaching people how to produce impactful ideas, there are two primary success factors when it comes to generating ideas on your way to becoming a visionary. The first is making the time to think and come up with enough ideas. The second is knowing which questions to ask yourself that help trigger those ideas.

There are two primary success factors when it comes to generating ideas on your way to becoming a visionary. The first is making the time to think and come up with enough ideas. The second is knowing which questions to ask yourself that help trigger those ideas.

I'm sure you would agree, it's easier to review someone else's idea than generate your own. That's why most corporations are nothing more than copycats of other companies' ideas. Most products in the market are simply different versions of the same things.

I considered Keith's question in relation to these success factors. My answer to him was, "Coming up with great ideas is a function of desire, not ability. It's much like personal growth and change that way. If you want to change yourself, it's not about your ability. It's a function of emotion, drive, and a willingness to put in the effort."

For you, regardless of where you are in your profession, you can generate brilliant ideas with the proper mindset, formula, and time.

You can do it the 1 percent way or the Warren Buffet way...

To oversimplify, visionaries essentially come about from one of two paths. You have a 1 percent chance of being born from the first path and a 99 percent chance of being born from the second path.

The 1 percent-group, so to speak, are those individuals who come up with a truly contrarian or unique idea. It's something so new and something others simply cannot or will never be able to see. Of course, these visionaries also need to be correct about their ideas. That is, it needs to be something the world actually—eventually—embraces. Interestingly, these first two elements aren't even the most difficult part. What's even more special about the one-percenters is they not only need to be able to see the contrarian idea and be correct, but also need to work it and work it and work it to bring it to life. Oftentimes, they're not only struggling with the sizable number of iterations and failures, but they're also dealing with the skepticism from whomever they've shared their ideas with as well as anyone in the public who laughs off their absurdity.

Then there are the rest of the visionaries. The 99 percent group is often born through consistency and grit. These individuals simply take swing after swing and hit a homerun every now and then. This is how most ideas are brought to life. You might not realize this because you don't see the first 999 attempts. You watched, purchased, or are playing with the thousandth attempt.

Take Warren Buffet for example. The Berkshire Hathaway chief and probably the greatest investor of my lifetime (if not ever) said, in a recent annual letter to the shareholders, his company's "satisfactory results" in investing were attributed to "about a dozen truly good decisions—that would be one every five years." He continued, "Over time, it takes just a few winners to work wonders [...] and, yes, it helps to start early and live into your nineties as well."

Along these same lines, Adam Grant, organizational psychologist and author of *Originals: How Non-Conformists Move the World*, determined through his experiments, "When it comes to idea generation, quantity is the most predictable path to quality."

Additionally, Stanford Professor Robert Sutton attests, "Original thinkers will come up with many ideas that are strange mutations, dead ends, and utter failures. The cost is worthwhile because they also generate a large pool of ideas—especially novel ideas."

This stands to reason primarily because it often takes many ideas and iterations of those ideas to reach great heights. Thomas Edison had 1,093 patents in his lifetime that in some way supported a number of inventions. How many of those inventions can you name? Off the top of my head, I remember the light bulb, phonograph, motion picture camera, alkaline battery, and microphone. That's only five. Imagine how many ideas he must have generated and solutions he tried to bring these inventions to life. I'm sure his "yes" pile of ideas was substantially smaller than his "no" pile.

Open your eyes and stretch your ears.

Taking a lot of swings is one prerequisite to generating creative ideas. Of course, it'll take more than swing after swing. We need to swing at good pitches, not bad pitches! That helps if we start our thinking in a place that leads us to beneficial ideas. What do our companies, customers, teams, communities, and people in this world need to make their lives better?

This question reminds me of something my grandfather used to say to me. "Andy, open your eyes and stretch your ears." Never mind the fact he'd say this during our Pinochle grudge matches against my dad and Uncle Frank. Papa and I were always partners and he didn't like to lose, so occasionally he'd send me a few signals to make sure that didn't happen. A little underhanded for sure, but the expression, as it relates to paying attention, is still a good one.

Generating great ideas starts with being observant. This takes no experience whatsoever. It takes keeping your eyes and ears open. It requires focusing. I mentioned before, your greatest opportunities will be found in the sounds of other people's complaints. Solve their problems and you're their hero.

You can take this a step further if you believe, as I do, everything in our world is connected. Look for the connections and relationships. This association will lead to valuable ideas that can improve your company's product or team's processes. It's one of the best first steps to take before formulating the tactics to bring your ideas to life.

I genuinely believe everything is connected in your mind and in this world. Everything you've done in your life can be applied to another aspect of your life or someone else's. If you're attentive to this, you'll start noticing analogies which will lead to ideas.

Here's a little example from my life as it relates to the book you're now holding. When authors want to get their books published, they develop book proposals they pitch to literary agents and publishing houses. These proposals include their idea, an overview of the book, outline, marketing approach, and host of other information publishers need to know so they can decide whether it's a worthwhile investment to bring the author's book to life. As I wrote the proposal for this book, it occurred to me, the sections I included are essentially the same steps job seekers would take to market themselves for a new job. That thought led me to creating a lesson I shared with my community. I used the analogy to help them think through and execute their job searches. Analogies like this are constantly around us and lead to great ideas that provide value to our companies, customers, friends, and colleagues. You simply need to be on alert to recognize and capture them. Nothing in this world exists in a vacuum.

To take this a step further, ideas will flow when you observe the world around you. When you're constantly asking yourself, "Why is that? How is that connected? What could happen next?" you will discover causes and effects that lead to great ideas. Again, we're all connected.

When you're constantly asking yourself, "Why is that? How is that connected? What could happen next?" you will discover causes and effects that lead to great ideas.

I remember when I first realized the Covid-19 pandemic would expand throughout the world. As a career coach, I wanted to do everything I could to help my community of professionals. It was apparent, many of them would soon be unemployed because they worked for companies in industries that would be negatively affected. Conversely, other industries would begin to thrive out of necessity for their products and services. I wanted to make sure I offered lessons to my community so they became aware of the potential impacts and what to do to take care of themselves.

Each morning, I have a brainstorming session with myself (more details on this in a bit). During one of these sessions, I sat in my "brain-storming chair," and mentally walked through my house to consider which industries would thrive and which ones would decline. I didn't turn to Google yet. I just sat and thought! I envisioned each room including my home office, kitchen, bedroom, basement, and the rest. I thought about the products in my home. People would remain in their homes as opposed to going to places they visited daily. The pandemic would require people to avoid frequently visited places such as their office buildings and health clubs as well as less-visited places like movie theatres.

I started writing down my ideas. If people can't go to their offices, they'll start buying home office equipment. If they can't go to their health clubs, they'll start buying exercise equipment. They'll be cooking at home more frequently than going to restaurants.

Then, I thought about the other primary activities people do outside their home. They can't go shopping for clothes or groceries. They'll order online. Amazon will become more prominent than it already is. What does Amazon need to support its customers? It needs boxes. What companies make boxes? What material is used to make the boxes? They're made of cardboard!

From this "exercise," I identified thirty-six industries that would thrive. I know there are more, but I had what I needed to create a lesson for my community to help them understand the causes and effects of what would happen. Once they understood this, they could take steps to ensure they managed well during this incredibly difficult time. This entire activity took me less than fifteen minutes. That's the point. I just needed to carve out the time to sit down and think.

Once you realize everything is connected and start looking for the relationships, ideas will flow. With that mindset, let's get into the formula and techniques I use on a daily basis to generate creative ideas.

Success has its own timetable. Stick with it so you're there to see it when it decides to show up.

The reason so few people reach visionary status is not related to lack of ability. It's because they don't make the time or put in the effort. Here's a novel thought. Let's plan the time to come up with creative ideas. I want to be really clear. I did not say, "Let's plan the time to be creative." I plan the time to execute a practice that leads to creative ideas. I show up and work the process and work the process and work the process. The creative idea has its own timetable. If you stick with it, you'll be there when it decides to show up.

Let's plan the time to come up with creative ideas. I want to be really clear. I did not say, "Let's plan the time to be creative." I plan the time to execute a practice that leads to creative ideas.

First, let's cover why this works. Have you ever "gotten into the zone"? Perhaps you refer to it as "being in a state of flow." Whatever you call it, this happens when we feel energized doing something we enjoy. We are doing it skillfully and without much conscious thought. We tend to lose track of time.

Have you ever gotten into the state of flow before you started your activity? Of course, you didn't because that's not how "flow" works. You need to be doing the activity first and then the state of flow occurs because it's not possible to be totally immersed in an activity unless you're actually doing the activity!

I'm writing these words on a Tuesday morning at exactly 4:52 AM. I assure you, at 4:30 AM, I was not in a state of flow like I am now. I didn't have any momentum until approximately 4:42 AM. I certainly didn't have it at 4:20 AM when I rolled out of bed.

The most important factor that helped me get into the state of flow as quickly as possible had to do with my daily planner. Last night, when I checked my morning schedule, there was an activity on the schedule that essentially told me I would begin writing at 4:35 AM. I showed up. I knew I would be writing this section of the book. I started writing. I kept writing and it started to flow.

Creation of any kind is like this. You can certainly have a brilliant idea regarding one of your projects at 2:27 PM while you're working on another project. If you want to generate lots of great ideas, however, you can't rely on thoughts popping into your head while you're in the middle of another activity.

You might be wondering what time of day you'll tend to be most creative, how much time to spend generating ideas, and how frequently to perform this exercise. First, we all have different schedules. If you have a one-hour commute each morning, that might not leave you a lot of time before work. Schedule the time whenever you can. Second, I have reviewed several studies and found them inconclusive as to when humans are most creative during the day. I also polled members of my Leadership Coaching Program regarding when they feel most creative. The results were all over the clock so to speak. Some were early-morning thinkers. Others were late-night thinkers. Experiment to see what works for you. The magic isn't in the "when." It's in putting in the time whenever.

When it comes to frequency, this is a bit more important. Generally, no matter what you do, whether it's writing or playing a sport or musical instrument, the more frequently you do it, the better. When it comes to an activity of this nature, where you're thinking extensively, it's beneficial to practice it and revisit it as frequently as possible. Your ideas have a way of percolating as you stay connected to them consciously and subconsciously.

For me, I tend to be most creative after I sleep and when I can think without interruption. This is early in the morning when it's quiet. It's also the time I'm least likely to get distracted, which is why I have my idea-generation sessions in the morning before I start my "normal" workday. I also perform them for twenty minutes each day Monday through Friday. I realize not everyone can do that, so you need to figure out a schedule that works for you. Can you do it three times each week? If not, can you manage one session per week?

To put this in perspective, I generate ideas for approximately one hour and forty minutes each week. If I do that throughout most of the year, that's approximately eighty-six hours of nothing but thinking! How many great ideas can you come up with given that amount of time? Even if you spent twenty minutes each week, that's seventeen hours each year. That would be a great start.

*I studied Spanish in high school because I wasn't sure what
I would do with Latin, until now.*

We know what gets scheduled gets done. Let's say you're willing to spend time generating ideas and getting into the practice of brainstorming. How exactly would you come up with those ideas? Where would they come from? What would help you get started besides opening your eyes and stretching your ears and listening to your coworkers complain?

Earlier, I mentioned the two critical success factors were making the time to think and knowing which questions to ask yourself that help trigger those ideas. When it comes to generating ideas, I like to focus on just that—generating ideas. I like to keep the development and implementation of the ideas separate. I do this because I want to generate a lot of ideas and sift through them later based on my corporate strategy, timing of my projects, and other factors. I don't want to bog down my twenty-minute exercise with trying to think through how I would accomplish that idea. I can do that later.

Over the years, I've tinkered with various techniques to maximize my idea-generating sessions. I've settled in with two simple, but powerful formulas I use during my sessions. I've named one Ex Nihilo, which, in Latin, translates to "out of nothing." I've named the other Ex Aliqua, which translates to "out of something."

Ex Nihilo: Out of Nothing

Using the Ex Nihilo technique, I put myself through a series of questions and answer them only with ideas. Keep in mind, if you venture into idea-development mode or solutioning, you'll take yourself off the brainstorming path, get bogged down in the details, and ruin your flow. I essentially plant the seeds during this exercise and leave all the planning and execution for a different time. This also helps me avoid "judging" the idea at this moment.

As owner of a company, I ask myself questions centered on improving my business and customer service. The specific questions are:

- What can I do to better serve my customers?
- What can I do to better serve my community?
- What can I do to become more well-known or discovered?
- What can I do to optimize my internal systems?
- What do I need to stop doing?

These have worked so well for me over the years because they focus on the most vital aspects of running a healthy business.

For you, there will be analogous questions or you can develop your own. As an example, your customers might be your company's actual customers or an internal group within your organization. Your community could be your team or partners or networking group. Whereas I look to market my services by becoming more well known, you might look for ways to help your company better attract its customers. While I use many technology systems to manage my business, you might streamline your team's processes. Of course, we can all review ways to forego activities we shouldn't be doing. Whether these are completely wasteful or non-value added or whether you can delegate or outsource them.

The most important factor is to design questions that are relevant for you and spend time asking yourself these questions to elicit great ideas. As Graham Wallas, the English social psychologist and co-founder of the London School of Economics, wrote in *The Art of Thought* (1926), "Our mind is not likely to give us a clear answer to any particular problem unless we set it a clear question, and we are more likely to notice the significance of any new piece of evidence, or new association of ideas, if we have formed a definite conception of a case to be proved or disproved."

Ex Aliqua: Out of Something

While the Ex Nihilo technique enables me to generate ideas somewhat "out of thin air," I use the Ex Aliqua approach whenever I'm triggered by something else. On any given day, I'll read books, watch videos, listen to podcasts, and scan social media posts. Other times, I might be researching a topic.

Regardless of how or when I consume the material, it's natural for me, and anyone, to have thoughts, opinions, and ideas. The important factor is to capture my ideas immediately and in an orderly fashion.

With the Ex Nihilo method, I ask myself direct questions to generate ideas. With the Ex Aliqua approach, I complete sentences to create a "new" idea. It's new, essentially, because it's a variation of what I noticed. Depending on how I feel about what I just saw, heard, or read, I'll complete one of these three sentences:

- No, I think this instead...
- Yes, that's true, but...
- Yes, that's true, and...

No, I think this instead...

I complete this sentence whenever I generally disagree with what I noticed. It's important for me to capture my rationale and evidence and other important factors I might need to call out in the future.

Yes, that's true, but...

I complete this sentence whenever I agree in large part, but view one or more aspects differently.

Yes, that's true, and...

I complete this sentence whenever I agree wholly, but want to add elements.

This technique is very effective whenever you're performing research for a project. As you read or watch videos, keep your notepad handy because this technique will enable you to brainstorm ideas and variations of the information you're reviewing.

I also find this technique to be helpful for individuals who think *that's been done already* or *I'm no different* or other thoughts of this ilk. It has a way of helping them get over this mindset. When they practice this technique, they're able to unlock and gain momentum in generating regardless of what they're creating.

There is no such thing as an overnight sensation. I know if I keep singing, one of my songs will be a hit.

I have news for you, that new song you just heard and loved by that "brand new" artist was a long time coming. It's that plain and simple. That singer worked long and hard for many years on writing, singing, and a host of other skills required to bring that song, album, concert, and tour to life. You just discovered the music now.

Ideas, funny enough, are the same way. They might not require years of rumination, but they don't just pop into your head. The brilliant ones, too, were a long time coming. You can accelerate generating, and ultimately bringing to life, new ideas by practicing more frequently. That, in turn, will help you produce more ideas, which increases the probability you'll discover a brilliant one.

I think it warrants a moment to share how ideas comes about. Earlier, when we were discussing communication techniques and crafting compelling messages, I shared my iterative development process aligned to "standard clocks" I've created for my communications. I have been massaging my approach for years, and without much thought to the formula itself, I crafted what works for me to deliver my best messages across the mediums I use.

It's worth noting the creative stages as formulaically as we can, so you might adapt these concepts to what works for you. I love Graham Wallas' description of creative stages in *The Art of Thought*. Interestingly enough, the evolution he explains came to light when he heard German Physicist, Hermann von Helmholtz share how his thoughts came to him. (Perhaps Graham Wallas used his version of my Ex Aliqua technique!) von Helmholtz said his ideas came to him in three stages, which Wallas concisely labeled preparation, incubation, and illumination. Wallas then added, there needs to be a fourth stage called verification. My interpretation of Wallas' four stages is:

1. **Preparation:** This is the early stage of idea generating. It's very conscious as you gather, research, and directly think about a topic, subject, or solution.

2. **Incubation:** The second stage occurs when you "let your mind run." Here, you transition into the unconscious stage where you're not directly thinking about it, but you know it's running in the back of your mind.

3. **Illumination:** The third stage occurs when you have your Aha moment that probably isn't "a moment" at all. It probably occurred over a period of time, number of iterations, and additional elbow grease. Then, at a singular moment, it strikes you and you go with it.

4. **Verification:** The final stage is to bring your idea to life. This is the build-it, confirm-it, and validate-it stage. While, throughout this lesson, I've been focusing on the act of generating brilliant ideas, we both know, all the ideas in the world make no difference unless you bring them to life.

I've noticed, for me, my ability to incubate is enhanced when I bring myself back to the conscious state of mind at regular intervals. That is, when I "noodle" on ideas in the morning, I bring them out of "incubation" and back to "preparation" so I can work and rework them. When my brainstorming exercise is complete and I move into my regular workday, I transition back to an incubation stage for a period of twenty-four hours until I revisit those ideas the next morning. There are some instances where I might go through this cycle for weeks before I hit my Aha moment. Other times, I might implement an idea so I can get into the verification stage and then iterate to continue to make improvements. The approach I use is dependent on the size of the idea, effort, or project.

Now, it's your turn to get in motion and start generating those creative, needle-moving ideas. Let's head to the exercise!

GENERATING CREATIVE IDEAS EXERCISE

Thought-Provokers

1. I generally come up with the best ideas during this time of day...
2. Based on my primary work areas, the best questions to ask myself are...
3. I can remove the following items from my calendar to create space to think...
4. Ideas I've had in the past I should revisit are...
5. The limiting beliefs that have been standing in my way of creating are...

Challenge

Week One: Perform ten minutes of idea generation each day. During week one, find ten minutes in your calendar—anywhere—to brainstorm the questions you cited in the second thought-provoker question. Jot down the ideas. Do not judge your ideas. Simply capture them.

Week Two: Incorporate the Ex Aliqua-technique to your week. Continue with you daily ten-minute brainstorming sessions. Additionally, identify a project or effort you're currently working on. It should be something of substance. For anything you review, read, or watch—basically any research—capture your thoughts related to 1) No, I think this instead... 2) Yes, that's true, but... 3) Yes, that's true and...

Week Three: Pick one idea to bring to fruition and plan it out. You should now have two weeks' worth of ideas. Using the appropriate planning process best suited for building out your idea, put the plan together!

Week Four: Take the first step. The first step toward implementing your project is usually the hardest. We typically make it harder than it ought to be because we're trying to eat an entire elephant in one bite. Just take the first step. Get in motion. Repeat!

PART EIGHT

The Satellite View

CHAPTER 19

Self-Diagnostic

Where did I leave my stethoscope?

Y ou're probably wondering, *Now what?* That's what I'd be wondering if I didn't write this book.

I suppose you can dive right in and start working on those fifteen lessons I just shared, but I think it's a good idea to get a birds-eye-view of where you are before you build your development plan and start working it.

This isn't something that's easy for most people. For starters, they don't know what to measure. They don't have a grading scale. Even if they did, they wouldn't know which grades matter or what to do with the report card.

To help you gauge how effective you are within each tier of my skill-building methodology, I've created a seventy-five-question "leadership" assessment for you to take so you can get a quantifiable view of where your strengths and opportunities for development are.

It's quick. There are no right or wrong answers. There's a 100 percent probability you'll pass. It's easy to assess yourself and you can complete this entire assessment in ten minutes. You can also double your fun if you want to ask your boss or colleagues to join you and offer their feedback.

Simply read each question and rate yourself as follows: 1 (Never), 2 (Somewhat), 3 (Sometimes), 4 (Often), and 5 (Always).

At the end of each section, add up your total points to see where you stack up against the "perfect score" of seventy-five total points. Then, carry your totals for each section to the summary chart and capture whatever additional thoughts you have related to the assessment.

Producer Section

Question	1 Never	2 Rarely	3 Sometimes	4 Often	5 Always
1. I can easily concentrate on one task without allowing myself to get interrupted.					
2. I perform one activity at a time and do not "multi-task."					
3. When I give someone my "word," I always follow through on my promise.					
4. When I perform a task, I do not stop until I finish it.					
5. I do more than is expected on each task.					
6. I feel vibrant each day (and am rarely tired).					
7. I like my environments in order (house, desk, etc.).					
8. I enjoy operating by myself so I can think.					

9. I get excited when there's a new project for me to do.

10. I prepare a plan for everything I do.

11. I can easily bring order out of chaos.

12. I enjoy taking complex problems and creating my own step-by-step outline.

13. When I plan, I see both the vision and the details of the goal.

14. I am goal oriented.

15. I stay on track toward my goals no matter how long they take to achieve.

Producer Score: _____

Communicator Section

Question	1 Never	2 Rarely	3 Sometimes	4 Often	5 Always
1. I am able to concentrate when someone else is speaking to me.					
2. I am willing to listen to someone's viewpoint if it's different from mine.					
3. I do not get upset when someone has a different opinion from mine.					
4. I'm easily able to determine someone's true message regardless of their chosen words.					
5. I am organized in the way I express myself verbally.					
6. I get energized when given an opportunity to present to a large group.					
7. I don't need to write out my thoughts in detail before speaking to a group.					
8. I think first about the purpose and goal of my written communication before I start.					
9. I often use examples and stories to make my point when communicating with someone.					

10. I get energized when there's an opportunity to meet new people.					
11. I am able to easily build rapport with new people I meet.					
12. I get excited when I go to large meetings, conferences, and get-togethers.					
13. When something unexpected occurs, I pause and consider the situation before reacting.					
14. When a problem arises, my first reaction is, *How can I make the best of it?*					
15. I have a positive outlook regarding my past situations.					

Communicator Score: _____

Influencer Section

Question	1 Never	2 Rarely	3 Sometimes	4 Often	5 Always
1. I have a detailed plan to grow my overall career.					
1. I am considered a subject matter expert in my field by my peers.					
2. I have a collection of mentors and teachers I follow and study to build my skills.					
3. I enjoy debating with others to share my point of view when it's different from theirs.					
4. I am able to easily convince other people to do things my way.					
5. I prepare an outline before I write anything lengthy or give a presentation.					
6. I am comfortable presenting to a large group.					
7. I like creating solutions by working with a team.					
8. I am easily able to guide large groups to accomplish their goals.					

9. I am comfortable asking for what I want and making a strong case for it.				
10. I consistently reach out to people to build new relationships.				
11. I frequently contact my acquaintances to see if they need help with anything.				
12. I won't take "No" for an answer irrespective of the situation.				
13. Whenever I encounter a rough situation, I look on the bright side.				
14. I am willing to focus on whatever I need to do to improve a situation or find a solution.				

Influencer Score: _____

Developer Section

Question	1 Never	2 Rarely	3 Sometimes	4 Often	5 Always
1. I'm required to develop the resource plan to build my team.					
2. I'm responsible for hiring the people who work on my team.					
3. When I manage people, I use a detailed approach that includes their individual growth plans.					
4. I spend time learning the behaviors and interests of my team members so I am able to effectively motivate them.					
5. I am comfortable managing large teams.					
6. I enjoy teaching other people the steps they need to take to accomplish their job.					
7. I provide detailed feedback to my team members regarding opportunities for growth.					
8. I feel every employee should be an ambassador for their team and company.					

9. I promote new ideas throughout my company.						
10. I like when my company changes because it means we're improving.						
11. I am able to easily adapt to corporate change.						
12. I explain major corporate changes to help people understand how it will benefit them.						
13. When my teammates disagree with me or each other, my first inclination is to understand their viewpoints.						
14. I am comfortable putting large-scale workplans together to accomplish major projects.						
15. I use a risk-management plan to account for known and potential risks.						

Developer Score: _____

Visionary Section

Question	1 Never	2 Rarely	3 Sometimes	4 Often	5 Always
1. I am a naturally perceptive and curious.					
2. I get excited when tasked with a project never done before.					
3. I am the person my company taps to tackle the toughest problems.					
4. I often see hidden potential opportunities before others identify them.					
5. I am able to easily connect the dots on subjects and come up with innovative solutions.					
6. I continually experiment with and implement techniques I've not seen used before.					
7. I frequently automate processes or build systems when they do not exist.					
8. I continually implement improvements even if they are small.					
9. I allocate time every week to identify improvements for my team and company.					

10. I am willing to try new approaches and techniques even if they might fail.					
11. When an approach fails, I consider it a lesson rather than a failure.					
12. I am able to see changes in the industry or market well-before they actually happen.					
13. I plan my team's and company's expected performance using proven formulas versus gut-feels.					
14. When I evaluate problems, I'm able to determine the solution without reviewing the analytical details.					
15. I build strategic models and approaches my company implements.					

Visionary Score: _____

Assessment Summary

Tier	Score (Max 75)	Initial Notes on Growth Opportunities
Producer		
Communicator		
Influencer		
Development		
Visionary		
Total (375 points)		

Let's look in the mirror!

Now that you've had a chance to take the assessment, consider whether your total scores in each section seem reasonable. Do they make sense to you based on your quick, instinctive assessment of yourself?

The assessment is intended to serve as a guide, not a test. It's a starting point for you and those who might help you develop your professional skills. Consider sharing your results with your coach, mentor, boss, peers, and people who know you best. Ask them if the results seem correct to them. If you and they are a little confused by the results, revisit each question to see which ones contributed to the lower- or higher-than-expected results.

The goal of the assessment is not to label you as much as it is to surface areas you want to develop. It's about becoming clear on your growth opportunities.

Now that you have a starting point of areas you might want to focus on, let's turn to the next step and begin building your professional development action plan!

PART NINE

Draw Your Own Map

CHAPTER 20

Build Your Plan

Life doesn't come with a map. You need to build yours, of course,
but the only way to complete it is to get lost a few times.

Hopefully the skills assessment provided you with insight into where you are on the map I've given you. From where you're starting, you can use my skill-building system to design your developmental path to reach your professional goals.

While I've given you my map, so to speak, I'd love for you to draw your own. You can add "cartographer" to your résumé if you'd like!

An effective map will serve as your best environment to operate within. It'll have goals ("destinations") along the way. You can put your flags down wherever you'd like. As you charter your route—your plan—to get to your goals, you can add in the terrain, hills, and track your detours on your journey.

Every map has a title, body, scale, legend, and compass to help you make sense of it. They even have insets, smaller maps blown up inside the larger map, to give you a closer view of particular areas. Your map needs analogous components so you know where you are at any moment as well as which direction you're heading. I recommend including these seven components to create the best structure:

Goals: We need to have something to work toward. Life's more fun and fulfilling that way. Goals come in a variety of forms and can include work assignments such as delivering a presentation or self-imposed

283

objectives like opening your own business. The purpose of these goals is to use them to guide your personal and professional development as you identify the skills required to achieve them.

Skills: Identify the skills you want to build to become a master of your profession. I provided you with fifteen lessons to get started. In Chapter 3, The Career Syllabus, I shared forty-five skills I believe most professionals need to become a "zebra" and not only stand out from the crowd, but also enjoy their careers to the fullest. Your goals will serve as the best clues to know which skills to build.

Lessons: You need detailed instruction to effectively build the skills. That includes the steps to develop, practice, evaluate, iterate, and grow them. That's where lessons in this book come in handy. I chose the fifteen lessons inside this book to get you started because I believe they'll provide the greatest immediate return and accelerate your ability to learn the remaining skills. Additional lessons can also come in the form of training and certification courses, manuals, books, or any mediums where you're learning in an organized fashion.

Tools: As you learn the steps to build each skill, you'll become more proficient in developing them if you use the proper tools. Tools come in different forms. There will be tools to practice the skills and tools to execute the skills. Reading about how to chop the tree down is one thing. If you don't have an axe, you won't be able to practice or complete the act.

Coaches: Getting proper instruction will expedite your growth. Getting the proper instruction from actual gurus will improve your growth exponentially. Your choices in selecting the right experts to learn from is no less important than the effort you put into developing your skills.

Calendar: All the intention in the world means nothing if you don't have the space in your life to do what you intend to do. We generally focus on the urgent. Building your skills, especially those that don't appear immediately necessary or come with a short-term payoff are often pushed to the side. Consistently planning time in your calendar to develop your skills—and sticking to it—will pay tremendous dividends throughout your career.

Tracker: Without recording what you've completed, how far you've come, or how much further you need to go, you won't know where you are on your map or how much progress you've truly made. This is especially important for your psyche. As we pursue long-term goals, we don't realize how far we've come because our attention is typically on how far we need to go. Trackers can be as simple as capturing notes in your journal or a worksheet to identify your accomplishments. They can be as sophisticated as corporate career development models or systems that label your progress on a graph.

Metrics: The measurements you select are as important to your success as the work you put in to achieve that success. Improper metrics can be a great source of strain. If you're measuring outcomes you cannot control or designating target goals without fully understanding the effort and variables required to achieve them, you'll be susceptible to throwing in the towel. If you've never run a 26.2-mile marathon and are setting a specific race finishing time as a goal, you'll likely be disappointed. For that matter, you might be shocked by how much training is required to be able to cross the finish line upright and with a smile on your face.

You're measuring it with a micrometer, marking it with chalk, and cutting it with an ax. Do your best.

Now that you have an understanding of the components to build your development plan, I want to cover some considerations to make you successful when building and operating your plan.

The expression, "What gets scheduled gets done," has never been truer than for skill building, practicing any craft, or anything else that is not urgent nor shows immediate output. Consider the tactic I shared in the lesson on Planning and Running Your Day. Each week, as I inventory my activities for the upcoming week, I explicitly add the skills I'll be practicing that week. That way, they are visible as I schedule my activities. This helps ensure I schedule the time to work on my craft each and every week.

This is akin to building up your savings account. Some people get their paychecks and start spending on luxuries. I'm not talking about paying for food and rent. It's a great idea to immediately account for your true essentials like the roof over your head and making sure the kids are fed. (I've got four dogs to feed. I know whereof I speak.) After the necessities are taken care of, it's beneficial to put some of the money into your savings account so you're investing in your future. After you've saved and invested first, then treat yourself to the extras if it's financially possible. Your skill-building activities and the compounding effect they'll have on your career are exactly like this investing analogy. If you don't take the time to allocate some of your waking hours each week to building and practicing your skills, you won't be able to develop them. Your "skills account" will be thin and it won't grow.

Let's say you're willing to create the space in your calendar to develop your skills and invest in yourself. If you're still reading this book, I'm fairly certain, at this moment, your intentions are high. You wouldn't otherwise still be with me. Even so, you still need to know what to work on, when to work on it, and how to work on it. It would also be helpful to know the most economical way to build your skills so you can, as quickly as possible, practice them in real-life situations and get immediate, observable feedback. This practical experience will help you make the proper adjustments and grow faster.

There are key steps to develop your initial plan including the components to help you work your plan. Once you've completed the first iteration of these steps, you can start building your skills in an organized fashion.

Your plan, and the execution of it, will be highly fluid and require constant attention to stay on track. Realize, your plan is living, breathing, and ever evolving. It must grow with you.

As you use your plan to work toward your long-term goals, which might span multiple years, you can avoid overwhelm by planning your skill-building efforts in manageable time horizons. This will help you remain focused and, as importantly, make it easier for you to see your progress.

When I determine my goals and the skills required to accomplish them, I work in one-year blocks and break them down into three-month periods. I plan my business and projects during each calendar year. I also review my initiatives in quarterly and monthly timeframes, so this enables me to align my skill-building efforts with the deliverables and services I'll be creating and offering. Regardless of your position or profession, many businesses work this way. Additionally, many companies conduct annual reviews and appraisals for their employees, so these timeframes might also offer convenient opportunities for you to evaluate your previous and upcoming years. Use the most easy-to-manage periods based on your particular situation and what makes the most sense for you.

Evaluating annual and quarterly periods also allows me to identify the areas I want to upskill to help me make incremental improvements from previous versions or iterations of my projects. For example, each January, I run a goal setting or productivity workshop. Each time I plan that year's version of the workshop, I identify opportunities to improve the previous versions. Is there a better way to teach the material? What skills can I improve to make the communication and presentation of the lessons more effective for the students? Is there a better way to market the program? What marketing skills could I build to improve that aspect of the program? Can I improve my execution of the sales process? Would better storytelling or email copywriting increase my sales?

Thinking this way not only allows me to make incremental improvements of my programs and identify opportunities to grow my skills in accordance with my goals, but the schedule of my events also helps me pace when to practice those immediately applicable skills.

These are some key considerations that will help you build a practical development plan that pays dividends sooner than later. As you see your results, you'll stay charged and interested in continuing your growth.

Don't fall in love with the plan.
Fall in love with the planning process.

Taking into account the elements that make up a great development plan, we can address them in a number of steps to get you started in the right direction. I stress "get you started in the right direction," because, although I've laid out the pillars of a great plan serially, you'll likely be bouncing back and forth among the steps as you take on new challenges, are given new assignments, discover new coaches, and revisit your goals.

I also want you to create your own design using the tools you favor. Whether you're capturing this in a journal, Word document, or fancy system, your success will be found in the execution of the steps more so than how you lay it out.

For illustrative purposes, I provided a Skill-Building Plan Example in Appendix Two. If you want to see what each step in your plan might look like, review that sample for additional perspective.

Now, let's get to it!

1. REVIEW ASSESSMENT

Review your leadership assessment results.

Take a closer look at your leadership assessment results and note your tendencies. Based on your strengths, opportunities to improve, interests, and professional goals, capture the areas you feel are most critical to your success. At this point, you're simply trying to **identify a handful of most-impactful skills** that will accelerate your ability to reach your goals.

Think in terms of Pareto's principle. 80 percent of the consequences will come from 20 percent of the causes. For example, carrying forward my annual workshop example, if my primary goal was to increase sales, my main skills to improve would be copywriting, presenting, and selling. There will likely be a handful of related skills that will be the keys to putting you on a faster path to reach your goals.

Ask yourself questions such as…

- What skills will have the greatest impact on my longer-term, overall professional development?
- What skills will have the most immediate impact on my immediate professional results?
- What's the ONE skill I can develop right now that makes building the other skills easier?

Goal of this step:

- Gain a general understanding of your strengths and opportunities for improvement at each tier level.

- Understand your most important, most impactful areas of development so you have a centerpiece to guide you.
- Consider the "accelerator" skill that will make your development and outputs easier.

_____

_____

_____

2. RATE SKILLS

Perform an overall skills review using the Track Your Progress Worksheet in Appendix One.

Even though you identified key skills in step one to accelerate your growth, it's beneficial to get a complete review before you build and execute your plan. You might notice other skillsets that require immediate attention because you have deliverables due soon. You might also discover there are related skills which can be built synergistically. That is, you can build multiple, related skills by economizing your time invested in their development.

This is the opportunity to take into account your unique situation. If you are just starting your professional career, I'd suggest starting with the skills in the Producer Tier and progress your way up the skill-building pyramid. Of course, we're each at different points in our careers and have different job functions, so we want to accommodate for where we are currently and where we want to head.

Performing a complete skills review will help you benchmark where you are and give you a chance to **take your interests and timing into account** based on your personal situation. In the Track Your Progress Worksheet, there are three major considerations to help you with this:

Rate yourself for each skill. For all skills within each Skill-Building Tier (Producer, Communicator, Influencer, Developer, Visionary), give yourself a rating. You'll notice I included additional skills, beyond the fifteen I covered in the book, to help you grow in each tier. On a scale of 1–10, with 10 being the strongest, how effective are you—currently—at each skill? This is an opportunity to create an initial benchmark for yourself to note which skills you want to invest time in developing. The intent is for you to clarify which areas require the most-immediate attention.

Identify the professional relevance of each skill. Not all the skills I cited will be applicable to you or require a significant level of adeptness. In the professional relevance column, make notes for yourself regarding whether each skill is very important (high), mildly important (medium), and not really important (low). For example, someone who markets or sells a product will have very high relevance to the skills in the Influencer section.

Determine the timing and urgency of the skills. While certain skills might be important for your long-term growth, other skills might require your attention in the short term. This is an opportunity to think through and prioritize when you want to work on each particular skill. At this point, simply make a few notes. You'll align these more specifically to your calendar in step number five of this process.

The Track Your Progress Worksheet can also serve as an initial **tracking mechanism** as you evolve your skills. It's a simple way to keep your inventory. You can use the worksheet, in conjunction with any additional company-specific or personalized development plans you're using to track your growth.

Goals of this step:

- Identify a starting point and initial level of proficiency of your skills.
- Clarify which skills will be most important for your professional development.
- Pinpoint which skills to work on in the short-term based on upcoming professional needs.

3. LIST GOALS

Identify your current-year and long-term goals.

Make a list of the high-level goals you'd like to accomplish during the upcoming and future years. Capture these at the highest level as well as the intermediary, stepping-stone goals you'll need to accomplish along the way.

These goals can be anything you'd like to achieve such as delivering a presentation at the company's quarterly meeting, gaining a promotion, speaking at an event, opening your own business, or starting a side hustle.

As you develop your plans to attain your goals, you'll identify the intermediary and pre-requisite steps for those goals. For example, to attain your promotion, you might need to cite certain skill proficiencies or deliverables required to achieve it. For opening your own business, you might have goals of attaining funding or building a product platform or some other necessary goals that enable you to build and sell your product.

Each goal will ultimately have its own plan. Included in each plan will be the skills you'll need to develop to achieve the goal. You can use any goal-setting plan or sheet you'd like as it relates to attaining your goal. You're welcome to check out my Goal Setting Masterclass at the milewalk Academy® site for more information on my goal-setting techniques and tools.

Based on the target timing of your goal attainment, you can determine how much skill-building effort will be required each week and month to achieve it. The intent of this step is to provide you with a designated timeframe so you can manage the steps you'll need to take along the way to hit your target goal date. Give yourself something to shoot for!

Ask yourself questions such as...

- What key work deliverables do I have this upcoming year?
- What additional personal goals do I want to shoot for this year?
- What are ALL the skills required to attain each of these deliverables and goals?
- Which of the skills I identified will require the most attention and development to achieve the deliverables and goals?

Goals of this step:

- Create a list of upcoming goals (i.e., work assignments due, professional goals, etc.).
- Create a list of corresponding skillsets required to achieve those goals.

_____

_____

4. INVENTORY SKILLS

List the skills you need to build to achieve your current-year and long-term goals.

For the goals you identified in the previous step, you identified the associated skills you'll need to develop. In this step, **collect them so you have a consolidated inventory**. It'll be easier to manage your skill-building time if you have a singular list to manage. If you don't have specific professional goals, but would like to start building skills you know will pay dividends over time, you can use the suggested skills I cited within each tier (see the Track Your Progress Worksheet in Appendix One) as a starting point. I believe this structure can be universally applied no matter what your profession or goals are.

Goal of this step:

- Build a consolidated list of your skills to develop to aid in planning.

_____

_____

_____

5. ALIGN CALENDAR

Align your skill-building activities so they coincide with when you need them most.

From the previous steps, you have your goals and inventory of skills to build to achieve those goals. Technically, this might just look like a giant to-do list. You know how I feel about to-do lists!

Let's turn this information into an actionable plan by **thinking in terms of time and due dates for your skill-building efforts**. This will help you pace yourself and clarify which skills to work on and when to work on them.

Ideally, you'll plan these efforts to coincide with your **real-life situations. These real-life situations will serve as "beacons" to guide and pace you**. More importantly, they'll help you feel engaged, purposeful, and get the best results from your skill-building efforts because you'll be able to get immediate, observable feedback on your progress.

When I coach individuals who are building their development plans, I have them prepare a **high-level, annual calendar** as a starting point to visualize the major milestones more easily for their years. This brings a level of order to the inventory of skills.

The purpose of this exercise is to get a **calendar view of major activities, deliverables, and target goals**. These can be recurring, annual efforts such as budgeting, performance review, or promotion attainment. They can be ongoing, every-week activities you want to improve such as your copywriting or presentations during your weekly status meetings. These are yours to cite however you want. The intent is to use real-life scenarios to serve as milestones and review how you're progressing.

Additionally, you'll include the specific skillsets to develop so you can improve your ability to produce the deliverables and accomplish your goals. This is an easy way to give yourself a time-based reference to make your planning easier.

In a few simple steps, you can see your plan come to life with activities and goals to use as guideposts for your skill development.

Annual calendar by month view: First, start with a calendar view of the entire year. I suggest drawing it before you move it into an electronic version or online tool because you're likely to do a lot of moving the pieces around. Perhaps use thirteen columns or boxes. Column one serves to note goals and skills. The remaining columns will include the months of the year. Make them large enough so you can write in them.

Personal, seasonal activities: Irrespective of what you do, generally, the beginning of the year is a great time to focus on goal setting, organizational, productivity, and planning skills. The end of the year is a great time to evaluate and reflect. You might also have a performance review, which requires you to improve your negotiation and influence skills. Think about the calendar in terms of your personal preferences and "seasonal" considerations.

Professional, cyclical activities: Your company or role might have recurring activities performed at similar times each year. If you already know, as an accountant, you'll be busy seasonally between January and April, you might target building your organizational skills during November and December. Perhaps, each year, your company does its annual planning and budgeting in November. You can focus on your planning and presentation skills in September and October. Think about the calendar in terms of your company's repetitive or cyclical tendencies.

Unique, major projects: Sometimes we need to develop deliverables or work on projects that are one-time efforts. While they'll require skills we can use on an ongoing basis, these particular projects have specific due dates. This book you're reading is a great example. The publisher and I agreed on a specific due date. Based on that date, I created time in my calendar during a few-months period where I was working on my book-writing skills. These skills are different from blog-writing or email-copywriting skills. You might have a big presentation coming up next month for which you want to focus on your communication skills. Think about the calendar in terms of any imposed or self-determined dates you'd like to use to guide your skill building efforts.

Ongoing activities: Many professionals perform similar activities week-in and week-out which are vital to their production and performance. These often don't have one big deadline, but rather have frequent, periodic deadlines. For example, I publish weekly newsletters on Tuesday and Thursday. I have more than 100 of these messages I prepare annually. That means, it's a good idea to develop and improve my email-copywriting skills on a continual basis. Think about your calendar in terms of these continual activities so you can balance your "big push" development with your all-the-time developmental needs.

Once you have an annual view, you can drill down into more detailed three-month, one-month, and one-week views to make the scheduling, planning, learning, and practicing of your skills more consistent and timelier.

If, for example, you are making a presentation in April, you can schedule time during February and March to practice your crafting compelling messages, communication, trust-building, and presentation skills. If you allocated two hours each week for eight weeks prior to your presentation, that would amount to two full workdays of practicing before you actually gave your presentation. Of course, you'll also be working on the actual presentation as part of your regular work schedule. Think of that entire effort as part of your skill development.

Additionally, there will be ongoing activities that have deliverables on a continual basis. These can be status reports you present to your management team each week or dozens of sales cold-calls you make each day. Activities such as these are your cues to note you can work on your presentation, communication, and organizational skills every month or perform more concentrated practice during the months when you don't have other big projects due. You can add these to the calendar each month if that's easier for you to track.

Here's a very high-level example of how you might identify goals and plan your skills development.

Example Annual View

MONTH	JAN	FEB	MAR	APR	MAY	JUN	JUL	AUG	SEP	OCT	NOV	DEC
GOALS, DELIVERABLES	Goal Setting, Time Management			Presentation to Management Team				Technical Certification Test		Annual Conference		Annual Performance Review
SKILL DEVELOPMENT	Focus, Habits, Planning Day		Persuasion, Craft Compelling Messages, Building Trust			Technical Skills Development			Personal Story Development, Networking		Self-Awareness, Negotiating, Goal Setting and Review	

Each week, as I mentioned in the Planning and Running Your Day lesson, I inventory the skills I want to focus on that week. I treat my skill-building efforts the exact same way I treat my work deliverables for my business. They get scheduled so they get done. They are also scheduled in accordance with my work project plans so I can immediately apply what I'm practicing.

During periods when I don't have major work deliverables, I'll allocate time to my every-day or every-week skills like the email-copywriting example I mentioned.

I realize considering all these factors might sound like a difficult effort to keep organized, but once you get in the habit of including skill-building activities as part of your every-day or every-week schedule, this will become as automatic as brushing your teeth each morning.

To start filling in your calendar, ask yourself questions such as...

- What are the personal, seasonal activities I do (or would like to do) each year?
- What would be the ideal time of year to perform the personal activities?
- What are the professional, reoccurring activities I'm required to perform each year?
- What are the one-time projects I'll be performing in the upcoming months and year?
- What are the ongoing activities I'd like to improve?

Remember, this is a systematic way to gather your goals and deliverables and, in turn, surface the most-practical opportunities to build your skills. As you plan your months and weeks, it'll become clear, from your annual calendar, which primary, high-value areas offer the greatest, immediate return for your time invested. If you actually carve out the time to work on those skills, you'll be amazed at your long-term results.

Goals of this step:

- Build a one-year calendar view that includes key milestones by month of corporate-set deliverables and professional goals.

297

- Assign target months to perform skill-building activities in advance of preparing deliverables and achieving your goals.

_____

_____

_____

6. CHOOSE COACHES

Select the right teachers, coaches, and mentors who will support you in your efforts.

As I mentioned in the Mastering Your Trade lesson, it's vital to choose the right teachers and coaches to help you learn the skills you need to build. There's no need to do everything on your own. Get guidance and input from experts. Be thoughtful in your selection process as you evaluate their knowledge, results, teaching style, dedication and love of their subjects, availability, generosity, and modality.

If you know some coaches you'd like to start following, you can list them here. In addition, list the skills here for which you'd like to start researching and following coaches.

As you become more familiar with them, you can evaluate whether to invest in yourself through their free, online material or premium training programs. These coaches will be crucial to your overall success, so make sure to choose them wisely.

In addition to the evaluation-based questions, make sure to consider your coaches from a scheduling perspective too.

Ask yourself questions such as…

- For the coaches I currently follow, are there specific coaching dates (e.g., monthly, group coaching sessions), conferences, or seminars I should consider attending and adding to my calendar?
- What additional coaches should I consider engaging?
- What other areas, in general, should I consider investigating to see whether there are coaches available?

Goals of this step:

- Create your starting "Franken-mentor" of coaches.
- Surface opportunities to schedule training in advance.
- Discover coaches' "training" content-release schedule (i.e., videos, podcasts, etc.).
- Build lists of skills and functions to research additional coaches.

_____

_____

_____

7. IDENTIFY LESSONS

Determine specific training formats (e.g., lessons, programs, books, podcasts, conferences).

Now that you have a starting list of coaches and teachers, you can start building your "structured" training program from the collection of relevant sources. Anything that helps you learn the way you enjoy is fair game.

You might wonder, *Why be so formal here?* Your ability to distill your focus and intake of content in any form is critical to your success. We spend a lot of time online. I hope your time online is productive. To make it so, let's make it directed by creating a list of potential assets to help you learn your subjects and develop your skills.

I use a combination of premium video-based training programs, subscription programs (where I get to attend monthly, private group coaching sessions), books, free weekly videos and podcasts, workshops, conferences, and seminars. You can use similar formats and mix in certification training programs, corporate-sponsored training programs, and any schooling you'd like.

The most important step is to start inventorying your ideas and potential avenues to learn so you can figure out what best supports your development.

Ask yourself questions such as...

- What are the premium training programs my coaches offer to help me with my skills development?
- What available books, blogs, speaking engagements, webinars, and seminars do my coaches offer?
- Does my company offer any internal and external training classes or support?
- Are there additional books, blogs, and podcasts which cover the subjects I need to build skills?

Goals of this step:

- Compile a list of various training lessons, instruction, and programs.
- Ensure you're following your coaches online and at their major events.
- Gather additional assets to investigate as potential resources.

_____

_____

_____

8. SELECT TOOLS

Select the tools to practice your skill building and execute your activities.

It's helpful to do some investigation regarding the tools you'll need. The intent of this step, at this point, is to research the best tools to help you practice and perform the skills you're developing.

For example, I deliver coaching services via online platforms. Any device that records me as I rehearse the show can be considered a tool to help me practice. Zoom, my iPhone, or any other medium will enable me to review my practice and make adjustments.

When I offer my coaching, I need tools such as a camera, microphone, visual aids, and other tools to actually provide the services. I might conduct the session on YouTube, Zoom, or our proprietary training platform. This entire collection of tools and software is required to "operate my skills."

Your evaluation will be an ongoing process, not a one-time occurrence. I have one word of caution. No tool is effective if there's an operator error. You can have the fanciest sales tracking system, for example, but if you're not entering the necessary data, you can't track and adjust properly. Focus on the processes first and then determine which tools will best help you execute them.

Ask yourself questions such as...

- What is the minimum toolset required to develop the skills and deliver the outputs?
- Are there inexpensive options of these tools so I can learn them and determine what's necessary?
- Are there skills I'm developing "manually" that I can accelerate with tools?

Goals of this step:

- Identify (and purchase or access) tools to help with your skills practice and execution.
- Create of list of additional tools to research or level-up in the future.
- Discover opportunities to test tools to automate or streamline your ability to execute.

_____

_____

_____

9. DETERMINE METRICS

Identify the right criteria to evaluate your progress.

There are two important steps to correctly gauge whether you're growing. The first is identifying and using the correct success metrics to measure your progress. The second is taking the time to reflect and review what and how you've done in relation to your metrics. Even if you take the time to reflect, it's vital to use the correct metrics. Otherwise, you might misconstrue you're not making progress when you actually are.

Generally, the **best success metrics** will be ones **you can completely control**. For example, you might not control whether you get your promotion, but you can control your attitude, work effort, and whether the quality of your work product is improving. These are all elements that contribute to your promotion. Your promotion is something someone else decides.

You might not be able to control the final sale of your company's product, but you can research well, prospect effectively, make the sales calls, develop and practice an effective sales pitch, respond well to customer objections, evaluate what's working, and other contributing factors.

As you're evaluating your long-term goals and development, it's better to measure (and enjoy) the process than the outcome. There's nothing wrong with having specific outcome goals. It's nice to have something to shoot for as long as you don't let your actual outcomes, or lack thereof, control your happiness and take away from the joy you get "in the doing."

I want you to choose the best success metrics based on your goals and skills you're developing. To provide guidance into how to think about metrics and which ones to consider, here are a few examples you can use. Keep in mind, tailor these and add whichever ones are most appropriate for you.

Increased productivity and project completion: Measure how much more, how much better, or how much faster you can accomplish the same task. If you're able to do more within the same time limit, you know your skills are improving. As an example, it used to take me one hour to shoot a ten-minute video. Now, I can shoot a ten-minute video in eleven minutes.

Quality improvement: Measure the quality of your work product. This can be decreased error rate, increased customer satisfaction, or anything related to whichever skill you're building and task you're completing. Continuing with my video example, the quality of my lesson delivery, aesthetics in the video, sound, "eye-contact," and a host of other factors have improved which make my videos more engaging.

Process-goal attainment: Measure your progress of long-term skills development, as well as designated outcome goals, by achieving intermediary goals required to attain the larger goals. If you are a salesperson given a $1,000,000 revenue goal for the year, you might initially get overwhelmed. That's the large, outcome goal. Your process goals, for example, might include learning the product, getting the sales pitch down, making ten cold calls each day, getting invited to write two proposals each week, win one client each month, and so on. Breaking down the larger goal by providing yourself intermediate target goals makes it easier to focus on the process and attain those stepping-stone goals. The accumulation of achieving these intermediate goals is what ultimately helps you hit the larger, outcome goals.

Feedback from colleagues and managers: Measure your progress via feedback from your colleagues, managers, customers, and others. This information will provide valuable insight into your professional skills development. The feedback can be verbal from your manager via informal conversations or performance reviews. Feedback can also come in the form of surveys such as customer satisfaction surveys or 360-degree-style surveys.

Increased confidence: How you feel can be, in and of itself, a success metric. While maybe hard to tangibly measure, how you feel will have a great deal to do with your ability to keep forging ahead in whatever development or goals you're trying to attain. The more time you spend reflecting and focusing on what you *did* accomplish and what went well that day, the better you'll feel. Do you feel more confident giving a presentation? Are you more confident in your ability to perform the task?

There will be instances when you want to measure your progress in situations where you're interacting with others. This becomes more prominent as you reach the Communicator and Influencer Tiers. After all, you are building relationships and trying to motivate others. In these situations, it might not be as straightforward as to whether you're more easily able to accomplish a task. How will you gauge whether you're becoming better at these communication and interaction skills? Here are a few ideas.

Improved relationships: Is your relationship improving? Are you communicating more effectively? Are you able to come to agreements or resolve your issues more quickly? Is the person more receptive to your ideas? These are only a few questions you might consider when evaluating whether you are more effectively communicating and building relationships.

Reduced misunderstandings: When you're communicating more clearly, you'll find there are fewer misunderstandings in your interactions. This is one aspect to measure whether your communications intelligence (CQ) is increasing.

Improved listening ability: Your ability to listen will be dependent on your ability to focus. Are you able to concentrate on what someone else is saying? While our interpretation of whether we're listening isn't necessarily a reality of whether we're listening, there's no question you should be able to evaluate whether you can understand and retain what someone is sharing.

Feedback from others: Similarly, as I mentioned when it comes to performing tasks, feedback can be valuable when it comes to building relationships too. Get feedback from people you communicate with regularly, such as your boss, teammates, and customers. Their insight can help you determine whether you are communicating effectively.

Increased confidence: Confidence is helpful in not only performing tasks, but also in interacting with others. Do you feel more confident when communicating with others? Are you able to express your thoughts more easily? These are great signs you're improving.

These five examples are a good starting point when it comes to evaluating your progress related to communication and interaction skills.

Now, it's your turn to start collecting your success metrics. Based on the skills you'd like to build in the upcoming year, what are the success metrics you'll use to know whether you are making progress?

Ask yourself questions such as:

- What are my best indicators of productivity improvement (i.e., faster, more, etc.)?
- What are my best indicators of quality improvement?
- For each goal/skill, what are the intermediary milestone-goals I need to hit to show progress?
- In addition to my boss, who can I get feedback from regarding my progress and performance?
- Do I feel more comfortable performing this particular activity?
- Are my relationships with my coworkers, boss, customers, and others improving?

Goals of this step:

- Assemble the primary success indicators for each goal.
- Clarify the stepping-stone goals or intermediary steps required to achieve each larger goal.
- Prompt yourself to reflect with the appropriate questions.

---

10. TRACK PROGRESS

Record your improvements and iterate.

In step two, you used the Track Your Progress Worksheet in Appendix One to rate your proficiency for the relevant skills. This is not a one-time occurrence because, on a weekly basis, you'll get better if you're putting in the time to properly develop your skills.

To track your progress effectively, monitor your growth, and make adjustments, it's helpful to **review your progress** and priorities (that is, upcoming projects, due dates) on a **monthly basis** at a minimum. Depending on how much time you're putting into skill building, you might want to reflect and evaluate on a weekly basis.

These consistent, periodic reviews will provide opportunities for you to truly assess what's working and ensure you keep your skill-building efforts in alignment with your highest-priority work projects.

Goals of this step:

- Update the tracking worksheet (checkmarks, new ratings, additional notations) to record your progress.
- Reevaluate your goals and required skills development on an ongoing basis to ensure you are perpetually learning.
- Identify new ways to improve your skills and techniques by iterating and leveling-up your practice.

PART TEN

Before You Go

CHAPTER 21

My Gift to Find Your Gift

The gift is in the giving.

Before you head out to build your skills and practice them, I'd like to give you a parting gift. This isn't the kind you unwrap and instantly know what it is. That wouldn't be as fun as you might think. This gift is the kind that requires you to give. Indulge me for a few more minutes.

Imagine all the events that needed to take place for you to be reading these very words. I'm not talking about how you surfed Amazon or walked into a store to buy this book. I mean all the events that needed to take place for your parents to meet, date, get married, and bring you to life. Of course, the same goes for me. You can go back further to Grandma and Grandpa and so on and so forth.

Think of the struggles you've gone through in your life and career. Consider all the aspirations you have that motivated you to get this book. How about my aspirations that set me on a path to learn these lessons and build these techniques for you? How about the effort it took to write the book and get it published so you can buy it and read it when you need it most?

We could go on for days regarding everything that led to your and my convergence. It wasn't a straight line and I'm guessing it's been quite an odyssey for both of us. Even so, however you size it up, it was meant to be. How do I know?

Have you ever woken up on any given day and asked yourself, "How the heck did I get here?" I did that this morning as one of my four dogs was licking my face! *How on Earth do I now have a wife and four dogs when I was single until I was forty-nine years old?*

Take a moment to think back on your life. Go as far back as you possibly can and consider it as objectively as you can. Think about your entire evolution. It makes no difference how old you are. Whether you're twenty years old or seventy years old, look back at the common thread or theme that seems to permeate through every single thing you've done. It's there. I promise you.

Here's an analogy from my life to help you with this. When I think back to my childhood, I remember school and playing organized sports. I was a good student, but I didn't really care about the subjects all that much. What I remember most was not the lessons and the grades, but helping other students with their homework. What I remember most about playing sports was hanging out with my friends and teaching them my practice routines and how I developed my game.

Ohm's Law this ain't.

When I got to college, this is where I recollect my first big "mistake." Since this was the first thing I ever got to choose in my life, it would stand to reason I'd have a hiccup or two. Instead of studying the subject matter I loved, such as something people oriented, I enrolled in electrical engineering because I was strong in math and science and figured this was a good way to pay my inevitable bills. Today, I'm not sure it's possible for me to care any less about Ohm's Law other than I want the electricity in my house to work.

As I graduated and was about to embark on my professional career, I realized I didn't want to be an engineer. I knew, from a self-awareness standpoint, this wouldn't be congruent with what would make me happy. I decided becoming a technology consultant would offer me a chance to leverage my degree to get a job and also enable me to focus on what I enjoyed most. That would be helping people and companies. I went on to rationalize how it would give me a chance to see a variety of companies and industries and meet a lot of diverse people. In hindsight, I never cared about the technology I implemented. The joy, for me, was always in the counseling part. Helping people and companies improve are what really energized me.

I had that wake-up-one-day-and-wonder episode seventeen years later. I could no longer stomach being a technology consultant. It was time for a change. That's when I decided to start my recruitment firm, milewalk®. This brought me one step closer to making helping people my primary focus. It's what also led to me eventually becoming a career coach, which is perhaps the capacity in which you know me.

Lightning in a bottle.

When I look back at my entire life, there was one constant for me. That is, helping people and getting them to where they want to go. Whether that relates to their career or opening a business or living a more fulfilled personal life. This is my gift.

When you look back on your life, what is the common thread that permeates every single thing you've done?

Now, I want to help you find your gift. When you look back on your life, what is the common thread that permeates every single thing you've done? Keep in mind, your gift is something you give this world to make it a better place!

If it isn't yet apparent to you, let's take another step and focus on your present. This will offer you another clue to finding your gift. It relates to passion and energy.

First, let's not confuse your gift with your passion. Of course, I want you to be passionate about what you do and what you offer this world. I'm passionate about what I do. I get enjoyment from helping you. That passion, in the act of helping you, is actually *for me*. My ability and desire to help you is my gift *to you*.

I also don't want you to just "follow your passion." That's some of the worst advice ever and typically a recipe for disaster for most people. Instead, let's work our way into becoming passionate through exploration and what energizes you.

**I also don't want you to just "follow your passion."
That's some of the worst advice ever and typically a recipe
for disaster for most people. Instead, let's work our way
into becoming passionate through exploration
and what energizes you.**

Second, understand, one is not born with passion. I didn't come out of my mother's womb and then all of a sudden want to be a career coach. Passion is something you discover between the time you were born and now. It's something you found, and through repeated interaction with it, you fell in love and developed a passion for it. Perhaps you enjoyed it instantaneously. To develop a real passion, however, requires you to do it or be in touch with it over and over again.

The easiest way to find your passion is to consider the parts of your life that energize you. If you focus on what gives you energy, you'll likely discover your passion. In turn, this discovery has a way of helping you notice your gift.

You'll also notice you won't tire of what gives you energy. For example, I do a weekly, free live coaching show on my YouTube channel every Thursday. Each month, I perform many more group and individual coaching sessions for members of my paid programs. I've been doing this for several years. There's no way I could fake this in front of a camera for that many hours every month. I'd be miserable if I did!

Has anyone seen my mirror?

Much like my coaching sessions, you've got something that energizes you and keeps you motivated. I'd also be willing to bet you love the fact it benefits others. That's a key part of your gift—you keep going because others pull you toward your gift. Whether it's your customer or a person you serve or your loved ones, these people will see you differently than you see yourself.

We can be our own worst critics and we don't always recognize how good we are at something or how valuable it is to someone else. The reason we don't recognize how valuable our experiences and gifts are is because we forget what it's like not to know what we know. We don't think what we offer is valuable because we consider the value to ourselves instead of thinking about the value it'll have to someone else!

As a final clue to helping you find your gift, let's pay attention to external feedback. Do people tell you, "You're really great at this" or "Thank you! That helped me so much"? If you're hearing remarks like this, it's a pretty good indication you have a gift.

Where do I find out what the latest inheritance tax is?

Nothing helps you live a more vibrant life than dying. I know. That's a splash of cold water, but it's certainly out of love. Have you thought about what kind of legacy you want to leave? What do you want to be known for?

Most people I work with think of these questions in terms of their families, children, and grandchildren. You can have that for free. It's a given.

If you're reading these words, I'm talking to you and not most people. If you're reading these final pages, I know you have major aspirations and want to leave something behind from a career standpoint. I know you want to make a positive impact on this world.

For me, I'm indifferent about being known as a consultant who helped companies put in technology systems. I want to be known as someone who went all-in on helping people build better careers and lives. I do that day in and day out and I give it everything I have every day. I constantly remind myself my words will echo in places I will never visit, but I have faith they will have a positive impact on the people who hear them directly as well as the people to whom they pass on the lessons.

Does anyone actually know how many TV shows
Steve Harvey hosts?

If you put in the effort to find your gift and give it to this world, I know it will be a huge success for you and have a major impact on others. No major positive impact exists, however, without needing to overcome big hurdles. You will encounter challenges.

You will have failures. Keep going. When you trip, remember a (single) failure does not make you a (complete) failure. I hope you embrace these bumps along the way as part of the process.

You'll need to put in the invisible work that no one will ever see. Have faith that true champions are made in the darkness. They're the ones that practice before the sun rises. They treasure that time and know their effort is what will help them make a better life for themselves and others.

Steve Harvey, the comedian and TV host of a bajillion shows, said, "Your gift is the thing you do the best with the least amount of effort." In part, I agree with his statement. It's yet another clue to helping you find your gift, but I want to challenge you.

If you want to manifest your gift to the level it deserves, the least amount of effort won't get you there. It will take more. Instead of asking, "What's the least I can do?" ask yourself, "What's the most I can endure?" What are you willing to work hard for? What are you willing to sacrifice for? This will be an even better clue leading to your gift.

I didn't want to learn how to use a camera or what it takes to build a podcast or any of the other mediums I needed to learn to make my lessons available to the world. I'd rather sit in my pajamas all day and write books. Even so, helping you, to me, is worth taking the time to learn new tools and other vehicles, which are uncomfortable for me. That's because I'm willing to endure that to offer my gift to the world because I'm passionate about helping people.

This world needs more of you, not less. There are people who need you to do what you ache to do. That's the part of you, you need to give them. That's the part of you I'd love to see. That's the part of you the world wants.

This world needs more of you, not less. There are people who need you to do what you ache to do. That's the part of you, you need to give them. That's the part of you I'd love to see. That's the part of you the world wants.

Appendices

Track Your Progress

You can use this worksheet to assess, update, and review your skill-building progress as well as keep your efforts in alignment with your upcoming projects.

The lessons in the book cover fifteen skillsets I feel are vital for career success. This worksheet contains an additional thirty skillsets to support your professional growth. These skillsets are broken down by their respective tiers.

To initially complete this worksheet and use it on an ongoing basis to monitor your progress, perform the following three steps:

1. **Skill-Building Tier, Completion Status, and Skills Rating Column:** Give yourself a (current) rating for each skill on a scale of 1–10, with 10 being the highest. For those skills you want to develop, do your research, read the lessons available in this book, and seek additional guidance. You're welcome to check out my Leadership Coaching Program if you're interested in my video-based lessons on any of these skills. Seek out any additional programs, tools, and courses to support your development as appropriate. Revise your ratings as you progress through the lessons, practice, and implement these skills.

2. **Professional Relevance Column:** Gauge how applicable the skills within each tier are for your profession. In the professional relevance column, make notes for yourself regarding whether each skill is very important (high), mildly important (medium), and not really important (low). For example, someone who markets or sells a product will have very high relevance in the Influencer section.

3. **Urgency, Timing Column:** Note timing considerations to help prioritize when you want to work on each particular skill. For example, early in the year tends to be a great time to work on goal setting. You might have a big presentation coming up in which you want to accelerate the time you spend learning those skills. Take into account YOUR personal situation when scheduling your plan!

Skill-Building Tier + Completion Status (Done, Scheduled Date/Week, etc.) + Skills Rating (1 Low to 10 High)	Professional Relevance (High, Med, Low)	Urgency, Timing (Now, Q1)
PRODUCER (TIER 1) Operating independently. Becoming proficient at managing oneself and delivering outputs of value. **Assessment (Completed Lesson, Individual Skills Rating)** ☐ Focus _____ ☐ Planning _____ ☐ Integrity _____ ☐ Decision Making _____ ☐ Habits _____ ☐ Goal Setting _____ ☐ Willpower _____ ☐ Productivity _____ ☐ Energy _____ ☐ Patience _____ ☐ Confidence _____ ☐ Self-Awareness _____		
COMMUNICATOR (TIER 2) Interacting with others. Learning behaviors and using communication vehicles to build powerful relationships. **Assessment (Completed Lesson, Individual Skills Rating)** ☐ Empathy _____ ☐ Storytelling _____ ☐ Listening _____ ☐ Building Trust _____ ☐ Speaking _____ ☐ Relationship Build _____ ☐ Writing _____ ☐ Reaction _____		

Skill-Building Tier + Completion Status (Done, Scheduled Date/Week, etc.) + Skills Rating (1 Low to 10 High)	Professional Relevance (High, Med, Low)	Urgency, Timing (Now, Q1)
INFLUENCER (TIER 3) Inspiring others. Using communication vehicles to deploy logical and emotional tactics to inspire positive behavior in others. **Assessment (Completed Lesson, Individual Skills Rating)** ☐ Master Trade _____ ☐ Collaboration _____ ☐ Influence _____ ☐ Facilitation _____ ☐ Persuasion _____ ☐ Negotiation _____ ☐ Compelling ☐ Networking _____ Messages _____ ☐ Perseverance _____ ☐ Presentation _____		
DEVELOPER (TIER 4) Leading teams and coaching people. Motivating and guiding a team or individual to achieve a desired outcome. **Assessment (Completed Lesson, Individual Skills Rating)** ☐ Hiring _____ ☐ Delegating _____ ☐ Team Build _____ ☐ Promote Culture _____ ☐ Managing _____ ☐ Manage Change _____ ☐ Motivating _____ ☐ Resolve Conflict _____ ☐ Coaching _____ ☐ Manage Risks _____		
VISIONARY (TIER 5) Creating and predicting. Using expertise to create and implement market-moving ideas and predict trends. **Assessment (Completed Lesson, Individual Skills Rating)** ☐ Strategy _____ ☐ Forecasting _____ ☐ Idea Gen _____ ☐ Prediction _____ ☐ Creativity _____		

Skill-Building Plan Example

I realize it's easier to develop something when you have an example or can see someone else do it first. To help you, I've prepared an abridged sample of how professionals might consider each stage of building their plans.

Remember, everyone is unique. While I've given you the framework, add your own touches and take into account your specific job function, goals, and schedule. The most important factor isn't to do everything exactly the way I've laid it out, but to provide yourself with a personalized structured to help you remain consistent. This structure will also enable you to maintain visibility to the skills that'll pay dividends and align your efforts to real-life targets so you learn and practice in a beneficial, timely fashion.

I hope this example helps illustrate how you might develop your own plan. For conciseness, I've included a handful of goals and skills and carried them through select steps for demonstrative purposes. The sample is not intended to be this professional's complete plan, but to provide you with a walk-through of how you'd navigate your plan. Also, for brevity, I omitted stages such as taking the assessment, rating skills, and drafting a pictorial-view of the annual calendar where I've provided examples and templates throughout the book.

If you'd like more information on how to develop your plan and detailed lessons on building specific skills, check out my Leadership Coaching Program at milewalkacademy.com. The team and I are continually innovating new ways to make your career and life easier and more fun. We're already working on new tools that will be released by the time you finish this book!

SKILL DEVELOPMENT PLAN

Here's my skill development plan as a project manager with aspirations of growing my capabilities and getting promoted to the next level in the upcoming year. It's also important for me to ensure my customer's project runs smoothly and my entire team is growing in their professional development.

1. Review Assessment

Review leadership assessment results.

The qualitative review of my assessment shows me...

The areas I consider will have the <u>greatest impact</u> on my professional development and performance are: customer service, relationship building, effective communication, project planning, time management, and delegation.

A few skills that will help me improve my <u>immediate results</u> are: effective communication, project planning, delegation.

The <u>ONE skill</u> I can develop right now that will make building the other skills easier to build is: effective communication at all levels including executive-level, group discussions, collaboration-style, and facilitation methods.

2. Rate Skills

Perform overall skills review using the Track Your Progress Worksheet.

(Provided Tier 3 section for illustrative purposes.)

Skill-Building Tier + Completion Status (Done, Scheduled Date/Week, etc.) + Skills Rating (1 Low to 10 High)	Professional Relevance (High, Med, Low)	Urgency, Timing (Now, Q1)
INFLUENCER (TIER 3) Inspiring others. Using communication vehicles to deploy logical and emotional tactics to inspire positive behavior in others. **Assessment (Completed Lesson, Individual Skills Rating)** ☐ Master Trade __5__ ☐ Collaboration __6__ ☐ Influence __4__ ☐ Facilitation __5__ ☐ Persuasion __4__ ☐ Negotiation __3__ ☐ Compelling ☐ Networking __2__ Messages __4__ ☐ Perseverance __6__ ☐ Presentation __6__	All 10 skillsets are HIGH in professional relevance.	Focus on presentation skills, collaboration, and facilitation for this tier for quarter one based on project kickoff, planning, and team building deliverables.

3. List Goals

Identify current-year and long-term goals.

The most important primary and secondary goals for this upcoming year and the skills required to achieve them are:

Goals	Associated Skills
Successfully complete project on time and within budget.	Communication, trust building, relationship building, project management (my craft), influence, collaboration, facilitation, team building, managing people, coaching, resolving conflict, managing risk, forecasting, creativity.
Attain a client satisfaction score of 10 out of 10.	Customer relationship building, communication, empathy.
Attain promotion to senior project manager.	Proficiency in all skills cited for project completion goal.
Attain 100 percent promotion rate for all staff members on my team who are eligible for promotions.	Managing people, motivating people, coaching, delegation, empathy, influence.
Renew client's contract for follow on work once the project is completed.	Customer relationship building, trust building, influence, negotiation.

(To Do: Review the milewalk Academy Goal Setting Masterclass and use the Goal Setting Worksheet to capture details for each goal or review other online options to help me keep this in order. Capture metrics related to my progress in attaining those goals in their respective worksheets.)

4. Inventory Skills

Consolidate list of skills to achieve current-year goals.

Collectively, there are <u>eighteen</u> skills I need to focus on to attain my goals this year:

Coaching, collaboration, communication, creativity, relationship building, delegation, empathy, facilitation, forecasting, influence, managing people, managing risk, motivating people, negotiation, project management (my craft), relationship building, resolving conflict, team building, trust building.

I'll assemble them into a <u>handful of groups</u> to make it easier and more efficient for me to learn and practice. Effective communication will be the number one skill that permeates most of these.

Communication: Communication, influence, resolving conflict, empathy.

"Trade" Skills: Project management, managing risk, forecasting, collaboration, facilitation.

Managing People: Coaching, managing people, motivating people, team building, delegation.

Relationships: Relationship building, trust building.

Ideas: Creativity.

Sales: Negotiation.

5. Align Calendar

Align skill-building activities so there's a time-based view of what to work on and when to work on it.

I'll start with the key activities and list them to create a quarterly calendar and break it down to the monthly version in the next iteration.

Quarter One: January, February, March

Goals, Deliverables: Project kickoff (Jan), plan initial phases completely (Jan), complete risk management plan (Jan), build elite team (Jan-Feb), Client Satisfaction Survey (Mar).

Skills: Primary skills to allocate time developing during this quarter are project planning, communication, facilitation, managing people, relationship-building (customers and team), empathy.

Quarter Two: April, May, June

Goals, Deliverables: Operate project on time/budget (entire Q2), plan sub-sequent project phases and develop proposal for follow on services (Jun), Client Satisfaction Survey (Jun). Improve creativity skills and implement weekly brainstorming process to help with solutions for follow on proposal.

    Skills: Project execution, trust-building, collaboration, resolving conflict, forecasting, selling/negotiating, communication.

Quarter Three: July, August, September

Goals, Deliverables: Complete project on time/budget (Sep), secure sale of follow-on work to start in October, conduct preliminary discussions with boss regarding my end-of-year promotion (Sep), conduct informal staff reviews for their end-of-year promotions (Sep), Client Satisfaction Survey (Sep).

    Skills: Project post-audit, resolving conflict, managing risk, forecasting, coaching/motivating people, relationship-building, trust-building.

Quarter Four: October, November, December

Goals, Deliverables: Project phase 2 kickoff (Oct), finalize post-audit and submit report to management (Oct), Client Satisfaction Survey (Dec), year-end-promotion (Dec), annual review reflection and salary negotiation (Dec), staff year-end promotions (Dec).

    Skills: Creativity (new ideas based on previous learning and project post-audit), coaching/motivating people, negotiation, relationship building, trust building, communication.

6. Choose Coaches

List teachers, coaches, and mentors and functions/skills to investigate to support my growth.

    For starters, this Andy guy seems like he knows what he's talking about. I should join his leadership program so I can work with him each month and get access to all his lessons on these skills.

    Coaches, trainers, and authors I currently follow and areas to investigate related to the skills I need to improve are:

Communication: Vanessa Van Edwards, Robert Cialdini, Zoe Chance, Tasha Eurich

Project Management "Trade" skills: Laura Vanderkam, Jim Collins

Managing People: Brené Brown, Tony Robbins

Relationships: Kelly McGonigal, John Maxwell

Ideas: Adam Grant, Malcolm Gladwell

Negotiation/Sales: Chris Voss

[These coaches are for illustrative purposely only with no affiliations or rewards to me or the milewalk Academy® should you invest in their programs.]

7. Identify Lessons

Potential resources and training to help build the skills.

There are many related lessons in *The Zebra Code* and I can start with the respective exercises and challenges for the skills I need to build.

This year, I'll be able to cover some of my trade skill development through on-the-job training and the "Master Your Trade" challenge inside this book.

Some additional thoughts regarding coaches, lessons, podcasts...

Communication: Vanessa Van Edwards' People School. Get her books *Captivate: The Science of Succeeding with People* and *Cues: Master the Secret Language of Charismatic Communication.*

Managing/Motivating People: Tony Robbins, various programs.

Relationship Building: Investigate Business Relationship Management (BPM) course options.

Ideas: Use *The Zebra Code* lesson and "challenge exercise" on Generating Creative Ideas to brainstorm ideas. Follow Adam Grant's podcasts "ReThinking" and "Work Life."

Negotiation: Chris Voss' Black Swan and Art of Negotiation programs. Get his book *Never Split the Difference.*

[These coaches and programs are for illustrative purposely only with no affiliations or rewards to me or the milewalk Academy® should you invest in their programs.]

8. Select Tools

Select the tools to practice your skill building and execute your activities.

I have work-supplied tools for my project management skills. I'll investigate "relationship management builders" once my organigram (network map) starts to grow. Initially, I'll use Excel and my calendar to manage.

9. Determine Metrics

Identify the right criteria to evaluate your progress as it relates to building skills.

I'll reflect on my progress for the skills I practiced on a weekly, monthly, and quarterly basis.

My main focus will be to ensure I'm following the correct process and working on what I can control as it relates to building my skills. I'll use the goal worksheets to manage progress on each goal.

As a starting point, I'll use these metrics as I start to implement my training and "grade" myself on how well I adhere to the steps.

I'll add additional metrics as I progress through the year and spend more time training the additional skills.

Quarter One: Primary areas are project planning/management, communication, relationship building, empathy, and managing people.

PROJECT PLANNING

Assess metrics based on my company's development plan and what's expected of me. Confirm these metrics with my boss.

COMMUNICATION

- **Timeliness:** Communicate clearly and in a timely fashion so my team and customers are up-to-date and there are no misunderstandings.
- **Clarity:** Express my ideas and instructions in a way the other parties can easily understand. Practice "proactive intent checks" and get them to reiterate back to me as well.

- **Engagement:** Ensure conversations are engaging—meaning both parties are involved. Strive to keep their attention and interest proactively as well as use questions to prompt their ideas.

- **Feedback:** Get feedback and welcome ideas on my communications. Learn the other parties "communication languages" and what registers best with them.

- **Action:** Ensure my communication leads to appropriate action if others are carrying out instruction.

- **Rapport:** Build rapport with others so we have good relationships and they trust me.

RELATIONSHIP BUILDING

- **Communication:** Communicate clearly and effectively with others—meaning in an open, honest, timely, and respectful manner.

- **Listen:** Listen actively and concentrate on what someone is sharing; show them I am listening.

- **Support:** Provide my support and help when they need it.

- **Respect:** Show them respect regardless of who they are or whether I agree with their ideas. Have constructive conversations when working through issues or resolving conflict.

- **Recognition:** Recognize others for their contributions and offer encouragement when they need it. Show appreciation for their work.

- **Perspective:** Remain open and supportive to new or different perspectives.

- **Follow-up:** Follow up with others after interactions to check on progress and maintain the relationship. Be responsive to their messages and requests for communication.

- **Trust:** Show others you trust them and be reliable and consistent with my intentions towards them.

EMPATHY

There will be similar or overlapping metrics with empathy as with building relationships. In addition to communicating effectively, listening, being respectful, and maintaining proper perspective, I'll monitor the steps I can take to put myself in a better position to be empathetic. These are:

- **Pre-routine:** Consistently performing my pre-step routine to consider others before I'm speaking with them.
- **Practice:** Practice listening with perspective so I maintain an open mind and am accepting of differences.
- **Reflect:** Reflect on my finished conversations to determine if I was empathetic and how I can be more empathetic in the future.
- **Feedback:** Get feedback from colleagues.
- **Check-ins:** Become more aware of others' emotions by proactively "checking in" with them.

MANAGING PEOPLE

There will be similar or overlapping metrics with communication, empathy, and building relationships when it comes to effectively managing my team. In addition to the metrics cited for those areas, I'll monitor the steps I can take to put myself in a better position to be empathetic. These are:

- **Conversations:** Conduct initial conversations regarding their goals, interests, "feedback language" and other success factors for a great relationship.
- **Labels:** Determine appropriate beginner, intermediate, expert, master label for each person.
- **Set targets:** Work with each team member to set their target achievement dates for their skill development.
- **Communicate feedback:** Communicate their progress informally on an ongoing basis and be clear on areas they're doing well as well as opportunities for improvement. Additionally, perform quarterly reviews on a formal basis with adherence to their scheduled "sit-down" checkpoints.
- **Socratic method:** Use Socratic method to enhance engagement and ownership when working on the projects.
- **Support:** Make sure to be patient and welcoming as they need support throughout the projects.

Additional metrics and areas to consider throughout the year:

CREATIVITY

- **Ex Nihilo:** Consistently performing Ex Nihilo (out of nothing) technique daily/weekly brainstorming session.
- **Ex Aliqua:** On a daily basis, use Ex Aliqua (out of something) technique as I read, watch, listen, and observe.
- **New ideas:** Generate fifty new ideas and variations to improve (service, product, operations, etc.) each week.
- **Standard clocks:** Consistently use my "standard clocks" when writing or developing any major piece of content.

COLLABORATION

- **Mindset:** Remain open to new ideas.
- **Process:** Put process in place to ensure group can collaborate on frequent (perhaps weekly) basis.
- **Team:** Optimize team based on their experience and knowledge, creativity, and diversity.
- **Schedule adherence:** Adhere to the periodic collaboration meetings (shoot for 100 percent adherence).
- **Preliminary steps:** Formulate and distribute questions to members to stimulate thinking.
- **Brainstorming:** Perform individual brainstorming to generate preliminary ideas.
- **Goals:** Clearly communicate goals and educate participants of the collaboration.
- **Technique:** Concentrate on THE idea, not the source of the idea to ensure impartiality.
- **Support:** Be supportive of ideas when team is enthusiastic even if I'm not completely sold.

FORECASTING

- **Forecast:** Complete project budget, forecast, progress vs. expected, post-audit and cite, in detail, all assumptions, risks, etc.

- **Delivery:** Ensure on-time and on-budget delivery of phase one.
- **Accuracy:** Evaluate accuracy of initial projection against completion figures to determine variance and rationale in the event it's not on-time or on-budget.
- **Post-Audit:** Revise work estimates for phase two based on actual completion figures for phase one.

MANAGING RISK

- **Identification:** Effectively complete the risk matrix with all identifiable and considerable risks.
- **Meetings:** Be prepared weekly at the Steering Committee meetings with risk updates, mitigating plans, and contingency plans based on newest information.
- **Communication:** Communicate immediately in the event a risk arises that needs management decision.

NEGOTIATION

- **Proposal development:** Put together effective proposal that outlines all major areas and various cost options.
- **Solutions:** Challenge myself to provide creative solutions at attractive prices.
- **Perspective:** Challenge myself to consider the client's viewpoints as I prepare the presentation and proposal details.
- **Presentation delivery:** Effectively present proposal to client.
- **Preparation and readiness:** Prepare inventory of client's potential objections and our rebuttals.
- **Agreement:** Reach a mutually beneficial agreement.
- **Relationship:** Enhance positive relationship and communicate respectfully.
- **Composure:** Maintain professional composure throughout entire process and remember this is not personal.
- **Trust:** Regardless of outcome, make sure to establish and build more trust.

Afterword

It doesn't need to be perfect. It needs to be breathing.

Anytime you create something of value, three things occur. First, you need to gain experience that enables you to create the value. Then, you need to take time to package your experience into a format others can actually use. Finally, people take it in and, hopefully, do something that positively affects their lives. The real value is in the ripples. The magic happens in the echoes.

Writing this book didn't take me a few months. It took me three decades to gain the experience to learn the concepts I shared in this book. It took me a few months to write it and another year to get it fully published so you can use it.

The value to me, in writing this book, has nothing to do with what happens to me and everything to do with what happens for you when you integrate these concepts into your life. As I mentioned, I write books so, in a matter of hours, someone can add my years of experience and wisdom to their own. I hope you're willing to write and share your "book" with the world.

Remember this concept whenever you want to build something that can help others. Create those minimum viable products and share them. Iterate and iterate some more. The world doesn't need your perfection. It needs your persistence. Don't wait around for your A-game to show up when your B-game will change lives. You are already good enough. What you create will be good enough. Get it out there. It doesn't need to be perfect. It needs to be breathing.

More Resources

If you love the concepts and lessons in this book, they are only a taste of what's inside my **Leadership Coaching Program**!

As a member of the program, I'll help you take your development and production to the next level with monthly, live, interactive sessions on these topics. You'll build and sustain serious momentum, stay focused, overcome challenges, and truly enjoy your career as you leave a hugely positive mark on this world.

You'll have access to lessons not only related to the skills I detailed inside *The Zebra Code*, but also the dozens more I mentioned as part of my skill-building framework. As of this book's release, there are nearly 100 recorded video lessons available inside the leadership library. Along with those videos, you'll get access to booklets and assets to help you work the lessons much like the exercises inside this book.

You'll learn more about lifestyle and wellness, organization and productivity, success and high performance, communication and influence, building relationships, building teams and promoting culture, goal setting, and other related career development topics.

If you'd like to get more information on becoming a member of this program, check out the milewalkacademy.com!

Acknowledgments

This is the part of the book where the author graciously claims that no one writes a book by himself. On he goes to name all the people who wrote the book with him. Well, since I didn't see any other blurry-eyed humans at my desk pecking the keyboard in the wee hours of the mornings, I'm simply going to thank myself for somehow managing to function at that hour of the day. I will, however, toss in a shout-out to my Dachshund posse, Harley, Ginger, Rocket, and Starla for their remarkably consistent, seven-days-per-week, 4:15 AM barks for breakfast. Thank you for helping me save money on alarm clocks.

For the rest of world, I do have a few people I'd like to thank. By their gifts of time, observation, and wisdom, I was able to collect many nuggets that found their way into this book.

First and foremost, I want to thank the members of my Leadership Coaching Program for letting me test-drive these lessons and concepts. Your level of attention and dedication to your and my professional growth has not only made this book better, but also made me a better teacher. For that, I am truly grateful.

I owe a very special debt of gratitude to my Kara (yes, you still can't have her). Any words I put in here as a thank-you to her couldn't possibly justify the level of dedication and help she's given me in this book project or any other effort she and I have completed together to make this world a better place. I can't imagine my professional life without you.

Of course, no book project is done without a publisher and editor. To the entire gang at Post Hill Press, thank you so much for having faith in me as one of your authors and bringing my book project to life. A special shout-out to my Acquisitions Editor, Alex Novak, for his direction throughout this entire effort. I can't thank you enough for your guidance from the inception of this idea through the final product. This book is

Acknowledgments

a better product because of you and your advice throughout this entire journey will live on in my future efforts.

Finally, here's the mushy stuff. I am grateful to my wife and best friend, Lynda LaCivita. Thank you for all your patience and encouragement throughout what you know was my most challenging effort. There's simply no way I could have pulled this off without your love and support. For that, and for you, I am eternally grateful.

Let's Connect

Andrew LaCivita, a globally-renowned career and leadership coach, is the founder of the milewalk Academy®. During the course of his distinguished career, he has impacted over 350 companies, more than 100,000 individuals, and spanned nearly 200 countries, helping them unlock their full potential. He is an award-winning author who gained international recognition with his groundbreaking books, *Interview Intervention: Communication That Gets You Hired* and *The Hiring Prophecies: Psychology behind Recruiting Successful Employees*. Both of these seminal works, along with his celebrated vlog, *Tips for Work and Life*®, consistently earn top spots on reputable, worldwide lists which rank the best career advice books and blogs.

You can join him for more training at the milewalk Academy® (milewalkacademy.com), catch him on Thursdays for his free Live Office Hours on YouTube (@andylacivita), or listen to his weekly Tips for Work and Life® podcast. You can also connect with him on social media at @andrewlacivita on LinkedIn, Instagram, TikTok, and Facebook and @arlacivita on Twitter.